D0079179

The Painful Field

Recent Titles in
Contributions in Military Studies
Colin Gray: Series Advisor

Contemporary Studies in Combat Psychiatry
Gregory Belenky, editor

Perspectives on Nuclear War and Peace Education
Robert Ehrlich, editor

Arms Control and Nuclear Weapons: U.S. Policies and the National Interest
W. Gary Nichols and Milton L. Boykin, editors

New Weapons and NATO: Solutions or Irritants?
Robert Kromer

The American War in Vietnam: Lessons, Legacies, and Implications for Future
Conflicts
Lawrence E. Grinter and Peter M. Dunn, editors

Nuclear War and Nuclear Strategy: Unfinished Business
Stephen Cimbala

The Anglo-American Winter War with Russia, 1918–1919:
A Diplomatic and Military Tragicomedy
Benjamin D. Rhodes

The Last Gaiter Button:
A Study of the Mobilization and Concentration of the French Army in the War
of 1870
Thomas J. Adriance

NATO Strategy and Nuclear Defense
Carl H. Amme

A Nuclear-Weapon-Free Zone in the Middle East: Problems and Prospects
Mahmoud Karem

Gentlemen of the Blade: A Social and Literary History of the British Army
Since 1660
G. W. Stephen Brodsky

China's Military Modernization: International Implications
Larry M. Wortzel

THE PAINFUL
FIELD

THE
PSYCHIATRIC
DIMENSION OF
MODERN WAR

Richard A. Gabriel

Contributions in Military Studies, Number 75

GREENWOOD PRESS

NEW YORK · WESTPORT, CONNECTICUT · LONDON

Library of Congress Cataloging-in-Publication Data

Gabriel, Richard A.
   The painful field : the psychiatric dimension of modern war /
Richard A. Gabriel.
       p. cm.—(Contributions in military studies, ISSN 0883-6884 ;
no. 75)
  Bibliography: p.
  Includes index.
  ISBN 0-313-24718-8 (lib. bdg. : alk. paper)
  1. Psychiatry, Military. 2. War—Psychological aspects.
I. Title. II. Series.
U22.3.G333 1988
355'.001'9—dc19   87-31785

#17295837

British Library Cataloguing in Publication Data is available.

Library of Congress Catalog Card Number: 87-31785
ISBN: 0-313-24718-8
ISSN: 0883-6884

First published in 1988

Greenwood Press, Inc.
88 Post Road West, Westport, Connecticut 06881

Printed in the United States of America

The paper used in this book complies with the
Permanent Paper Standard issued by the National
Information Standards Organization (Z39.48-1984).

10 9 8 7 6 5 4 3 2 1

To Erin Gerry,
my beautiful godchild

Contents

Tables

The Painful
Field

Introduction

Surveying the extant literature dealing with war, one cannot but be struck by the lack of studies on the psychiatric dimension of warfare. To be sure, there are a number of works on the psychology of war, works that tend to focus on the larger question of why men fight. Whenever military establishments have addressed the psychology of war, their analyses have stressed such things as morale and discipline. Indeed, it seems an unproven axiom of armies that soldiers who have high morale and strong discipline will almost always carry the day on the battlefield. The few books and articles on the psychiatry of war are overwhelmingly clinical in orientation, no doubt because military psychiatrists write these reports and tend to minimize or even ignore the larger human questions that are necessarily involved. What is clearly needed is a book that addresses the psychiatric dimension of war in the larger and more important context of whether men can continue to plan and fight wars while remaining truly human.

Armies all over the world, no doubt with the support of their political leadership and the unquestioning adherence of their civilian populations, continue to propagate a number of myths about their soldiers' ability to wage war and remain sane. In contrast to nuclear war, most civilians regard conventional war as little different from World War II. Moreover, the belief persists that soldiers can learn to withstand the stresses of battle; that with a few weeks of training most civilians can make sound and sane fighting men. Finally, the saddest myth of all is that only the weak or cowardly will break under the strain imposed by the horror of modern conventional combat. Media establishments in both the United States and the Soviet Union, one government-controlled the other uncontrolled, sustain these myths with television screenplays and motion pictures in which heroes always triumph over fear. Psychiatric collapse is at most portrayed only occasionally and then almost always as a rare and temporary occurrence. With the citizens of both superpowers fed a constant diet of such visions of heroism, they can hardly be blamed for believing that psychiatric collapse in battle is a rarity reserved for the weak and cowardly. Like all myths, these too are false.

The simple and horrifying truth is that human beings are very fragile psychic beings. A historical review of psychiatric collapse in battle shows clearly that no matter how well trained the soldier is, no matter how cohesive battle units are, no matter how good and technically proficient the soldiers' leaders are, no matter how motivated the soldier, men under fire will succumb to the stresses and strains inflicted upon their psyche by the horribly destructive environment of the battlefield. Given enough exposure to combat, every soldier will eventually suffer mental collapse and be unable to continue. It is this truth of inevitable collapse of the soldier under conditions of combat that must be juxtaposed with the myth of psychiatric invulnerability that sustains the military establishments of the world.

As this book demonstrates in its first two chapters, one finds instances of psychiatric collapse among soldiers of the armies of ancient Babylon, Egypt, Greece, and Rome. Madness has always been the constant companion of the soldier regardless of the time in history in which he fought. Indeed, until modern times, most battles were not decided by the rate of killing but by the rapidity with which one side simply lost its nerve, broke, and ran. It was after the collapse of battle units that most physical casualties were incurred. During the American Civil War, the highest rate of discharges was not for physical wounds, but for psychiatric reasons. The same was true for the British and German armies in World War I. Indeed, among American soldiers in World War I the rate of psychiatric casualties was almost twice as high as the number of dead. During World War II, the American army—not including naval, marine, and air forces—lost 504,000 men, enough for fifty combat divisions, from the fighting effort because of psychiatric collapse. In the 1973 Arab-Israeli War almost one third of all casualties on both the Israeli and Egyptian sides were psychiatric. In the 1982 incursion into Lebanon, Israeli psychiatric casualties were twice as high as the number of dead and accounted for 27 percent of the total wounded casualties. Indeed, the number of psychiatric casualties in every war in this century—beginning with the Russo-Japanese War in 1905—have exceeded the number of soldiers killed by hostile fire by 100 percent. To sustain the myth that only the weak and cowardly collapse under the strain of combat requires ignoring a great deal of contrary evidence.

These numbers count only those psychiatric casualties that were severe enough to require hospitalization and evacuation from the war zone. They do not count those soldiers who required only a few days' rest at the battalion aid station before being returned to the fighting. If these figures are added, the number of men lost to the fighting effort for psychiatric reasons would at least double. In addition, such figures do not include the very large numbers of men who become so paralyzed by fear they can make no significant contribution to the fighting effort at all and thus are, for all intents and purposes, lost to the fighting unit. By far the great majority of soldiers fall into this category. For example, during World War II, no more than 15 percent of the soldiers in American frontline combat battalions ever fired their weapons at the enemy regardless of whether they were attacking or being attacked. Most soldiers were simply so afraid that they did nothing but stay in their holes. One percent of American fighter pilots accounted for 49 percent of the total enemy kills. The rest refused to engage the enemy even when they had the chance.

If the numbers of men psychiatrically debilitated during war is staggeringly high, so is the inevitability of psychiatric reactions to combat stress. It is categorically false that only the weak and cowardly suffer debilitating fear and collapse. The truth is that all sane soldiers eventually suffer these conditions. During World War I and II, the American army extensively screened soldiers for psychiatric predispositions to stress breakdown. By the time the soldier was exposed to combat, he had been screened upon induction, during training, and before deployment. Thus, only the "strong" were actually sent into battle; the "weak" had already been eliminated from combat units. Still, the rate of psychiatric collapse was enormous. Moreover, studies by the American army indicate that fully half the psychiatric casualties occurred within the first five to seven days of exposure to battle. Among the Israelis in Lebanon, 100 percent of the psychiatric casualties were taken within the first seven days of the war. Further studies by the American military after the war demonstrated that after thirty days' exposure to combat, no less than 98 percent of the soldiers had manifested severe psychiatric reactions. The remaining 2 percent? They were found to be already psychiatrically ill; they had been aggressive psychopathic personalities before being drafted and somehow had managed to slip through the induction screening. In a functional sense, the stress of combat psychiatrically debilitated all those exposed to it for more than a single month, hardly evidence that only the weak or cowardly are subject to psychiatric collapse.

These figures would, one would think, be sufficient to give pause to those military planners whose task is to plan for the next conventional war. After all, if World War II levels of combat produced such psychiatric casualty rates, what can modern conventional wars be expected to produce? The fact is that the intensity of combat in World War II is as far removed from modern conventional combat as Waterloo is removed from Normandy. The American (and Soviet) estimates of the intensity of modern conventional war assert that modern war will be at least seven to fourteen times as intense—even barring limited battlefield nuclear weapons—as was World War II combat. A modern Soviet and American mechanized division can deliver ten times the firepower at three times the rate as their respective World War II counterparts. Projections for purely conventional war scenarios involving Soviet and NATO (North Atlantic Treaty Organization) forces in central Europe suggest that the number of psychiatric casualties could reach between 40 and 50 percent of total casualties on both sides within a single week of combat. The loss of men from psychiatric debilitation is fast reaching crisis proportions. As each new generation of weapons makes war more destructive and the battlefield more lethal, the number of men lost to the fighting effort as a result of mental collapse grows, rapidly threatening to reduce the combat power of the fighting forces drastically and, in some instances, overwhelming it altogether. The problem of psychiatric collapse in battle is rising to central importance for any military force that can expect to see battle in future.

How are the Soviet and American military establishments dealing with this problem? What is the state of military psychiatry in the Soviet and American armies? As might be expected, both armies have strategies, plans, and medical facilities to deal with the problem. Yet, the field of military psychiatry is still a developing discipline—more so in the United States than in the Soviet Union—and there remain tremendous problems in working out which mechanisms and treatments work best if at all. While there is little doubt that the military planners of both armies are making some effort to solve the problem, the effort seems less than systematic and complete.

Moreover, the doctrines and practices of each army are quite naturally far more the result of its own battle experiences and the direction of the broader field of psychiatry within its own country than of any systematic attempt to study and incorporate information available from military history or the experiences of other armies. Consequently, there is no comprehensive written history of military psychiatry that addresses the development of combat psychiatry cross-culturally, nor are there books that offer a comparative in-depth treatment of the subject against the background of historical experience. One of the major objectives of this book is to fill this void by providing a comparative analysis of the Soviet and American system of military psychiatry rooted in the historical experience of both armies while, at the same time, placing it within the larger historical experience that armies have endured for two millennia.

One conclusion that emerges from this analysis of Soviet and American battlefield psychiatry is that neither side expects its present system of treatment and prevention to work very well. Accordingly, both armies have embarked upon efforts to explore more direct ways of preventing psychiatric collapse among fighting men. Inevitably, this has led both sides to open the Pandora's box of trying to prevent psychiatric collapse by chemically altering the mental processes of the soldier. Both sides are presently engaged in a number of research projects that seek to develop a "magic bullet"—technically a nondepleting neurotrope—that will control the soldier's anxiety while leaving him mentally alert to conduct combat operations and to sleep normally. In short, both sides aim at no less a chemical revolution than banishing fear from the mind of the soldier. This chemical revolution has staggering implications for the nature of future conventional war and even more tragic implications for the nature of man. Chapter 8 discusses the subject in detail.

In an era of high-intensity warfare of greatly increased lethality and stress some thought must be given to how military psychiatry will accommodate the very harsh realities within the battle zone. The sad truth is that soldiers have always to some extent been dispensable in war. Certainly, loss rates are somewhat predictable for certain kinds of combat operations, and success requires that commanders be willing to accept these losses. Perhaps we have reached a point in the development of warfare where the reality is that soldiers who suffer psychiatric difficulties are more dispensable than others, a cruel proposition at best, especially in light of the overwhelming evidence that there are no significant personality traits that immunize a soldier against psychiatric breakdown. All men are at risk of mental collapse when placed in the environment of modern war.

In the end, of course, there is no answer; there are only victims. The cruel realities of past wars have grown exponentially more cruel as armies face the future. The human material of war has not changed nor is it likely to do so unless medical research is allowed to cross the chemical frontier and alter human psychic nature as we have known it from the beginning of time. In this sense we stand at the brink of a new and frightening advance in medical science, the ability to chemically prevent fear in the soldier. If we cross that frontier, as well we might, we will be plunged into a long dark night, and there will be no way back. For the present, the men who stood at Meggido or Cannae or Waterloo were no different from those who will be asked to stand on future battlefields. They will have the same hopes and the same fears, and all too many will suffer the same fate. What has changed, of course, is the nature and lethality of war. And the disturbing truth is that without chemical assistance, the human psyche can no longer withstand the stress of modern war without seeking refuge in insanity.

1 ───────────────────────────────

War and Madness in History

To understand modern conventional war is to recognize a single indisputable fact: War is not only becoming more lethal in terms of its ability to kill and maim; it is far more destructive in its ability to drive soldiers mad. Indeed, as the warriors among us improve the technology of killing arithmetically, the power to drive combatants crazy, to debilitate them through fear and mental collapse, is growing at an even faster rate.

People today seem to have a tendency to regard the past as somehow more idyllic than it was and to endow it with the quality of a golden age in which many of the human problems we now face were somehow absent or not very important. Lt.-Col. L. H. Ingraham and Maj. Frederick Manning, both members of the staff of the Department of Military Psychiatry at the Walter Reed Army Institute of Research, have written, "psychiatric battle casualties are a phenomenon new with 20th-century warfare."[1] Accounts of past battles so often seem to offer examples of individual heroism and courage and all too seldom recall acts of cowardice and fear. It is as if we were the first generation to question our ability to endure the horror of battle. At the very least military histories seem to simplify all aspects of battle, so that the complications attendant to modern war often seem absent or minimized in accounts of past wars. One result is to convey the impression that men who fought in earlier times were somehow different from those who will fight the battles of the future. This seems to be especially true of accounts of performance and endurance under fire. Nothing could be further from the truth.

Fear and madness have been man's companions in war since the beginning of recorded history and, most probably, before that. There is clear evidence that men recognized very early that the ability to conquer fear was crucial to achieving victory over one's enemies. Xenophon, himself an experienced soldier and troop commander, wrote almost 2500 years ago,

"I am sure that not numbers or strength bring victory in war; but which-
ever army goes into battle stronger in its soul."[2] There is no good reason
to believe that soldiers in past times were any less fearful of dying or being
maimed than their modern-day counterparts. Moreover, that battle has
driven men of the past just as mad as it has driven modern soldiers seems
a historical fact. The forms that madness has taken in the past are identical
to those of modern soldiers. The degree to which earlier armies and their
primitive medical corps were able to identify these symptoms as madness
has changed greatly as have the names that military physicians have assigned to them. The willingness of modern armies to tolerate such symptoms has also changed. What has not changed is that battle drives a considerable number of its participants crazy.

At least as far back as ancient Egypt, we have written accounts that
testify to the fear that men must endure in battle. In a letter written almost
3000 years ago an Egyptian combat veteran, Hori, writes to an inexperienced young officer, "You determine to go forward. . . . Shuddering seizes
you, the hair of your head stands on end, your soul lies in your hand."[3]
The importance of fear in deciding military victory cannot be overestimated. Until the nineteenth century battles were usually over fairly quickly,
commonly in less than a single day. As a rule such battles were not decided
by the amount of killing and wounding, which was almost always considerable on both sides, but by fear and panic. Usually after a short period of
engagement—often minutes or hours—one side broke and ran, leaving the
other to pursue and slaughter it. In an age of primitive weaponry with
limited range the human factor was paramount in the equation of combat
effectiveness. Thus, it is little wonder that the writers of Greece and Rome
should spend so much time on the subject in their accounts of military
operations.

That men broke and ran was a fact of military life, and it still is. But an
experienced commander even then had to have the sensitivity to recognize
what Farley Mowatt has called "the worm of fear" in his men and to take
steps to prevent their succumbing to it. In 480 B.C., Leonidas was in command of a force of Spartan soldiers whose task was to defend the pass of
Thermopylae. As an astute commander he recognized that some of his
troops had been shaken in earlier action and were likely to break completely if engaged again. Herodotus, the Greek historian, records that
Leonidas "dismissed them when he realized that they had no heart for the
fight and were unwilling to take their share of the danger."[4] Here is a
clear example of an early commander's recognition that units can become
mentally exhausted and when they do, are at risk of breaking down. Then,
as now, the only solution to the problem was to pull the men from the
line. Since World War I it has been common practice in all armies of the
West to rotate combat soldiers and units out of the line on regular sched-
ules to prevent them from collapsing and becoming psychiatric casualties.

Every modern commander is educated in military schools to recognize the signs that a unit is near its mental limits and to understand that from such men nothing further can be reasonably asked. It is a stark reality of war that men have limits of psychological endurance.

If fear has been a constant companion in war, so has madness. Even a cursory reading of the accounts of battles over the ages provides numerous examples of men manifesting various forms of psychiatric and emotional symptoms brought on by the fear and stress of war. Today we recognize such symptoms for what they are and call them "combat reactions." Their occurrence was as well known to soldiers of earlier times as to the modern soldier although their dynamics were not understood. History illustrates how remarkably consistent the occurrence of battle reactions has been.

Herodotus records that as the battle for the pass of Thermopylae was about to begin, two soldiers of the hand-picked elite Spartan unit of 300 reported to the surgeon and claimed that they were suffering from an "acute inflammation of the eyes." That two soldiers should acquire the same ailment at the precise point when the fighting was about to start is, to say the least, suspicious. The soldiers asked for permission to retire to the rear. When the battle began, one of the Spartan soldiers, Aristodemus, "finding his heart failed him," remained safely in the rear and did not join the fight although the other soldier did. After the battle, the Spartans gave Aristodemus the name "the trembler" for his refusal to fight, and Aristodemus "found himself in such disgrace that he hanged himself."[5] Studies of soldiers in World War I and II demonstrate clearly that they often suffered psychosomatically induced ailments prior to an engagement and often used them as an excuse to avoid combat. Indeed, one of the major tasks of today's unit psychiatrist is to distinguish such stress-induced ailments from genuine ones. It is also evident from prior studies that some soldiers who succeed in evading combat through a contrived illness—although they may not always consciously know that it is contrived—sometimes have great difficulty coming to grips with their own emotions. This problem seems to be greatest when their unit meets disaster as was the case of the Spartans at Thermopylae. Like Aristodemus, soldiers with similar experiences often suffer severe depression, psychosis, and, all too often, suicide. There is nothing in the story of Aristodemus that would be unfamiliar to a psychiatrist who dealt with psychiatric casualties in World War II or Vietnam.

In another instance, Plutarch notes that in the Roman siege of Syracuse in 211 B.C. in which Archimedes, the great Greek inventor and mathematician, was killed, a number of the soldiers defending the city "were stricken dumb with terror."[6] If we may take Plutarch literally, he is surely recording an example of the psychiatric condition called surdomutism, an inability to speak induced by great fear. Russian psychiatrists stationed at the front in the Russo-Japanese War of 1905 were the first to make a clinical diagnosis of this condition as resulting directly from the trauma of battle stress. Russians in World War I and II saw countless cases of the same condition, and they developed the Kaufmann method of strong electrical shock to deal with it. Surdomutism was diagnosed by American, British, and French doctors in World War I, and it occurred in World War II as well although apparently somewhat less frequently. Today it is recognized as a common, though serious, conversion reaction to the stress of battle.

Roman military medicine made its institutional appearance during the Punic Wars (264–146 B.C.). The removal of the wounded and shocked from the battle to hospitals in cities and ports far to the rear was difficult. The trip to the hospitals was often long and rugged, and many of the wounded died before they reached medical help. Then, as now, medical evacuation to the rear was likely to make more difficult the task of returning the slightly wounded soldier to his unit, as the slightly wounded were often mistakenly evacuated as well. The Romans established a series of military hospitals staffed by Greek physicians along the roads leading to the battle, thus inventing a major principle of modern military medicine, the principle of proximity of treatment. Evacuation of the wounded was accomplished on a modern basis with the most severely wounded given the last priority of movement while the less severe cases were treated as close to the battle as possible. The principle of Roman military medicine was the same as that which guides modern military medicine and psychiatry: to return as many men as quickly as possible to the battle. Over time, the Romans established a network of military hospitals that extended throughout the empire.

One result of this institutionalized permanent military medical system was the compiling of excellent records of wounds suffered by Roman soldiers. Among these records, as expected, there are examples of conditions brought on by combat stress. Among the most interesting of these are the records dealing with self-inflicted wounds. Polibius, the Roman military historian, records that as early as 168 B.C. the Romans were familiar with soldiers who deliberately injured themselves in order to avoid battle. The problem must have reached some importance because this highly bureaucratized permanent standing army published in its standing regulations the punishment for self-inflicted wounds: the punishment was death.[7] The phenomenon of self-inflicted wounds appears again and again throughout military history, including the Vietnam War. In one instance, a medic in Vietnam actually anesthetized the limbs of soldiers who planned to shoot themselves to obtain an honorable discharge for a war-related injury. In World War II a ring of sergeants at embarkation ports were arrested for selling instructions to new recruits on how to escape being shipped out. One of the recommended ways was "accidentally" to shoot one's self in the foot. Psychiatrists now recognize that many of the "accidents" involving soldiers about to go to war are in reality secondary reactions to fear and stress. Another category of "accidents" occurs when the soldier is so emotionally fatigued that he can no longer process mental information. The American army regards high incidence of trench-foot and frostbite in a unit as clear indication of emotional stress approaching breakdown. Interestingly, frostbite almost always occurs on the hand that the soldier uses to pull the trigger. Whether or not the Romans were familiar with such a range of stress reactions is unclear. That they had to deal with the problem of self-inflicted wounds is beyond dispute.

An interesting account of an acute fear reaction which produced debilitating symptoms that made further military action impossible is found in the Anglo-Saxon Chronicles, which recount a battle in 1003 between English and Danish armies. The English commander, Aelfric, leading his men toward the enemy, suddenly became violently ill and began to vomit. He was so sick that he couldn't continue, and the Danes easily routed their adversaries. It may be that Aelfric had suffered this condition in similar circumstances before, for the Chronicles note that "he was up to his old tricks" and that Aelfric "once again betrayed the people whom he should have led."[8] That fear in or before battle can cause symptomatic reactions that can debilitate a soldier is clear from studies during and since World War II. In a study of American soldiers assigned to a combat division in France in 1944, over half admitted that they became sick to their stomachs, felt faint, lost control of their bowels (thus the old expression "scared shitless"), or broke out in cold sweats during battle. About a third reported that these symptoms had a significant effect on their ability to do their duty.[9] Almost all of us has had some direct experience with this feeling of illness induced by fear. Many athletes vomit before a game. Anyone who has felt weakness in the knees from witnessing the carnage of an auto accident or the paralyzing adrenalin rush that results from a near miss on the highway understands what Aelfric felt.

In 1346 on the field of Crécy a unit of Genoese bowmen simply came apart under stress. They had marched all day and were physically worn out. Their commander told the king that "they were not in a fit condition to do any great things that day in battle."[10] Despite this warning, they were committed to action first. They engaged in a small skirmishing action and when they were subject to counterfire from the enemy, they completely collapsed, and "some of them cut the strings of their crossbows" (no doubt the medieval equivalent of the jammed rifle of later years), "others flung them on the ground, and all turned about and retreated."[11] Modern experience has clearly taught that fatigued troops—hungry, thirsty, tired—will very readily break under even moderate stress. It has also taught us that there are objective limits to human endurance that cannot be exceeded; the only treatment is rest and relief from the line.

One interesting aspect of combat reaction symptoms is the "million-dollar wound," or "blighty," a term apparently coined in World War I but reflecting a reality that is much older. Soldiers exposed to battle almost all wish to escape the horror (about 2 percent seem to enjoy it). But a number of myths that function to protect the ego demand that some "legitimate" way be found to gain relief. A legitimate escape is one that will not be seen by one's peers, family, or friends as cowardice. The "million-dollar wound" is a physical injury that is not severe enough to be life-threatening or even physically debilitating at the time it is inflicted, but provides an adequate excuse to gain relief from the battlefield. Once wounded, however slightly, most combat soldiers feel that they have done their share and have honorably earned the right to be removed from the fight. In the siege of Constantinople in 1453 at least one soldier understood the usefulness of such a wound.

Captain John Justiniani commanded a unit in defense of a section of the city wall. From all accounts he and his unit had fought well throughout the day. Near day's end Justiniani was slightly wounded in the hand by an arrow. He immediately left his post to seek a surgeon. The emperor Palaeologus, who was acting as commander-in-chief of the defense of the city, saw Justiniani leave his post and ran to intercept him on his way to the rear. The emperor entreated him not to retire for "the danger is pressing." Justiniani, trembling with fear, refused to be stopped and continued his flight to the rear even though his wound was minor and was not disabling.[12] As is often the case in modern war, men will fight well until given an excuse by circumstance—a slight wound is a perfect excuse—to leave the fight. During Custer's last battle, for example, soldiers under Maj. Marcus Reno's command, surrounded and under attack for two days, left their defensive positions for the hospital area with minor injuries even though the hospital area offered no cover and was exposed continuously to hostile fire and was no safer—and perhaps considerably less so—than positions at the perimeter of the battle.

Almost anyone who has served a stint in military service in almost any army (and, no doubt, at almost any time in history) has received what is known as a "Dear John" letter. Especially when men are at war a soldier who learns that he has lost his girlfriend or wife to another man—one who is safe in the rear area—will become despondent and succumb to a stress-related illness. Some men deliberately place themselves at risk to the point of overtly courting death. Such men are really committing suicide. Lord Falkland seems to have been just such a case at the Battle of Newbury in November 1643. As a chronicler of the battle notes, Falkland "being there, and having nothing to do decided to charge; as the two armies were engaging, rode like a madman (as he was) between them, and was shot. . . . Some would needs have the reason of this mad action of throwing away his life. It was the grief of the death of Mrs. Moray . . . who was his mistress and whom he loved above all creatures."[13] Farley Mowat, in his account of his own battle experiences in Italy in World War II, recounts the story of a soldier in his unit who received a "Dear John" letter and then squandered his life in similar fashion. Mowat also recounts that his father had told him the same thing happened to men in his unit in World War I.[14] While many things will cause despondency among men in war, studies of psychiatric casualties in the Vietnam War indicate that a "Dear John" letter was often a major element in precipitating nostaligia-related emotional problems.

The stress of war can make itself felt in a number of physical ways. Lord de Ros recorded an interesting incident of battle stress symptoms involving the czar of Russia, Peter the Great. At the sack of the city of Narva in 1704 Peter's officers apparently lost control of their men, and they began a bloody slaughter of the civilians of the town. Although Peter ordered the slaughter stopped, the troops were in such a frenzy that it continued unabated. Finally, in an act of desperation, the czar waded into the fray with sword drawn to cut down his own soldiers. He came upon an officer who had literally gone beserk in the slaughter and who, "in the heat of the carnage, was rendered deaf" to his commander's order to stop.[15] Peter killed him with his sword. Examples of men going beserk under fire—a term derived from the drug-induced madness that overtook Viking troops in their battles of the ninth and tenth centuries—are too numerous in modern times to require documentation. This state of extreme physical and psychological excitement made the Viking soldiers capable of acts of great "courage," which often got them killed.

Deafness of soldiers in modern wars has been recognized, at least since the end of World War I, as due far more often to hysterical conversion reactions caused by emotional turbulence than to physiological damage. During World War I and before that in the American Civil War and the Franco-Prussian War of 1870, deafness on the part of combat soldiers had been explained primarily as a function of concussion and contusion to the brain or eardrums caused by artillery fire. It was this belief which led to the use of the term "shell shock" to explain a number of battle reactions, which we now know to be due to emotional turbulence. During World War I hundreds of autopsies were performed on soldiers who had become deaf and who later died. Accompanying damage to brain or eardrums was not usually found, a fact that did much to reverse the then current physiological explanations for conversion reactions such as deafness, paralysis, blindness, and surdomutism. Today, such incidents among combat soldiers are usually treated as emotional and not physical problems.

A particularly interesting reaction to battle stress is the way soldiers react to the increased fear of being killed as a consequence of the perceived incompetence of their superiors, usually officers and noncommissioned officers (NCOs). Studies by the Israeli Defense Force have found that among the most important elements for warding off emotional breakdown in bat-

tle—and increasing the battlefield performance of the individual soldier—
is the degree to which soldiers trust their officers and believe that they will
not squander their men foolishly.[16]

When forced to serve under officers they believe to be incompetent and
therefore dangerous, soldiers throughout history have resorted to the simple yet effective device of killing them. Assassination involving one of
Marlborough's officers at the Battle of Gross Hepach in 1704 is a typical
example. As one eyewitness recorded the event, an officer, fearing he might
be shot by his own men once the battle began, assembled his men and told
them that if he survived the day, he would mend his ways. After the battle,
the officer again called his men together "to call for a cheer." As he took
off his hat, he was struck between the eyes with a bullet and "there was
decided suspicion that the bullet was no accident."[17]

While there are documented cases of officers being assassinated by their
men in World War I, World War II, and Korea, in the Vietnam War the
assassination of officers and sergeants reached major proportions. At least
1,013 documented cases of killing or attempted killing of superiors by
fearful troops were reported.[18] In general, the reasons behind these assas-
sinations were the fear of officers and NCOs whom the troops perceived
to be incompetent or too aggressive, or whom they did not trust. Lack of
trust was a direct result of an individual system of troop replacement,
which made it impossible for whole units to serve together long enough to
trust one another. The fact that officers served combat tours of six months
while their troops were required to serve "in the bush" for twelve months
no doubt also contributed. In any case, killing one's officers as a way of
dealing with a terrible fear of what he will cause to be done to you once
the shooting starts has a long, if not so noble, history.

During the British siege of Gibraltar in 1727 a soldier who was part of
the defense of the city recounted several incidents in his diary that are
textbook examples of reactions to combat stress. The soldier records a
disciplinary action against another soldier on April 12. The diarist recalls
that the soldier was whipped for the fifth time. He had refused to work,
fight in defense of the city, or eat and drink.[19] Such symptoms clearly
define what later became known as "nostalgia," a psychiatric reaction to
stress and fatigue that was reported thousands of times during the American Civil War, World War I, and World War II. During the Vietnam War,
American soldiers suffered a comparatively high rate of psychiatric casualties, many of them diagnosed as involving "nostalgia-like" symptoms. In
Vietnam, the soldier's emotional turbulence was reflected in a range of
symptoms that included alcohol and drug abuse, temporary desertion to a
local bar or brothel, and high rates of venereal disease—all considered by
military psychiatrists as secondary symptoms of the stress induced by combat or military life. In extreme cases the soldier's condition can degenerate
further to the point where he suffers extreme physical fatigue all the time

regardless of how much rest he has had. This is often accompanied by an inability to understand and process even the simplest instructions.

In another entry the same diarist, describing the same battle, notes that a soldier "withdrew a bit from the fighting line" and inflicted a wound upon himself with his rifle in order to avoid having to continue fighting—an example of the same condition addressed by the Romans and seen by the American army in Vietnam. Finally, another entry records the case of a soldier who quite deliberately put down his rifle, climbed to the belfrey of a church steeple, and jumped off, committing suicide.[20] Such incidents are well-known reactions to combat stress, and they occurred while the city was under siege and great stress was being imposed upon the defenders. These same symptoms appear again and again in modern wars.

Nostalgia is a cluster of symptoms marked by excessive physical fatigue, an inability to concentrate, an unwillingness to eat or drink leading at times to anorexia, a feeling of isolation and total frustration leading to a general inability to function in a military environment. It was first diagnosed and described by military physicians among Swiss soldiers in 1678.[21] It was also diagnosed among German troops of the same period by German doctors who called the condition *Heimweh* or homesickness. It was thought that the symptoms resulted from the soldier's longing to return home, a very accurate observation confirmed by more modern military psychiatry. French military doctors termed the same symptoms *maladie du pays,* and the Spanish, who noted an outbreak among their soldiers, called it *estar roto*—literally, "to be broken." Even earlier examples of nostalgia appeared among the soldiers of the Spanish Army of Flanders during the Thirty Years War. There exists a report from 1643 of soldiers in the Spanish army being discharged for the same illness. Military physicians recognized even then that the source of the symptoms was emotional and not physical, noting that "imagination alone can cause all this."[22] During the Civil War autopsies performed on nostalgia patients who died confirmed that nostalgia producing emotional turbulence was quite capable of producing physiological symptoms of disease. Tragically, nostalgia in itself was often fatal, especially if the soldier had his mental resistance weakened by a wound. When it did not kill, it often drove the soldier to insanity. The recognized cure, then and now, was simply to relieve the soldier from the fighting and send him home on furlough.

Nostalgia was recognized as a mental condition afflicting soldiers during the eighteenth century among the armies of France, Italy, Germany, and Austria, all of which recorded numerous incidents of the problem. In one instance reported in 1799, a unit of Scottish Highland troops succumbed to the condition almost to a man. All that was needed to trigger the onset of nostalgia, the report notes, was for the Highlanders to hear the sound of the bagpipes. Nostalgia was reported among Napoleon's troops at Waterloo and again during accounts of the French retreat from Moscow, where the diary of an officer notes numerous incidents of soldiers perishing from the illness as well as being killed because they were unable to defend themselves. In the first year of the American Civil War, 5,213 cases of nostalgia were diagnosed, or 2.34 cases per thousand.[23] By the end of the war, almost 10,000 cases had been diagnosed among Northern soldiers alone. Nostalgia has remained a constant affliction of soldiers and appeared repeatedly in World Wars I and II. One study of psychiatric casualties during the Vietnam War found that the major category of war-related neurosis that emerged in that war was probably nostalgia and its accompanying symptoms.[24]

Sometimes soldiers develop combat reactions very quickly—indeed, within minutes or even seconds. This type of reaction is called *acute battle shock*, since the soldier develops it without having had long periods of exposure to combat that serve to wear down his emotional resistance and invite reaction symptoms. A classic case of acute battle shock leading to temporary paralysis occurred at the Battle of Eylau in 1807. A French officer leading his men in an attack against the Russians had a near miss when a Russian cannonball ripped by, knocking off his shako but not hitting his head. Although the officer was not hit and suffered no head wounds, "I seemed to be blotted out of existence, but I did not fall from my horse. Nevertheless, I could still hear and see, and I preserved all my intellectual faculties, although my limbs were paralyzed to such an extent that I could not move a single finger."[25] While the officer remained paralyzed atop his horse, his unit clashed with the enemy trapping the officer in the middle of the fight. Being the only mounted man in the middle of an infantry engagement must have been frightening. The officer was unable to move and lacked even the ability "to press my legs so as to make the animal I rode understand my wish."[26] Eventually in what must have seemed like hours the battle moved elsewhere and the officer's horse calmly walked out of danger taking its paralyzed passenger to safety. The officer "came to his senses" somewhat later, and his paralysis abated.

Similar cases of acute hysterical paralysis were common on all sides in World War I, often accompanied by hysterical stupor. In some incidents the paralysis was localized in the arm, most frequently the arm needed to operate the firing bolt of the soldier's rifle. The frequency of contractive paralysis brought on by hysteria was relatively high, and French military physicians in World War I invented the technique of *torporlage*—administering electric current to the paralyzed limb—to treat it. German and Russian military physicians used a similar technique for treating the same condition. Once the soldier was removed from danger and given food and a few days' rest, the paralysis usually cured itself. This is exactly what appears to have happened to the French officer, since he recorded the events described in his diary.

Suicide is yet another reaction sometimes provoked by the stress of war, and it, too, appears quite often in military records of earlier battles. As the remnants of the French Grand Army fought their way out of Russia in 1812, an incident was recorded that had all the characteristics of a case of suicide resulting from emotional reaction to the stress of battle. A French officer in charge of an infantry battalion was hit in the thigh by a Russian cannonball that had ricocheted off the defensive pallisade and broke his leg. An eyewitness recorded in his diary that the officer "fell, and without the least hesitation, finding that his wound was mortal, he cooly drew his pistols and blew out his brains before his troops. Terrified at this act of despair, his soldiers were completely scared. All of them at once threw down their arms and fled in disorder."[27]

That soldiers can be provoked to suicide either by the loneliness of military life or by the fear and stress of battle is something that most combat officers knew well. Suicide in the American army is most common among new recruits who have difficulty adjusting to the separation that military life necessarily imposes. In the Soviet army the rigor of military life seems to have made suicide a major problem for Soviet commanders. In a recent study based on interviews with Soviet troops, 49.6 percent of the soldiers said that "while they were in the military someone in their unit committed suicide"; 53.1 percent reported that someone in their unit had attempted to commit suicide, and 84.1 percent reported that they had "heard stories about people committing suicide in other units."[28]

Among soldiers stationed on the American frontier in the 1860s suicide was almost epidemic. In 1867 the suicide rate among U.S. Army recruits posted to the western frontier was almost 6 percent, three times higher than the rate for British army recruits stationed in similar circumstances.[29] Six of every hundred new recruits could be expected to destroy themselves by their own hand before their tour of duty was over. Suicide under fire, especially when things look desperate, occurs with a startling frequency. It happened among Custer's men at the Battle of the Little Big Horn. In one well-documented case a group of Indians chased a fleeing soldier on horseback for nearly six miles. At the end of the chase the frightened soldier glanced back at the one remaining Indian warrior still giving chase, drew his pistol and shot himself in the head.[30] In an even more macabre incident, Indian warriors who took part in the attack against Custer and his men told journalists that as the Indians began to overrun a group of soldiers who had taken cover behind their dead horses on a hillock, the soldiers began to shoot themselves and even each other. The Indians were so amazed at this self-destructive behavior that they broke off the attack and simply watched as the men killed themselves.[31]

During the Civil War there were no psychiatrists posted to the battlefront. Such a development would not come in the West until 1905 when the Russians began the practice. However, military physicians diagnosed cases of functional disability from fear of battle and the stress of military life. They diagnosed a range of illnesses that are now known to be caused by emotional turbulence. These included "exhausted hearts," paralysis, severe palpitations (called "soldier's heart" at the time), war tremors, self-inflicted wounds, and nostalgia.[32] The only effective treatment for these disorders seemed to be relief from the line, rest, and sometimes a furlough for the soldier. Interestingly, soldiers on normal home leave often collapsed with emotional illness at home even when they had shown no symptoms of mental debilitation before they left the fighting. Similar incidents were found among Israeli soldiers who had returned home for a brief respite from the 1983 war in Lebanon between Israel and the Palestine Liberation Organization (PLO). In a great many cases, the brief "rest cure" prescribed by Civil War doctors resulted in the abatement of symptoms.

Union Army doctors diagnosed some severe conditions as "insanity"—a condition that today is called psychosis—and insanity accounted for 6 percent of the medical discharges granted by the Union Army.[33] These physicians also dealt with a number of cases that they diagnosed as "feigned insanity," a condition where emotional turbulence produced severe physiological symptoms but for which a physiological cause could not be found. These conditions included lameness, blindness, deafness, and lower back pain.[34] Today, psychiatrists diagnose such illnesses as conversion reactions. Emotional stress builds up in the soldier, and if no permissible emotional outlet is allowed, the soldier will "convert" his symptoms into physiological conditions. During World War II Soviet military psychiatrists refused to recognize debilitations resulting from purely emotional states, instead enforcing a strict rule that relief from battle was to be granted only to soldiers who had clearly defined physiological debilitations. Consequently, Soviet soldiers "converted" their emotional stress into "legitimate" physical ailments in order to gain relief from the stress of war. It seems clear that the Soviet army suffered disproportionately higher rates of conversion reactions in World War II than any other combat army.[35]

Even in peacetime minor conversion symptoms appear among troops under or about to endure stress. Medical doctors assigned to paratroop units, for example, routinely have to deal with psychosomatically induced complaints of lower back pain even in experienced paratroopers whenever the unit is scheduled to make a practice jump.

It seems, then, that in any war fear and psychiatric debilitation are constant companions. The experience of battle is one of the most threatening, stressful, and horrifying experiences that man is expected to endure. Moreover, even in relatively small engagements, large numbers of men are usually involved. Accordingly, it is very likely that in any given battle a number of instances of combat reaction will be repeated many times over even if they do not come to the attention of military doctors. Severe emotional response to battle is neither a rare nor an isolated event. Indeed, it is becoming so common that the ability of armies to sustain their manpower levels in future wars is being brought into serious question. Modern war may simply have become too stressful by its very nature for the soldier to tolerate for very long.

A CASE STUDY IN COMBAT PSYCHIATRY

In those battles for which adequate eyewitness accounts are available, even small ones, the full range of psychiatric responses to stress emerges clearly. An excellent example is the Battle of Little Big Horn in which George Armstrong Custer met defeat at the hands of Sioux and Cheyenne warriors.

As Custer was riding to his death against the main body of Sioux, a unit of about 300 men under the command of Maj. Marcus Reno was to act as a blocking force for the Custer attack. Reno's unit was trapped and forced to withdraw to a small bluff where he and his men fought a running defensive battle with the Indians for two days and a night. In this engagement Reno's men suffered almost every major symptom of combat reaction now known to military psychiatry. Reno himself became a psychiatric casualty when he succumbed to acute battle shock syndrome.

In the midst of the battle of Reno called his Indian scout, Yellow Knife, to his position in a clump of sagebrush. As bullets and arrows whistled overhead, Reno drew very near Yellow Knife's head probably to yell instructions in his ear. At this very instant Yellow Knife was struck squarely in the face by a bullet which sent his blood, flesh, and brains spattering all over Reno. Reno immediately went into shock. He began to foam at the mouth while his eyes rolled wildly in his head.[36] He was incapable of continuing his command or uttering any sounds that made sense. How long he remained in this condition is uncertain, but the diaries of witnesses report that he may have been out of action for at least a day.

Some of Reno's men were hysterically paralyzed with fear and were unable to function even to defend themselves. A small group of soldiers offered no resistance, so that the Indians thought them cowards and refused to kill them. Instead, they left these men to the young boys who dragged the soldiers away from each other and killed them without any resistance. In one case, a soldier was so terrified that the Indians refused to kill him, being content to strike him with pony whips. Meanwhile, Maj. Myles Moylan broke down completely and was unable to continue in command. The cavalry rescue force found him "blubbering like a whipped urchin, tears coursing down his cheeks."[37]

A very common reaction to the stress of battle and its anticipation is uncontrollable shaking, which can become so severe that men cannot fire their weapons, a condition called *war tremors*. A number of soldiers recorded in their diaries that some of Reno's men suffered from such uncontrollable shaking that they could neither aim nor fire their weapons. In one

case a soldier began shaking so violently that he eventually went into convulsions. His comrades had to bind him hand and foot to prevent him
from injuring himself. In yet another instance a soldier suffered such fear
that he lay in his rifle pit "crying like a child" unable to contribute to the
fighting. In probably the most macabre instance of paralyzing fear, one
soldier just sat on the ground continually rubbing his head with both hands
in abject confusion. Three Indians ran up to him, stretched him full length
on his back and decapitated him.[38] The poor soldier was unable to offer
any resistance to his fate.

Soldiers' fears often increase during night when their senses play tricks
on them. In Reno's command, some men began to hallucinate. One soldier
records, "Private James Pym believed he saw renegade whites circling the
rifle pits and shouting insults, challenging the troopers to come out. He
thought these renegades carried the little swallowtail flags called guidons,
and when Reno's bugler blew calls they would be exactly repeated. Other
men saw columns of soldiers approaching and distinctly heard the calls of
officers. Guns were fired to guide these rescuers and a trumpeter blew
'Stable Call.' "[39] Any soldier who has ever experienced night combat is
well aware of the things one "sees" in the shadows. In the case of Reno's
men, so many men "saw" the same thing that there is little doubt that
many were suffering combat reactions due to emotional tumult.

One soldier was suffering from acute neurasthenia and was lying face
down on the ground. He was so still that the other soldiers thought for
quite a while that he was dead. Two other soldiers maneuvering nearby
came upon him, saw that he was alive, and told him to move. Although
the soldier was conscious and looked right at them, he did not move. One
of the soldiers kicked him and he struggled to his feet insisting that he was
sick. Then "the man looked frightened to death. He walked a few steps
and fell to the ground heedless of the heat of the sun or anything else going
on around him."[40] Russian doctors in 1905 and again in World War I
encountered the same condition many times. The soldiers had entered an
asthenic fugue state approaching stupor caused by emotional exhaustion
generated by fear.

During the two-day siege of Reno's command some soldiers pretended
to be ill or wounded in order to get out of the fighting. As a practical
matter this was pointless, since the medical station was in the middle of
the battle area and offered neither cover nor concealment from enemy fire.
One soldier, Pvt. Billy Blake, pretended to be hurt, and another claimed to
be wounded and reported to the hospital area. A quick examination showed
only a slight burn on the stomach. The other wounded men laughed at
him and he was thrown out of the tent.[41] Soviet military doctors were
acutely aware of this tendency of soldiers under stress to develop physical
complaints and to use them to gain relief from battle. In World War II
common Soviet medical practice was to keep medical facilities at a dis-

tance from the troops to make it difficult for them to report with minor complaints. Even today Soviet doctors are instructed that they should not get too near the troops for fear that they will iatrogenically "cause" these complaints because access to medical relief would be so readily available.

About the only thing that did not happen to Reno's men in the short two-day battle was desertion, surely because there was no place to go. But desertion, which is now commonly recognized as a secondary reaction to emotional stress, distinct from the flight or panic response, was endemic among soldiers on the American frontier. Between October 1866 and October 1867 more than 500 soldiers deserted from the Seventh Cavalry (Custer's unit) alone; the desertion rate for the Seventh Cavalry reached 52 percent.[42] Despite severe punishments including flogging, jail, branding, and tattooing—to say nothing of the difficulty of reaching civilization once outside the gates of the army post—in 1867 no less than 25 percent of the entire American frontier army deserted. Military discipline, though harsh, was also ineffective in stopping antisocial behavior among soldiers. In 1867 there were 13,000 recorded court martials in a single year or about one for every two men in the frontier army.[43]

CONCLUSION

What this analysis suggests is that men have known fear for at least as long as they have known war. The often stated belief that men in the past were more willing to accept their own deaths in the service of one thing or another is little more than a naive act of faith for which there is precious little evidence. It also seems true that men have always had difficulty dealing with the nearness of death as it emerges full-face in battle. It seems clear that in a great many instances fear has reached such proportions that it has quite literally driven soldiers mad and debilitated them to the point where they could no longer go on. Moreover, as the example of Reno's men at Little Big Horn suggests, in any given battle men at war have manifested the full range of psychiatric reactions to fear. Only the historical naïveté of modern men, who often seem terribly ignorant of past human experiences, leads them to conclude that only they have known fear in war. Perhaps we need such myths to sustain the belief that somehow we are different from those who have gone before. If so, one must ignore a lot of historical reality if the myth is to be sustained.

On the other hand the fact that psychiatric casualties should appear so often throughout the ages should not come as a surprise. Man has changed little physically or psychologically in the 5000 years of recorded history. The awareness of madness in one form or another is well documented in ancient texts. Psychiatry as a way of dealing with madness has been with us in one form or another since very ancient times. What is perhaps most interesting is that the fear of death and maiming as manifested in psychiatric reactions to battle stress are remarkably consistent. One would have thought that the cultural conditioning of the soldier received in countless and vastly different societies would have changed the range of symptoms. It is clear, for example, from studies of psychiatric casualties in World War I that soldiers did in fact tend to manifest those psychiatric symptoms that had been defined by military medical authorities as "legitimate." Military psychiatry of the day defined "legitimate" psychiatric symptoms for Russian soldiers in purely physical terms. A soldier would not be allowed out of the fight until he had suffered some physical damage. If emotional causes were suspected, the Russians insisted that no soldier be relieved unless the emotional problem could be traced to some damaged physiology of the brain or central nervous system. As a result, Russian psychiatric casualties tended to manifest their emotional stress in precisely physical terms—paralysis, blindness, surdomutism, and others—at rates far greater than those in other armies.

While it is accurate to say that in any battle a range of psychiatric symptoms will appear, it is impossible to reconstruct the rates at which such symptoms appeared in the past. No one began keeping records on psychiatric casualties with any degree of precision until the Russo-Japanese War of 1905. Moreover, military psychiatry was not considered a legitimate field of study until World War I. Even psychiatry in general remained under the strong influence of neurology—an approach that attributed aberrant behavior to damaged physiology—until World War II when Freudian approaches for explaining emotional problems were first taken seriously by the American army. In the past, ignorance of trauma-producing events led genuine psychiatric problems to be regarded as cowardice or lack of character. In one instance, for example, a soldier who tried to commit suicide by leaping from a house roof broke his back. The attempt to kill himself was defined as cowardice, and he was hanged, broken back and all.

It seems likely that the rates of psychiatric debilitation among combatants must have been considerable if not always obvious. We know today, for example, that many more men suffer severe emotional reactions than ever reach the medical stations, especially if their problems result in only partial debilitation. In World War II studies of American soldiers engaged in combat revealed that more than three quarters of them never fired their rifles at the enemy when they were attacking or defending themselves. There are numerous examples from the Civil War of soldiers acting in a similar manner. In earlier battles when masses of men fought each other, usually only the front rank had to engage while those in the rear could safely do nothing. In engagements the size of Waterloo or Sedan, the opportunity for a soldier not to fire or to refuse to press the attack by merely falling down and remaining in the mud were too obvious for shaken men under fire to ignore. While there is no hard historical evidence to prove the point decisively, it seems nevertheless likely that armies of the past often lost at least some degree of combat power to the psychiatric reactions of emotionally disturbed soldiers.

It is important to understand the historical record of combat breakdown for the simple reason that while the technology of war may have changed considerably over the centuries, the raw material of war—the men who must fight it—has changed little if at all. This suggests that the technology of war, though important, is not the decisive factor in victory or defeat. As Xenophon made clear 3000 years ago, the "soul" of the soldier is still most important. Technology, no matter how sophisticated or deadly, will mean nothing if men cannot withstand the storm of battle.

Modern armies with their large staffs of technical experts tend all too readily to forget this lesson and to busy themselves with the details of "orchestrating" or "servicing" the battlefield through the employment of sophisticated technologies. They appear secure in the faith, historically quite unfounded, that soldiers can be made to do what the technology requires of them. Such military managers believe that today's soldier is somehow different from those who took the field in the past. What the lessons of the past ought to teach is that men break down in battle, technology not withstanding. Man, not his machines, sets the ultimate limits on battle performance. At the same time, however, there is no doubt that the technology of war has become so destructive that it has raised the question of whether any soldier except the already insane can endure the battlefields of the future. What evidence we have suggests that the limits of human endurance have already been reached.

NOTES

1. Lawrence Ingraham and Frederick Manning, "Psychiatric Battle Casualties: The Missing Column in the War Without Replacements," *Military Review* (August 1980), p. 21. The same authors make the same argument in "American Military Psychiatry," in Richard A. Gabriel, ed., *Military Psychiatry: A Comparative Perspective* (Westport, Conn.: Greenwood Press, 1986), Chap. 2.

2. Xenophon, *Anabasis*, Book III, Chapter 1, p. 42.

3. Gwynne Dyer, *War* (New York: Crown Publishers, 1985), p. 22.

4. Max Hastings, *Military Anecdotes* (New York: Oxford University Press, 1985), p. 18.

5. Ibid., pp. 20–21.

6. Ibid., p. 38.

7. Peter Connolly, *Greece and Rome at War* (Englewood Cliffs, N.J.: Prentice-Hall, 1981), pp. 139–140.

8. Hastings, *Military Anecdotes*, p. 64.

9. Dyer, *War*, p. 142.

10. Hastings, *Military Anecdotes*, p. 75.

11. Ibid.

12. Ibid., p. 98.

13. Ibid., p. 123.

14. Farley Mowatt, *And No Birds Sang* (Toronto: Bantam Books, 1979), p. 154.

15. Hastings, *Military Anecdotes,* p. 144.

16. Reuven Gal and Richard Gabriel, "Battlefield Heroism in the Israeli Defense Force," *International Social Science Review* (Autumn 1982), pp. 232–235.

17. Hastings, *Military Anecdotes,* p. 145.

18. Richard Gabriel and Paul Savage, *Crisis in Command* (New York: Hill and Wang, 1978), p. 182 (Table 3).

19. Hastings, *Military Anecdotes,* pp. 151–152.

20. Ibid.

21. George Rosen, "Nostalgia: A Forgotten Psychological Disorder," *Psychological Medicine,* Vol. 5 (1975), pp. 340–341.

22. Ibid., p. 342.

23. Albert Deutsche, "Military Psychiatry in the Civil War," *100 Years of American Psychiatry* (New York: Columbia University Press, 1944), p. 377.

24. Franklin Jones, interview with author, Walter Reed Army Institute, summer 1986.

25. Hastings, *Military Anecdotes,* p. 198.

26. Ibid.

27. Ibid., p. 220.

28. Richard Gabriel, *The Mind of the Soviet Fighting Man* (Wesport, Conn.: Greenwood Press, 1984), pp. 43–44.

29. Evan S. Connell, *Custer: Son of the Morning Star* (New York: Harper & Row, 1984), p. 155.

30. Ibid., p. 313.

31. Ibid., p. 419.

32. Deutsche, "Military Psychiatry," pp. 370–372.

33. Ibid., p. 377.

34. Ibid., p. 372.

35. Gabriel, *Soviet Military Psychiatry,* Chap. 4.

36. Connell, *Custer,* pp. 9–12.

37. Ibid., p. 30.

38. Ibid., p. 419.

39. Ibid., p. 55.

40. Ibid., p. 61.

41. Ibid.

42. Ibid., pp. 149–150.

43. Ibid., p. 173.

2

The Limits of Human Endurance

Although men have suffered psychiatric breakdown in war for centuries, military establishments have not been overly concerned with this subject. For much of military history psychiatric breakdown in war has been conveniently dismissed as isolated acts of cowards or the weak, a view that was generally held in the U.S. military through World War II. Nor has the general public been concerned or familiar with the subject. Most people who have not seen combat are conditioned by their perception of warfare in general, a view obtained mostly through the media and in wartime through a carefully controlled press. In World War I pictures and stories about troops at the front were carefully limited to reporting successes. Photographs were screened, so that that the civilian population would not be upset by too graphic a view of the realities of war.[1] While all governments commonly restrict information during war, Americans in particular, because of their lack of actual experience, have received their view of war mostly through motion pictures and television shows, a view that is all too often unrealistic and romantic.

However war is portrayed for mass audiences, soldiers breaking down under the strain of battle is rarely, if ever, shown. In those few instances that do portray a soldier in collapse, the condition comes through as rare, lasting only a minute or so, and then the soldier is brought around by a slap or some other minor treatment from an officer, sergeant, or comrade, usually accompanied by a lecture on military duty. This theme appears again and again in both American and Russian movies about World War II. The prevailing view is that soldiers who break under the strain of battle are weak or cowardly. This simplistic view is, unfortunately, often shared by military men as well.

The belief that only men who are cowards or innately weak, whose character and strength of personality dispose them to breaking down in battle, has led most military establishments for most of this century to adopt a grossly incorrect model of psychiatric breakdown. That model was based on the assumption that some men were more predisposed by their nature to break down. Thus, the model used by the U.S. military was predisposition plus stress equals psychiatric collapse.[2] This model was used for the first time in World War I when, after numerous complaints from commanders at the front about the mental quality and durability of their troops, military authorities instituted a more vigorous screening of recruits. Although the approach seemed logical, it didn't work very well when used during the last months of World War I. Despite this experience, during the interwar period (1918–1941) most military psychiatrists continued to believe that if too many soldiers were suffering mental collapse, then the answer was to select from the general populace only the strong who could be expected to endure the stress of war.

World War II saw the first large-scale systematic use of recruit screening for psychiatric disposition to mental collapse. In World War II the U.S. military examined 18 million men for military service. Of these, 5,250,000 (29 percent) were rejected as unfit for combat for physical reasons. The military rejected an additional 970,000 men for neuropsychiatric disorders and emotional problems. Thus, psychiatric exemptions accounted for 18.5 percent of the total rejections, a rate twenty times greater than that of the Soviet army, which employed no psychiatric screening.[3] The American soldiers who went to war, then, had been screened for potential psychiatric disposition to breakdown, and the "weak" were presumed to have been eliminated.

The results of this screening were disappointing. The rejection rate for recruits for World War II was almost seven times higher than for World War I. Yet, despite the attempt to eliminate the "weak" from the military manpower pool, psychiatric casualties were admitted to military hospitals at twice the World War I rate, and separations for mental and emotional reasons also showed a nearly sevenfold increase over the World War I rate. In fact, psychiatric casualties were the greatest single category of military disabilities granted by the American government in World War II.[4] Whatever else the psychiatric screening of conscripts accomplished, it had certainly not reduced the rate of psychiatric casualties on the battlefield.

Psychiatric breakdown has nothing to do with being "weak" or cowardly. It is an inevitable result of the nature of war. If one examines the extent of psychiatric collapse in America's wars in this century, no other conclusion is possible. During World War I, almost 2 million men were sent overseas to fight in Europe. Of these 116,516 died in battle; another 204,002 were wounded.[5] There were, however, 106,000 soldiers admitted to military medical facilities for psychiatric reasons, 69,394 of whom were so mentally shaken that they were evacuated and permanently lost to the fighting effort.[6] Some 36,600 represented a long-term loss to the fighting ability of the American army when they were hospitalized for periods lasting from several weeks to several months.[7] Many of those who returned to the fighting broke down again. Based on the number of soldiers who reported to medical facilities suffering from psychiatric problems but who were returned to the front almost immediately, that is, after a period of a few days, 53,000 additional soldiers were lost to the battle for a short period of time. The point is, however, that they suffered some degree of psychiatric debilitation. Again, many of these suffered relapses after they returned to the front. The data indicate that 158,994 soldiers were out of action for some period of time for purely psychiatric reasons.

Taken as a proportion of those soldiers who were killed in action, the number of psychiatric debilitations was actually 136 percent times greater than the number of dead. In fact, the chances of being put out of action by psychiatric symptoms was almost twice as great as being killed by enemy fire. Psychiatric casualties were only slightly fewer than the number of wounded. As shocking as these figures are, they do not show the true dimensions of the problem of psychiatric collapse. It must be remembered that in any combat unit, there are far more men in the rear and support areas than there are actually deployed in direct contact with the enemy. During World War I, for every soldier placed in direct contact with the enemy in an American division, there were at least eight additional soldiers in combat support roles. Accordingly, of the almost 2 million men sent to war by the American army in World War I, only about 250,000 or so saw direct combat. Of these combatants, 27.7 percent were evacuated out of the war zone because of psychiatric collapse. Another 14.6 percent were admitted to psychiatric medical facilities for periods ranging from days to months. What this suggests is that no less than 42.3 percent of the actual combat force suffered some degree of mental debilitation serious enough to merit treatment. It does not include those thousands who reported to a field medical facility for treatment and were not admitted because their symptoms were not considered serious enough.

If the evidence from World War I was insufficient to convince those still in doubt about the frequency and inevitability of psychiatric breakdown, the experience gained in World War II should certainly be more convincing. Over 1 million men—1,393,000—suffered psychiatric symptoms serious enough to debilitate them for some period. In the U.S. Army ground forces alone (not counting army air crews, marines, and navy) 504,000 men were lost permanently to the fighting effort for psychiatric reasons— enough manpower to outfit fifty combat divisions.[8] Of these, 330,000 men were lost to ground combat units in the European theater and received separations for psychiatric reasons. Another 596,000 were lost to the fighting effort for periods of weeks or months and eventually returned to the line. Still another 464,500 reported to medical facilities for treatment without being admitted and were returned to the line almost immediately.[9]

Once again these figures understate the magnitude of the problem. In

World War II the ratio of rear-area support troops to actual combatants was about twelve to one. In four years of war, no more than about 800,000 U.S. ground soldiers saw direct combat. Of these, 37.5 percent became such serious psychiatric cases that they were lost to the military effort for the duration of the war and were given discharges. Another 596,000, or about 74.0 percent, were admitted to medical facilities for psychiatric problems for periods ranging from days to months. Many were eventually returned to the combat effort. Although some casualties needed repeated treatments and thus reported or were admitted more than once, the fact is that in a statistical sense, every American soldier in the European theater was at risk of becoming a psychiatric casualty. It was not only the "weak" or the cowardly who were cracking under the strain of war.

It should be clear that while the strain of battle does not cause everyone to become a psychiatric casualty and not all men succumb as rapidly as others, combat does functionally debilitate great numbers of men who, even though they don't collapse and require treatment, are still functionally debilitated to the point where they cannot contribute to the fighting effort. The degree of functional debilitation is really much greater than the actual rate of psychiatric casualties would indicate. In World War II, interviews were conducted with more than 400 line companies who saw direct combat in both the European and Pacific theaters. All the soldiers had been in close combat. The results of that study indicate that in any given combat engagement no more than 15 percent of the soldiers ever fired their weapons at the enemy even if they were being attacked.[10] Even in elite companies with veteran soldiers and a reputation for aggressiveness, the number rarely rose to 25 percent.[11] The same findings emerged from a study of air force fighter pilots: less than 1 percent accounted for over 40 percent of enemy kills.[12] Most pilots never shot anyone down or even tried to because of fear. Fully 75 percent of experienced combat soldiers in World War II were too frightened to fire their weapons during an attack or even to defend themselves against an enemy attack. That all these men were cowards or "weak" hardly seems credible.

The Korean War produced fewer psychiatric casualties than either World War I or World War II although initially the rates of psychiatric debilitation were greater than in both world wars in the early days of the war as the front collapsed and there were few medical facilities to deal with the problem. In the first year of the war, the rate of psychiatric casualties was 250 per 1000 men or almost seven times higher than the average rate for World War II. As the war settled down, the lines stabilized, and medical psychiatric teams were dispatched to the battle zone, psychiatric casualties dropped to 70 per 1000 in 1951, 22 per 1000 in 1952, and 21 per 1000 in the first six months of 1953. The average rate was slightly lower than World War II at 32 per 1000.[13]

Once again, however, the raw data paint an even more dismal picture of psychiatric collapse in battle. Of the 1,587,040 men who served in Korea, 33,629 were killed by hostile fire and another 103,284 were wounded.[14] The number of psychiatric casualties admitted to military medical facilities for treatment was 48,002, a number greater than the total number of men killed in the war. In other words, the chances of becoming a psychiatric casualty were 145 percent greater than the chances of being killed. But of the 1,587,040 soldiers who served in the Korean war, only 198,380 saw actual combat. While only 12 percent of these combatants were killed, 24.4 percent became psychiatric casualties serious enough to require treatment for some period of time. The combatant in Korea was twice as likely to become a psychiatric casualty as to be killed by enemy fire.

The Vietnam War was, by normal standards, not an intense war. The degree of actual battle contact was low, and when contact did occur, it was relatively brief and not very intense. The number of psychiatric casualties during that ten-year war was relatively low at the beginning, increased to higher rates during the fierce fighting of the Tet Offensive of 1968, and then, paradoxically, as the intensity of battle fell off in 1970–1971, the number of psychiatric casualties rose even higher. Most of these later casualties were due to nostalgia, or what the U.S. military termed "disorders of loneliness." At the beginning of the war evacuations for psychiatric reasons reached only 6 percent of total medical evacuations. By 1971, this rate had increased to almost 50 percent.[15]

Of the 2.8 million men who saw service in Vietnam only a small proportion, as in other wars, actually faced battle with the enemy—about 280,000 men over a ten-year period. The average psychiatric casualty rate was 14 per 1000 men of the total force or 35,200 soldiers admitted to military medical facilities for psychiatric reasons. The war's lack of intensity can be seen in the fact that of the 2.8 million men deployed in-country, 45,735 men were killed by hostile enemy action or about .01 percent of the total force. However, when compared to the number of men who actually saw combat, the number of dead amount to 16 percent of the combat force while the number of psychiatric casualties reached 12.5 percent of the same force.

The Vietnam War was unique in America's military history, and the qualities that made it unique also worked to reduce battle intensity and thus the number of psychiatric casualties. These same circumstances produced another result of that war: the number of soldiers who suffered psychiatric symptoms and debilitation after the war was over and they were safely home. There are no precise data on the number of soldiers who suffered from post-traumatic stress disorders (PTSD) after the Vietnam War. Figures range from 500,000 to 1,500,000 PTSD cases, indicating that at least 18 percent and possibly as much as 54 percent of the force suffered psychiatric symptoms.[16] While there is disagreement on the exact numbers of such victims, there is widespread agreement that the Vietnam

War produced more victims of PTSD, in both relative and absolute numbers, than any other war in American history. While the chances that a soldier would become a psychiatric casualty in Vietnam were about the same as the chances of being killed in action, there is no doubt that the chances that he would eventually suffer delayed psychiatric symptoms as a direct consequence of his experiences were much greater than in any past war.

In every war in which American soldiers have fought in this century the chances of becoming a psychiatric casualty—of being debilitated for some period of time as a consequence of the stresses of military life—were greater than the chances of being killed by enemy fire. The only exception was the Vietnam War, where the chances were almost equal. If one includes those who suffered post-traumatic stress disorder, then once again more soldiers suffered psychiatric collapse than death from enemy fire. By way of comparison, it is worth pointing out that 30 percent of the casualties suffered by the Israeli Defense Force in the 1973 Yom Kippur War were psychiatric casualties. In the 1982 Lebanon invasion, not much of a war by any standard, the number of Israeli psychiatric casualties exceeded the number of dead by more than 150 percent.[17]

While the vulnerabilities of a particular people may cause their soldiers to crack more readily under the strain of combat, psychiatric collapse is due far more to the nature of modern warfare itself. In war, even those past wars that by modern standards of destruction were fairly low in intensity, the strain on the human psyche is often too much to bear. War, not man, is at fault. He has created a horror with which he cannot deal in a rational manner, and it threatens to destroy him. As a U.S. Army medical report written in World War II notes,

the key to an understanding of the psychiatric problem is the simple fact that the danger of being killed or maimed imposes a strain so great that it causes men to break down. One look at the shrunken, apathetic faces of psychiatric cases as they come stumbling into the medical station, sobbing, trembling, referring shudderingly to "them shells" and to buddies mutilated or dead is enough to convince most observers of this fact. There is no such thing as "getting used to combat." Each man "up there" knew that at any moment he may be killed, a fact kept constantly before his mind by the sight of the dead and mutilated buddies around him. Each moment of combat imposes a strain so great that men will break down in direct relation to the intensity and duration of their exposure. Thus, psychiatric casualties are as inevitable as gunshot and shrapnel wounds in warfare.[18]

There is, then, no evidence to support the commonly held view among the civilian populace, fostered by movies and television programs, that only the weak or the cowardly break down in battle. In reality, everyone is susceptible to psychiatric breakdown in war. Not only are there no personality or demographic factors associated with psychiatric collapse in war, but neither are there any factors associated with heroism. It is impossible to predict which soldiers will collapse and which will behave bravely.[19] All men seem equally at risk of becoming either heroes or psychiatric basket cases, and there is no way to predict which will become which. Worse still, a soldier who performs admirably one day may, quite unexpectedly, become a psychiatric casualty the next. Exposed to enough combat, there is no statistical difference between the rates of psychiatric breakdown between inexperienced troops and battle-hardened veterans. All are at risk in war.[20]

Where all men are equally at risk to be broken by the horror of battle, it seems ludicrous to talk of norms in war. When so many men, quite normal in any other way, succumb to psychiatric pressures and can no longer function, in what sense can such men be said to deviate from the norm of expected behavior? In what sense, if any, can breakdown in battle be considered abnormal? The rates at which soldiers become debilitated suggest quite strongly that psychiatric breakdown is precisely what normal men do when the strain becomes too great. It is the reaction of a sane man to want to escape the horror of war, and mental collapse is simply the means he chooses to escape.

There is enough evidence from studies done after World War II to suggest that the only people who do not succumb to the stress of war are those who are already mentally aberrant in a clinically defined sense. About 2 percent of soldiers exposed to combat over long periods of time do not break under the stress. An examination of these "heroes" reveals that their most commonly held trait was that they were "aggressive psychopathic personalities" who were this way before they entered the battle zone.[21] The lesson seems to be that only the sane break down. Those already mentally ill appear able to adjust to the horror of combat. Perhaps it is simply that while collective insanity can destroy normally sane men, it cannot reverse individual insanity.

THE DYNAMICS OF MENTAL COLLAPSE

In a physiological sense man is as biological as any other animal. He is equipped with all the normal physiological mechanisms of any animal that serve to prepare the body to deal with and survive under stress. As in other animals the normal accompaniment of emotion is muscular action as the autonomic system and endocrine glands bring the body to a heightened state of physical excitement to cope with danger. Man's inborn instincts are the same as any other animal: to recognize danger and to deal with it by "flight or fight."

Under severe stress the body automatically goes into action. The soldier's blood pressure rises, his heart beats rapidly, he begins to sweat, his muscles tense, his short-term muscular strength increases, his mind races, and the endocrine system activates all the biological mechanisms that contribute to increased sensory awareness and muscular power. Few soldiers have any real control of these physiological reactions to stress. Once the danger is removed, the body will gradually calm down as those biological systems that produced the stress response return to their normal state.

But what happens when the stressful situation—the perception of danger of death and mutilation on the battlefield—are of long duration? In these circumstances the body will maintain itself in a high state of readiness, since the presence of danger automatically sustains the physiological responses needed to deal with it. Unfortunately, no one can endure at this level of biological tension for very long without becoming physically exhausted. Moreover, if the danger produces a stress response long enough—days, for example—the body's biological systems that sustain the physiology of stress will become fixed to the point where only prolonged rest away from danger will enable it to reduce its state of readiness. A soldier in this state will eventually collapse from nervous exhaustion—the body will simply burn out.

But if man is part animal, he also has an intellect, the quality that allows him to make reasoned judgments about circumstances he must confront and to make choices about his actions. Thus, it makes no sense to attribute such qualities as heroism or cowardice to animals; they react in the only way they can, guided almost entirely by biological reactions and instinct. Because man can choose, only man passes judgment on the choices of his fellows in deciding whether they have acted bravely or not. And because he can choose, his mind can permit him to choose actions that overrule or contradict the impulses of physiology.

A soldier's body, exhausted by physiological reactions to stress, will affect the way his mind functions. One of the first faculties to degenerate under stress is the ability to process information and make decisions. Moreover, a physically fatigued body will surely collapse regardless of the amount of willpower the soldier exhibits. The old military maxim of basic training that "your body will do it if your mind makes you do it" is, for the most part, untrue. By the same token, the psyche can affect the physiological operations of the body in any number of ways. Psychosomatic illnesses, a condition of genuine physical debilitation, are brought on by affective mental states in which the mind produces genuine physical ailments and, in some cases, even causes the physical deterioration of body organs. One of the most interesting of these illnesses is nostalgia, mentioned earlier. In the Civil War, soldiers suffering from nostalgia quite often died from physical ailments that their mental states created. Civil War autopsies of soldiers suffering from "exhausted hearts" discovered clear evidence of physiological deterioration of the blood vessels when there was no other medical reason for them to deteriorate. Today's stomach ulcers and colitis and other diseases are commonly recognized as being brought on by continued stress. The mind and body coexist, and either may readily affect the ability of the other to function properly especially under conditions of great stress.

But the mind is not defenseless, and fortunately it is not autonomic in its reactions to stress. What men believe and think can have a great bearing on how they behave when confronted with danger. In this regard, Jules Masserman suggests that all human psychic defense rests on three key beliefs—"the Ur defenses of man"—which serve to shore up the psyche against danger.[22] The first of these beliefs is that there is a connection between a man's actions and what happens to him. Man simply cannot live in a purely random world (as battle often appears to be). He must believe that there is some connection between what he does and what eventually happens to him, especially in times of danger. Otherwise he will go insane.

The second belief needed to sustain the psyche in contact with reality is the faith that "someone will help me." Man is sustained by the belief (however unfounded at times) that he is not alone and that if he does all he can to survive and the danger still grows, someone—perhaps even God—will come to his aid and save him. It is precisely this belief that leads some men under great stress to develop physically debilitating illness. By becoming incapacitated, a condition that clearly does not improve his chances for survival, the individual shifts the responsibility for his survival to someone else. He retreats from reality and takes refuge in his belief that someone will keep him safe. Studies in World War I and World War II show that when prisoners of war and their guards were subjected to artillery attack or aerial bombardment, none of the prisoners—who had by being captured shifted the responsibility for their survival to their captors—suffered psychiatric reactions, while their captors did. Men sustain their sanity by the belief that when all else fails, someone will come to their aid, a fact that often accounts for extreme religiosity in soldiers in danger. When confronted with the fact that this belief may be false, men invariably come apart.

The third belief at the center of man's psychic survival is the belief that "I will live forever." Even under the most trying of circumstances, men must continue to believe that they will somehow survive the ordeal, or else they collapse. The desire to survive is so deeply embedded into our genetic makeup as to be self-evident. When confronted by the face of death from which there is no escape, few men can retain their sanity.

Men build their lives and social institutions upon these basic beliefs. What subcultures and social institutions like the military do is to buttress these beliefs by inculcating corollary beliefs in the individual soldier. Thus, all soldiers are taught about courage, the need to stand firm when battle begins, the need to keep faith with one's friends, and the need to be brave. The individual soldier comes to define himself in terms of these corollary beliefs, so that to be a good soldier is to act accordingly.

What happens to soldiers in combat is that they are constantly confronted with stark evidence that none of the basic assumptions upon which their mental stability is premised any longer holds. The evidence of the battle field—the noise, the randomness of death, its constancy, the shattered bodies—all combine to shake the individual's faith in his basic assumptions about life. He is left only with the corollaries developed by the military, and even these become subject to severe doubt as the evidence mounts daily that they do not offer any safety from the horror which surrounds him either.

A soldier in combat develops a constant severe conflict between his physiology's autonomic functions designed to keep him alive and the mental pull of his beliefs, which are already seriously eroded by the evidence of his senses. He wants to live up to the ideals of being a good soldier, but fear is pulling him in the other direction. To make matters worse, the soldier worries about what is happening, but he also fears what can happen. This ability to project fear produces a constant state of anxiety that grows with each hour and each day. Thus,

the soldier is suffering from a conflict between his fear of death and injury and his own ideals of duty. . . . With anxiety, however, since the fear is directed to what might happen and not to what is happening, there is nothing that can be done and the autonomic system runs riot . . . the commonest process by which relief is obtained is by the conversion of the anxiety state into a hysterical symptom . . . paralysis, blindness, deafness or indeed any illness gives him an honorable retreat from the situation, and his conflict is solved and his anxiety relieved."[23]

While the dynamics of mental collapse are clear enough, the onset of the soldier's breakdown can be rapid or gradual. A soldier debilitated by psychiatric breakdown is usually described as suffering from battle shock. Battle shock can be clinically described as acute (often called combat shock) or gradual (often called combat fatigue) depending upon the speed with which symptoms manifest themselves. In general, about 50 percent of all psychiatric casualties suffer acute onset of symptoms, usually within five days of being exposed to battle, while another 50 percent develop them gradually, within about thirty days.[24] In specific instances, of course, the distribution can vary. In the Israeli invasion of Lebanon in 1982, 100 percent of the Israeli psychiatric cases were battle shock, developing within six days of war or less.

Gradual combat shock (combat fatigue) develops in four stages. At any stage, however, the soldier's ability to function efficiently as a combat soldier is diminished to some degree. Almost from the moment of exposure to combat a soldier's effectiveness diminishes, and almost immediately his mental state is characterized by anxiety. During the first few days of combat most men enter a state of fluctuating fear. The symptoms of fear make themselves manifest in a number of ways including increased frequency and urgency of urination, a highly intense thirst, and a refusal to eat, often leading to anorexia in which food cannot be consumed or, if it is, it is vomited. There is an increasing fear of being alone or of being exposed to enemy fire even for a few seconds. Men will often defecate in their pants rather than leave the cover of their positions to relieve themselves. The old army adage about using one's helmet for a toilet has some basis in actual practice.

During various periods of tension, such as incoming artillery from harassing fire, soldiers manifest great increases in sweating, vasomotor instability, and other overt physiological signs of fear. Almost all soldiers develop muscular tremors to some degree, and many shake so uncontrollably that they cannot perform even the most rudimentary tasks such as loading their weapons. Although soldiers in the unit may have trained together, may have been deployed together, and may have become friends, there is a growing tendency among soldiers not to share articles such as blankets, shelter, food, or ammunition.[25] This first stage of combat fatigue usually lasts about five to seven days, and during this period a significant number of men will succumb to acute combat shock requiring evacuation.

Those who do not break down now enter a period where their confidence in themselves, their weapons, their comrades, and their own fighting ability increases. They are able to distinguish the sounds of enemy weapons from those of friendly forces, are able to react as trained in fire discipline and night concealment, watch for snipers, and otherwise perform as "battlewise" soldiers are expected to. In the first stage their physiological reactions had become so intense that they interfered with their ability to function. In the second stage these biological reactions, although certainly higher than those found among men in the civilian population, are at least reduced to a level where they no longer interfere with the soldier's ability to perform adequately.[26] During this period of about fourteen days on average the soldier reaches his maximum fighting capability. Then he begins to manifest the symptoms of combat fatigue to an even greater degree.

After three weeks on the line more serious symptoms of combat exhaustion begin to appear. The soldier becomes easily exhausted physically after only minor periods of exertion; he is always tired, and no amount of sleep or rest on the line will relieve the condition. Fatigue is no longer being caused by the soldier's physiology, but is being psychologically generated. The whole set of fear reactions that were evident in stage one reappear with increased intensity, and his ability to suppress them is less successful. The soldier again loses his military skills and is once again unable to distinguish friendly from enemy fire, outgoing artillery from incoming fire, and he becomes overcautious. He often will not come out from his position for any reason. He is unable to sleep and the more exhausted he becomes, the more unable he is to get any rest at all. When he does sleep, it is usually during the day because of the greater feeling of insecurity he feels at night. Irritability increases, and a number of soldiers manifest severe emotional outbursts of anger over minor matters. Tremors become constant, and often the soldier rushes around constantly changing his position to reduce the chances of being hit by enemy fire.[27] This period lasts about a week or so.

After being on the line for five weeks, the soldier enters the fourth phase of combat fatigue. The absence of old friends who have been killed or wounded and the mounting casualty toll engender in him a feeling of helplessness and hopelessness. He begins to believe he will either be killed or wounded and that he cannot go on. The soldier's mental processes begin to deteriorate and he becomes apathetic and unable to comprehend simple orders or directions. His memory begins to fail to such an extent that he can no longer be relied upon to remember simple instructions. His battle skills are manifestly absent, and he no longer remembers how to react to even minor situations. The soldier cannot concentrate on anything except thoughts of home and the constant thought of death in which the anxiety that he might be killed is replaced by certainty. Tremors disappear, and even the most threatening combat actions cannot rouse him from his general state of lassitude and listlessness.[28]

If the soldier is not evacuated at this point—about five to six weeks after his initial exposure to combat—he will likely enter a vegetative state where he is incapable of any action at all. Such states can and do approach catatonia. Very often, however, a soldier in this state will suddenly collapse under the impact of a specific incident such as the death of a close friend or a near miss. While the reactions to such an event vary, all too often soldiers undergo a violent, sudden emotional explosion and begin to run around wildly and aimlessly with total disregard for their safety. Some become amnesic; others become stuporous and unable to walk, see, or hear. Still others panic and run into artillery fire or even run at the enemy guns while others find a trench or hole and refuse to come out, remaining there crying or trembling out of control. Some men will fall on the ground and claw at the earth screaming. At this point, of course, the soldier has suffered a shattering emotional collapse and must be evacuated.

The simple fact is that men are crushed by the strain of modern war. Judging from the data presented earlier, all men are at risk of becoming psychiatric casualties, and, in fact, most men will collapse given enough exposure to battle stress. There is no such thing as getting used to combat. Nevertheless, studies of World War II soldiers revealed that about 2 percent of soldiers do not collapse. But they are already mad, for most of them were aggressive psychopathic personalities before they entered battle. Only the sane break down.

It is interesting to note that soldiers can break down in remarkable numbers at even the thought of being forced to go into battle. Of the men whom the U.S. Army rejected for military service for emotional reasons in World War II, many were suffering fear reactions from the very prospect of being sent into the military. Many had no history of emotional problems prior to being drafted. Moreover, of the men who were separated from military service for psychiatric reasons after they had been inducted and sent to training bases, a substantial number left even before they had either been deployed overseas or received orders to deploy.[29] In units that had been alerted for deployment to combat, psychiatric symptoms began to appear as much as eighty days before the unit actually shipped out.[30] And these symptoms were hardly minor. Once a unit was alerted for combat deployment, there was a great increase in the number of somatic complaints such as heart palpitations, dyspnea, general weakness, abdominal pain, vomiting, and backache. Many soldiers were hospitalized for these complaints and never returned to their units for deployment.[31] There were also large increases at this time in the number of self-inflicted wounds and accidents. Apparently, even the thought of going to war is sufficient to drive some men to develop psychiatric symptoms.

What must be kept in mind is that those soldiers who eventually became psychiatric casualties were not a representative cross section of the American army. Quite the contrary. They had been screened for psychiatric problems upon induction, again in stateside training, and again prior to deployment, again in their training bases overseas, and finally again before being sent into battle. The "weak" among them had already been removed or removed themselves by manifesting a range of psychiatric symptoms severe enough to debilitate them functionally. Those who finally went into battle were the strongest of the lot and many of them still succumbed to the stress of battle. War has simply become too stressful for even the strongest among us to stand for very long.

THE VICTIMS

To describe the dynamics of psychiatric breakdown in battle does little to describe the actual terrors that the psychiatric casualty undergoes. The soldier suffering from combat shock is, after all, a human being and often undergoes suffering that most civilians, save those incarcerated in mental institutions, cannot imagine. What battle does is to take a reasonably normal and sane individual and, sometimes in a matter of hours, transform him into a victim whose pain far exceeds anything most civilians ever suffer or witness. Nations often measure the "costs" of war in dollars, lost production, or the number of soldiers killed or wounded. Rarely do military establishments ever attempt to measure the costs of war in terms of human suffering of individuals. Psychiatric breakdowns remain one of the most costly items of war when expressed in human terms.

Since the end of World War I military medical establishments have outlined the major psychiatric conditions that soldiers suffer in war although it must be quickly added that the human mind seems infinite in its potential to produce widely different symptoms of battle shock. An examination of these categories of symptomologies reveals just how terrible the mental and physical condition of a battle-shocked soldier can be.

Fatigue Cases

A soldier suffering from "simple" fatigue is mentally and physically exhausted; his autonomic biological systems, after periods of hyperactivity in keeping his physiology at a heightened state in order to deal with danger, have collapsed. The physical exhaustion begins to erode his mental strength, and he is aware that his mental powers are deteriorating. The fatigue state is clinically "prodromal"; that is, it sets the stage for further and more complete collapse. If the soldier is not treated or evacuated, further collapse is inevitable. In a state of fatigue the soldier finds physical motion difficult if not impossible. If they are available, he will tend to indulge excessively in alcohol, tobacco, or, as in the Vietnam War, light and heavy drugs. He will begin to manifest a tendency to become unsociable and overly irritable. Eventually he will lose interest in all activities with his comrades and will seek to avoid any responsibility or activity involving effort. The soldier will be prone to emotional crises such as crying fits or fits of extreme anxiety or terror. There will also be accompanying somatic symptoms such as hypersensitivity to sound, increased sweating, palpitations, and cyanosis of the extremities.[32] If forced to remain in the battle zone, this state of fatigue will eventually develop into deeper psychiatric symptoms.

Confusional States

A soldier suffering from exhaustion can quickly shift into a confusional state, which is generally marked by a psychotic dissociation from reality. He no longer knows where he is. Unable to deal with his environment any more, he mentally removes himself from it. Often such states involve delirium of some sort and are eventually likely to produce schizophrenic states of dissociation. Frequently manic depressive psychosis develops with wild swings of mood and activity. One often noted response is the development of Ganzer syndrome. Confronted with the horror of war all around him, a soldier afflicted with Ganzer syndrome will begin to make jokes, act silly, and otherwise try to ward off the horror with humor and the ridiculous. The degree of affliction in confusional states ranges from the profoundly neurotic to the overtly psychotic.[33]

Conversion Hysteria

Conversion hysteria is one of the most pronounced and dramatic manifestations of battle shock. The soldier, torn between his fears and his socially derived notions of duty, "resolves" the extreme tension by "converting" his fears into some somatic symptom severe enough to incapacitate himself and thus gain relief from the terror he faces. The physical symptoms allow him to gain relief from the terror with a "legitimate" physical condition, thus preserving his self-respect in the eyes of himself and his peers.[34] After all, no one can rightly expect a soldier who has become blind or paralyzed to continue to fight.

Conversion hysteria can occur traumatically or in post-traumatic situations. Thus, a soldier can manifest hysteria after he has been knocked out by concussion, received a minor nondebilitating wound, or had a near miss. Hysteria can also manifest itself after a wounded soldier has been evacuated. Once in the hospital or safely in a rear area, hysteria begins to emerge most often as a defense against returning to the fight.[35] Wherever it occurs, it is the mind that is producing the physical symptoms of debilitation.

Conversion hysteria involves massive and partial dissociative states.[36] Massive dissociation manifests itself in fugue states—an inability to know where one is or to function at all—often accompanied by aimless wandering around the battlefield with complete disregard for evident dangers. Very often, a soldier in a fugue state is totally or partially amnesic, blocking out from his consciousness large parts of his past and present memory. The psychosis can also take the form of twilight states—a repeated passing in and out of consciousness—sometimes accompanied by severe and uncontrollable tremors. Often, hysteria degenerates into convulsive attacks in which the soldier rolls into the fetal position and begins to shake violently much as he would during an epileptic seizure. Finally, dissociation can manifest itself in complete catatonia or other states of physical rigidity in which it is impossible to move at all.

States of partial dissociation, while clinically less serious in principle, nonetheless produce horrible symptoms. Among the most common afflictions are hysterical paralysis, deafness, and blindness.[37] The mind literally forces the body to become incapacitated. In World War I and World War II, for example, cases of contractive paralysis of the arm were rather common. In this situation, the soldier's arm not only became paralyzed but often contracted, so that the hand became rigidly fixed to the shoulder. The psychosomatic nature of the condition was clearly evident; most often the arm that became paralyzed was the one used to operate the firing bolt mechanism of the rifle. Thus, in lefthanded men the paralysis occurred in the left arm while the opposite was true for righthanded soldiers. Sometimes the soldier suffered paralysis of one or both legs. There should be no doubt that although the physical symptoms are caused by the mind, they are no less real to the soldier. Soldiers suffering from partial dissociative hysterical states also manifest acute sensory disturbances including somatic pain. Often this manifests itself in the feeling that sections of his body are numb or the skin feels inflamed or the common occurrence of left infra-mammary pain simulating the conditions of a heart attack.[38]

Anxiety States

Generalized anxiety in soldiers suffering from combat shock is characterized by a feeling of total weariness and tenseness that cannot be relieved by sleep or rest, and that degenerates into an inability to concentrate. When the soldier can sleep, he is often awakened by terrible nightmares associated with battle experiences. Eventually, he becomes fixated on the idea of death and interprets the events of the battlefield as being personally directed at him. He becomes obsessed with death and the fear that he will fail or that the men in his unit will discover that he is frightened. If allowed to persist without relief, the soldier will develop phobic conditions, an extreme fear focused on some object. Thus, he might refuse to go near a tank for fear that it will draw enemy fire and he will be killed. Generalized anxiety can easily slip into hysteria.

Anxiety often shows up in a range of severe somatic neuroses such as effort syndrome, an abnormal physiological reaction to effort. Frequently it is accompanied by shortness of breath, weakness, precordial pain, blurred vision, giddiness, vasomotor abnormalities, and fainting. Another reaction is emotional hypertension in which the soldier's blood pressure rises dramatically with all the accompanying symptoms of weakness, sweating, nervousness, and so on. He may also develop severe palpitations (soldier's heart). A range of stress-related somatic problems frequently develops including peptic ulcers, stress dyspepsia, backache, and emotional diarrhea.

Obsessional and Compulsive States

These states of psychiatric breakdown are similar to those found in conversion hysteria except that in conversion states the soldier is often completely dissociated from his symptoms and is not aware of their being caused by his own fears and anxieties. In obsessional states, the soldier realizes the morbid nature of his symptoms, even that his fears are at their root.[39] The difference is that his tremors, palpitations, stammers, tics, and other symptoms cannot be controlled. Eventually the soldier is likely to take refuge in some type of hysterical reaction, which allows him the opportunity to escape psychic responsibility for his physical symptoms.

Character Disorders

This set of symptoms is somewhat misnamed, for it implies that somehow the soldier's character has been disordered by conscious action. This is not the case. What is implied is a condition in which the problems of stress have become so deeply seated that they have become part of the soldier's personality and are extremely difficult to reverse. Character disorders include stable obsessional traits in which the soldier becomes fixated on certain actions or things, paranoid trends accompanied by irascibility, depression and anxiety often threatening his safety, schizoid trends leading to hypersensitivity and isolation, epileptoid character reactions accompanied by periodic rages, the development of extreme dramatic religiosity, and finally degeneration into a psychopathic personality.[40] What has happened to the soldier is an altering of his fundamental personality. While some of these alterations can often be reversed, all too commonly they accompany the soldier for the rest of his life.

It is important to understand clearly that some symptoms of stress will develop in almost all soldiers in battle. Moreover, while not all soldiers will collapse from this stress, almost all will suffer some degree of combat debilitation—some lessening of their ability to fight—as a consequence. Table 1 presents a list of psychiatric symptoms and their approximate frequency of occurrence among Israeli soldiers in the 1982 Lebanon War. While many soldiers manifested multiple symptoms, it is clear from the available information that the range and frequency of symptoms is very great. It is also evident that soldiers tend to suffer clusters of symptoms induced by the stress of war. Interestingly, these clusters, while evident to some degree in every war for which there are available data, have tended to emerge in specific forms in different wars. Table 2 presents the most prevalent symptoms which have emerged in each conflict since World War I. While the data are not included in the table, many of the same clusters emerged in the Civil War as well although under different names. Tragically, the most common symptom in all wars, including those during Roman times for which there are no statistical data, is also the most serious. Conversion reactions, a condition where the soldier "converts" his fear into a physical debilitation such as blindness, paralysis, or other physical symptoms, remains the most common reaction to long-term exposure to battle stress.

CONCLUSIONS

This analysis of the symptoms of acute and gradual battle shock by no means exhausts the manifestations that show up among soldiers subjected

Table 1.
Psychiatric Symptoms Reported by Israeli Soldiers in the 1982 Lebanon War

Symptom	% Reporting
Anxiety	56%
Depressive Affect	38%
Sleep Disturbances	34%
Fear-focused and diffuse	34%
Social estrangement-detachment	24%
Conversion reactions	22%
Crying	21%
Decreased appetite	19%
Headaches	19%
Exhaustion, fatigue	17%
Psychomotor disturbances	17%
Disturbing dreams-memories	17%
Tremors	13%
Confusion, concentration problems	13%
Speech impairment	12%
Dissociative states	11%
Irritability	11%
Explosive aggressive behavior	11%
Memory impairment	11%
Noise sensitivity-startle reactions	10%

NOTE: Percentages reflect those soldiers in the IDF who reported each symptom. Since soldier's may have suffered more than one symptom, the percentages do not add to one hundred.

Source: Gregory Belenky, Israeli Battle Shock Casualties; 1973 and 1982 (Washington: Walter Reed Army Institute Of Research Report, 1979), p. 12.

to prolonged battle stress. The mind has shown itself infinitely capable of any number of combinations of symptoms and then, to make matters worse, burying them deep in the soldier's psyche, so that even their overt manifestations become symptoms of deeper symptoms of even deeper underlying causes.

What this all adds up to is the simple fact that war exacts a terrible cost in human emotions quite apart from the usual costs calculated in terms of dead, dollars, and damaged. And it is a cost which every soldier will eventually pay if he is exposed long enough to the horrors of the battlefield. Weakness or cowardice has nothing to do with the probability that a sol-

Table 2.
Symptom Clusters in Various Wars

				Arab-Israel Wars	
SYMPTOMS	WWI	WWII	Vietnam	1973	1982
Depressive affect	X			X	X
Fear; diffuse, foccussed	X			X	X
Noise sensitivity	X				
Tremors	X				
Psychomotor disturbance	X				
Conversion reaction	X	X		X	X
Confusion, Aprosexia	X				
Dissociative states	X			X	
Anxiety		X		X	X
Nightmares		X		X	
Exhaustion, Fatigue		X			
Decreased appetite		X			
Gastrointestinal		X			
Headaches		X			
Sleep disturbances		X		X	X
Constricted affect			X		
Social estrangement			X		X
Discipline problems			X		
Explosive behavior			X		
Drug abuse			X		

NOTE: Each X represents the most common symptoms reported by psychiatric casualties in each war.

Source: Gregory Belenky, Israeli Battle Shock Casualties; 1973 and 1982 (Washington; Walter Reed Army Institute for Research Report, 1979), p. 10.

dier will collapse under the strain of battle. It is not man that is too weak; it is the conduct of war that imposes too great a strain for the sane to endure. And there is no way to make the problem of battle shock go away; it is an inevitable part of the game. Indeed, what the statistical analysis of the frequency of battle shock clearly demonstrates is that it is a more frequently occurring factor even than death. Yet the myth persists among those who have never known combat that those who collapse under the strain of battle are somehow weak or cowardly or the exception to the rule. And that may be the worst delusion of all.

NOTES

1. Sometimes censorship from the horror of war reaches ridiculous proportions. Gen. Douglas Haig, the supreme commander of British forces in World War

I, forbade his staff officers to visit the front line. He believed that if they witnessed the horror personally, their ability to plan future military operations objectively would be lost.

2. Lawrence Ingraham and Frederick Manning, "American Military Psychiatry," in Richard Gabriel, *Military Psychiatry: A Comparative Perspective* (Westport, Conn.: Greenwood Press, 1986), p. 67.

3. Richard Gabriel, *Soviet Military Psychiatry* (Westport, Conn.: Greenwood Press, 1986), p. 123.

4. Ingraham and Manning, "American Military Psychiatry," pp. 67–68.

5. U.S. Department of Commerce, *Historical Statistics of the United States,* (Washington, D.C.: U. S. Government Printing Office, 1976), p. 1140.

6. Edward A. Strecker, "Military Psychiatry in World War I," in *100 Years of American Psychiatry* (New York: Columbia University Press, 1944), p. 403.

7. This figure is calculated by subtracting the number of psychiatric casualties recorded as permanently lost from the total number of psychiatric casualties admitted for treatment at military medical facilities.

8. Eli Ginsberg, *The Lost Divisions* (New York: Columbia University Press, 1950), pp. 91–92.

9. This figure is calculated by subtracting the total number of psychiatric casualties from the total of admissions to military medical facilities for psychiatric reasons.

10. Gynne Dyer, *War* (New York: Crown Publishers, 1985), p. 118.

11. Ibid.

12. Ibid.

13. Stewart L. Baker, Jr. "Traumatic War Disorders," (no further source given), p. 1831.

14. U. S. Department of Commerce, *Historical Statistics of the United States,* p. 1140.

15. Ingraham and Manning, "American Military Psychiatry," p. 88.

16. Ibid., p. 91.

17. Gregory Belenky, *Israeli Battle Shock Casualties: 1973 and 1982* (Washington, D. C.: Walter Reed Army Institute of Research, 1983), p. 26.

18. David Marlowe, *Cohesion, Anticipated Breakdown, and Endurance in Battle* (Washington, D. C.: Walter Reed Army Institute of Research, 1979), p. 3.

19. Richard Gabriel and Reuven Gal, "Battlefield Heroism in the Israeli Defense Force," *International Social Science Review,* vol. 57 (Autumn 1982), pp. 332–335.

20. Larry Ingraham and Frederick Manning, "Psychiatric Battle Casualties," *Military Review,* vol. (August 1980), p. 24.

21. Roy L. Swank and Walter E. Marchand, "Combat Neuroses: The Development of Combat Exhaustion," *Archives of Neurology and Psychiatry,* Vol. 55 (1946), p. 244.

22. Jules Massermann, *Principles of Dynamic Psychiatry* (Philadelphia: W. B. Saunders Co., 1961), pp. 180–182.

23. Emanuel Miller, *Neuroses in War* (New York: Macmillan, 1942), p. 87.

24. S.L.A. Marshall, as quoted in Marlowe, *Cohesion,* p. 31.

25. Swank and Marchand, "Combat Neuroses," p. 238.

26. Ibid.

27. Ibid., p. 240.

28. Ibid., pp. 240–241.
29. Ginsberg, *The Lost Divisions,* p. 91.
30. Swank and Marchand, "Combat Neuroses," p. 237.
31. Ibid.
32. Miller, *Neuroses in War,* p. 17.
33. Ibid., p. 229.
34. Ibid., p. 17.
35. Ibid.
36. Ibid., p. 229.
37. Ibid.
38. Ibid., p. 232.
39. Ibid., p. 18.
40. Ibid., p. 230.

3

The Face of Modern War

While only the truly insane would regard a nuclear war as tolerable, most people share the belief that a conventional war is acceptable. But the realities of today's wars make this belief questionable. Modern conventional weapons developed since the end of World War II are so lethal and destructive that, in the words of a U.S. Army manual, "conventional war has unconventional effects." As the famous British military analyst John Keegan has noted, there are any number of conventional weapons in use today whose destructive power is equal to or greater than nuclear weapons. The F-4 Phantom fighter plane, for example, can deliver destructive power greater than that afforded by a low-yield nuclear cruise missile.[1] When modern artillery is fired in mass, it is more destructive than nuclear artillery rounds. Even the destructive power of the neutron bomb can be readily exceeded by a squadron of aircraft dropping conventional Fuel Air Munitions. The conventional chemical-warfare capabilities of any number of military establishments, including those of the underdeveloped nations, can exterminate civilian and military populations much larger than those of Hiroshima or Dresden in only slightly more time than it took to destroy them with bombs. The horrible fact is that conventional war today is as far removed in its intensity, scope, and lethality from World War II as World War II was removed from the Battle of Waterloo.

GOOD-BYE WORLD WAR II

It seems logical to examine today's military capabilities in relation to those of World War II. There is an old military adage that when it comes to combat, "quantity has a quality all its own." In a conventional war in central Europe the numbers of men and equipment involved suggest that conventional war has changed qualitatively over the years.[2] If it is assumed that one side or the other gains some degree of surprise and thus reduces mobilization time to a minimum, on the first day of battle 1.7 million men on both sides will engage each other in combat. After two days when the ready reserves of the major combatants have been committed, the number of fighting men will increase to 2.8 million. If the fighting lasts ten full days, the number of combatants trying to kill each other would jump to almost 6 million men. In thirty days, after both sides had ample time to commit their substantial reserves, the number of men trying desperately to kill one another will increase to more than 15 million soldiers. No time in history has ever witnessed so many fighting men locked in combat in so short a time. If both sides understand that once war breaks out, the side that puts the most men in the field will have a decided advantage, it is difficult to see how the quantitative escalation in manpower can be stopped once it begins.

Modern armies have more machines of destruction at their disposal than at any time in history. There are, for example, 13,500 main battle tanks in the NATO inventory compared to 42,600 for the Warsaw Pact countries; 560 NATO attack helicopters to 960 for the Warsaw Pact; 32,000 antitank guided missile launchers for the Warsaw Pact compared to 12,300 for NATO forces; 33,000 NATO armed armored personnel carriers to 75,000 in the Warsaw Pact; 35,000 Warsaw Pact artillery pieces to 11,000 for NATO forces and 6,550 high-performance strike aircraft on the side of the Warsaw Pact compared to 3,100 similar aircraft in NATO. Whatever else conventional war in central Europe brings, it will result in the largest concentration of war machines ever committed to a single battle.

On the first day of fighting, both sides will be able to engage almost 20,000 modern main battle tanks. After thirty days, the number of tanks committed on both sides would increase to 56,000. Attempting to counter these armored battle cruisers will be antitank missile crews, who will be able to fire 530,000 guided missiles at one another. In the skies fighter aircraft will be as numerous as gnats. On the opening day of battle, each side could commit more than 4,000 strike aircraft, a figure that would double in less than a week as air reserves are committed.

All this manpower and machinery would be committed within a battle zone less than 700 miles long and 40 miles deep. Modern armies calculate that they need about 1400 soldiers per mile of battlefront, actually less than the 1700 maximum in World War II. However, in a modern conventional war it must be kept in mind that greater percentage of a unit's manpower actually will be engaged in the killing than ever before. Moreover, the ability of today's soldier to deliver and sustain firepower has grown exponentially since 1945. For example, a Soviet motorized rifle division can deliver ten times the firepower at three times the rate of a similar division in World War II. The same is true of NATO divisions. Compared to World War II, more men will be putting out far more firepower more lethally for longer periods over much greater distances.

This concentration of sheer military power is frightening enough, but it must be remembered that modern war is a war of speed, mobility, penetration, encirclement, and envelopment. Within a few days of the initial clash, the front line will flex, and one side or the other will have to give way. Once units begin to give ground, they will be pressed back against units deployed in the rear. In a phenomenon not unlike that of ancient Greek phalanxes crashing together, the battlefield will begin to shrink as the size of the battle zone becomes compressed. When this happens, the number of targets in the battle zone will actually increase creating a "target-rich environment," and the intensity of the battle will become even more ferocious.

In World War II combat occurred along a generally well-defined front line with usually safe rear areas. Areas twenty miles behind the line were almost totally secure as long as the balance of air power remained relatively intact. The enemy was clearly to the front at all times. Moreover, World War II was a tactical war in which most of the fighting was done by units of division size and below.

The conventional war of the future presents a far different set of circumstances. Linear tactics will be replaced by "swirling tactics." The combat reach of modern armies is so long and the mobility of combat vehicles so great that armies must now plan to fight three battles at once. Both U.S. and Soviet combat doctrine requires that units be able to fight the "direct" battle, that is, to engage units directly to their front. But it also requires that they can simultaneously fight the "deep" battle, to reach out and strike deeply behind the enemy's lines with large combat forces in order to disrupt timetables, supplies, and reinforcements. Of course, one side's deep battle is the other side's "rear" battle. Each army will have to deal with sizable enemy forces engaged in attacking its rear. Such forces will be inserted into rear areas by parachute drop or helicopter. Or they will break through the front lines and head for specific targets in the rear areas. Some idea of the ferocity of these "rear" battles can be gained from the fact that the units attacking the enemy's rear will be of division size or larger. Simultaneously modern attack aircraft and helicopters will roam hundreds of miles behind enemy lines wreaking havoc with their large-caliber multibarreled guns and guided rockets.

Accordingly, the entire battlefield will be highly unstable. It will not be a war of fixed lines, but of swirling combat in which units will be expected to fight isolated from parent units. Units will be trapped, decimated, bypassed, isolated, and often expected to stand and fight until they can no longer do so. In short, it will not be a war of offense and defense like World War II. It will be a war of meeting engagements in which all units will be expected to engage in a continuous offensive.

Modern conventional war will not be a tactical war in which relatively small units of division size or less do most of the fighting. Instead, it will be an operational-level war in which the scope of command and control will move back from the line divisions to the corps and theater commands. Corps will engage and fight battles as brigades did in World War II. Larger units will be committed at once for objectives of greater scope. More resources will be thrown at any one time into any given engagement. The shift from the tactical to the operational level of war will mean far more intense and destructive battles raging for longer periods of time over greater areas.

Under these conditions the zone of destruction—the area in which soldiers will be involved in combat and have a good chance of being killed or wounded—will increase. During World War I the zone of destruction extended a maximum of five miles from the front. By World War II it had increased to ten miles, and a division commander had to worry about the forces deployed about ten to fifteen miles to his front. Today, with the zone of destruction extending the depth of the front (about forty miles), he is responsible for locating and killing forces forty miles to his front, and his "area of tactical interest" extends to almost sixty miles. Moreover, he has at his command weapons systems that can reach sixty miles to his front to engage and destroy enemy forces. Of course, so does his opponent.

Another element that distinguishes modern conventional warfare from World War II is the amount of fighting that will take place at night. In World War II, the soldier's ability to fight at night was severely limited by his ability to see. Mechanical means for locating the enemy were almost nonexistent except for primitive radar that could locate large formations of aircraft. The World War II soldier generally had no better means of fighting at night than did the soldiers of ancient Rome. Consequently most military action, as it had for centuries before, came to a halt at nightfall. To be sure there were always nighttime probes and reconnaissance patrols, but what little fighting there was was confined to very small units, and the darkness itself reduced the effectiveness of weaponry. All that has changed.

Today's military forces are equipped with a wide range of electronic, laser, infrared, and optical devices that turn the nighttime battlefield into day. Modern tank sights can easily locate a target in complete darkness at 3500 yards, and the target is as easily visible as during daylight. Even when the target cannot be seen with optical enhancing devices, its outline and silhouette can be discerned by infrared and laser sights. Modern weaponry, especially antitank missiles, can home in with deadly accuracy on the heat emitted from the vehicle's engine. One optical device, the Starlight scope, the size of a small telescope, can even discern the difference between a male and female at over a thousand yards by the distinct differences in the heat of the pelvic areas given off by the two sexes. Furthermore, such night-sighting devices are not confined to the heavy machines of war like the armored personnel carrier or the tank. In addition, every infantryman will be equipped with night-vision goggles.

The increased ability of military forces to see at night makes it possible, indeed mandatory, for large combat units to continue military operations around the clock. Battles will rage continually. Once engaged, units of any size will find it very difficult to disengage, as the attacking force will be able to locate the enemy continually. The normal respite that soldiers for 2000 years have come to expect with the fall of night will come no more. War will be fought with almost the same intensity around the clock.

If the size, scope, and intensity of future conventional war has grown enormously, the reason, of course, is the weapons that are at the command of all truly modern armies. There are now weapons in the arsenal of the ordinary combat division that would turn even the most hardened of World War II commanders green with envy.

It is important to understand that the destructiveness of modern war and the tremendous stress it places upon the mind of the soldier do not depend upon bringing millions of men and machines to battle. Indeed, the most likely types of conventional wars of the future will be small "brush-fire wars" in which comparatively small numbers of combatants participate. However, the stress on the soldier will be the same, since the relative intensity of a division-sized battle will be the same as a corps-sized battle. The changes in the nature of warfare have made almost any conventional war among modern military forces horribly intense. The weapons have become more destructive, out of proportion to the ability of the soldier to withstand them.

ARTILLERY

Historically, artillery has always caused the most casualties to fighting troops, almost 60 percent, since the invention of gunpowder. In World War II, more than half of all combat casualties were caused by this fighting arm. And the capacity of artillery to destroy has grown frighteningly since 1945. The artillery firepower of a maneuver battalion has doubled in lethality since World War II while the "casualty effect" has increased by 400 percent. The range of artillery guns, on average, has increased by 60 percent since 1945 while the "lethality coverage area," the zone in which death can be expected to occur, has increased by 350 percent.

The explosive power of artillery rounds has increased almost seven times. In World War II most artillery rounds had thicker casings and delivered some variant of TNT. Today, with the revolution in chemical and plastic explosives, the casings are thinner, so that the same caliber shell can deliver many times the explosive power on the target. A single round fired by the M-110A2 self-propelled artillery cannon is approximately equal in explosive power to that of the MK-81 250-pound bomb. On impact, a single artillery round will produce a crater twenty-five feet in diameter and ten feet deep, displacing over 5000 cubic feet of earth. Such a round can penetrate up to three feet of concrete or five inches of steel, sending shrapnel out a radius of 300 feet. Almost all soldiers within a 200-foot radius of an exploding round would be killed by shrapnel or concussion. Newer artillery munitions, such as the Beehive round, are lethal at even greater distances. Developed during the Vietnam War to deal with mass enemy attacks, the Beehive round is filled with 5,000 flechettes, slender steel nail-like needles three inches long capable of pinning their targets to trees. If the Beehive round is set off above the heads of advancing troops, its lethality is even greater.

Modern artillery pieces are lighter, stronger, and far more mobile than they were in World War II, resulting in a revolution in mobile firepower. Today, a combat unit can take its artillery along with it as it advances. Moreover, an artillery unit can set up, bring its guns to bear, fire on a target, and move on to a new location in minutes, making it much more difficult for the enemy to destroy it by counterfire or air attack. Further, the rates of fire per gun have increased greatly, as the gun tubes are now made of stronger metal alloys. Projected rates of fire for modern artillery pieces approach 500 rounds per day over a four-hour period, or almost three times the World War II rate. The guns last longer, retain their sighting on target better, and don't overheat as badly. Less maintenance means more combat effectiveness.

The magnitude of artillery fire that modern armies can bring to bear staggers the imagination. If all artillery guns—from 81 mm mortars to tank guns are counted—the average combat division can mount almost 500 guns firing at once. In World War I the number of guns per thousand men in a division was six; during World War II it climbed to about twelve. Today, the number of guns per thousand men in a division exceeds thirty. To put this firepower in perspective, the Soviet Army is equipped to mass 300 artillery pieces per single mile of combat frontage. The magnitude of artillery fire is further increased by the use of different types of fuses, which increase its effectiveness. Thus, the variable time, or VT, fuse can be used to cause shells to burst over the heads of troops, greatly magnifying their killing capacity. Proximity fuses allow a shell to sense when it is near its target and explode close to it, causing great damage without having to hit the target directly. Delay fuses allow artillerymen to implant submunitions over wide areas and have them explode on a random or timed basis, thus denying large areas of the battlefield to the enemy.

And the range of artillery projectiles has increased enormously. Both the M-107 and M-110 are capable of hurling 175 mm shells and 203 mm shells twenty-three miles and twenty-two miles respectively. With rocket-assisted shells, these ranges exceed twenty-five miles. These self-propelled artillery pieces can move under their own power at speeds of thirty-five miles an hour with a range of 220 miles. The ability of mobile artillery to keep a retreating enemy easily within range far exceeds its World War II capabilities.

Artillery shells are also far more accurate, and thus far more deadly, than they were in World War II. This has been made possible by linking sophisticated electronic sensors with computers. Hardly any artillery is fired by manual calculations anymore. Information is fed to the guns from electronic sensors, sometimes dropped miles away by aircraft, while computers instantly do multiple range and deviation calculations. Rounds rarely miss their targets anymore. The rapidity of fire has increased as well. In World War II it would take an average gun crew about six minutes to zero in on its target. Today, an artillery battery can perform the same task in less than fifteen seconds, greatly reducing the chances that even a moving target will escape destruction. At the same time, of course, the means for delivering counterbattery fire on enemy artillery pieces have improved greatly. During World War II counterbattery fire was, at best, an uncertain thing. All artillery could do was fire in the direction of the roar or muzzle flashes of enemy guns and hope to saturate the area around the target sufficiently to knock out the gun. Today, electronic devices can compute the position of artillery fire almost instantly, commanding guns to return fire accurately on the battery. The days of the artillery being placed safely behind the lines are over.

While there have been great improvements in the accuracy of artillery weapons, the unguided artillery round used to saturate specific areas has truly come into its own. The Russians first introduced the idea of mass rocket artillery fired in salvo. Their Katusha rocket launchers in World War II were an ideal weapon for saturating large areas of the front while at the same time generating high rates of psychiatric casualties. Salvos of artillery rockets are ideal for achieving surprise, delivering chemical weapons, and spreading counterbattery fire. Today, a single Soviet battalion of eighteen BM-21 rocket launchers can fire 720 rounds almost seventeen miles in thirty seconds. Such a volley will put thirty-five tons of rockets on target and devastate an area 2000 yards by 500 yards. Not to be outdone, the Americans have developed the Multiple Launch Rocket System (MLRS). With this system a single three-man crew can launch twelve rockets in less than thirty seconds. After each rocket is launched in ripple fire, the on-board computer will recalculate the trajectory for the next rocket. A salvo of twelve rockets contains 8,000 M-77 antipersonnel weapons, which can be dispersed in mid-air above the target and saturate an area the size of six football fields in less than a minute. In another configuration, each rocket can dispense twenty-eight antitank mines. A third configuration allows each rocket to release almost ten SADARMs (Search And Destroy Armor Mines). Each of these SADARMs is a homing warhead, which can locate a tank, guide itself to the target, and destroy it. By the time the MRLS rockets have hit their targets, the crew has driven the launcher to a new position where it can reload and fire again.

The destructive power of artillery cannot be overestimated. Today, a division artillery complement can fire concentrations of artillery at three levels of intensity. If it fires at its lowest level (harassment), it can expect that 10 percent of the soldiers in the target area will be killed. At the second level of intensity (neutralization), it can kill 30 percent of the soldiers in the area of impact. If it fires at its most intense (destruction), it can kill 60 percent of the soldiers in the impact area.

Among the most bizarre, yet effective, artillery munitions is the Copperhead artillery round. This round can be fired from the M-109 155 mm artillery piece. Once fired, it follows its normal ballistic trajectory until it begins to descend in the general area of the target. At this point the round will home in on its target by laser illumination. The Copperhead has the ability to hit a moving tank nineteen miles away. In tests, the round actually found its way into the commander's open hatch of a moving tank.

Finally, artillery serves in air defense. During World War II division air defense artillery could expect to control the airspace above its position for about a mile in any direction. Today, it can control thirty-six times that space. In 1945, a typical American division carried sixty-four air defense weapons. Today, a division has 113, and Soviet divisions mount about 10 percent more. Almost all modern air defense artillery units have automatic guidance systems, radar, and optical sights. Some radar-controlled guns can fire sixty rounds in a single one-second burst. The M-163 Vulcan air defense gun, mounted on a self-propelled chassis, is a six-barreled 20 mm cannon capable of firing 3000 rounds a minute. It is equipped with an automatic telescope, a gyro-leading computing gunsight, and search radar with a range search time of one second. It can detect a target at almost two miles with 100 percent accuracy.

Advances in technology since World War II have been so great that there is no comparison between artillery of that era and that found on the modern battlefield. As in the past, artillery can be expected to cause the lion's share of battlefield casualties. It will surely generate the largest share of psychiatric casualties as rates and accuracy of firepower increase. The Russians, who suffered terribly from enemy artillery in the two world wars, are even greater proponents of artillery than are armies of the West. While Americans refer to artillery as "the king of battle," the Russians, who have been its greatest victims all the way back to Napoleonic times, have dubbed it "the hammer of god." Either way, it has revolutionized the battlefield.

TANKS AND ARMORED FIGHTING VEHICLES

Of great importance on the modern battlefield is the presence of large numbers of tanks and other armored vehicles, which complement the role of artillery in killing as many soldiers as possible. Modern tanks offer an unprecedented combination of firepower, shock action, and mobility. They can be expected to kill and be killed in numbers heretofore unseen in the history of warfare.

The modern battle tank is about one third heavier than its World War II counterpart, but its engines are twice as powerful. Accordingly, its horsepower-to-weight ratio is less, and its ground pressure is also less. This means that its range and speed are much greater than World War II tanks. Today's tank can cruise at speeds approaching forty miles an hour for more than 300 miles, a range three times that of World War II tanks. Development of stabilized turrets and highly sophisticated gun sights have given the modern tank the ability to shoot on the run with a greater probability of hitting its target than a World War II tank firing from a standing position. The accuracy of bigger guns has also improved tremendously. In World War II a tank firing at a target 1500 meters away had to fire thirteen rounds to achieve a 50-50 probability of hitting its target. Today, a modern tank will hit its target at that range with a single shot 98 percent of the time. Moreover, a World War II tank gun could penetrate only 4.8 inches of armor plate at 1500 yards. Today, a tank gun can easily penetrate 9.5 inches of armor plate at 6000 yards.

The size of tank guns has increased by at least one third while the muzzle velocity of tank rounds has doubled. The use of laser range finders has increased the range of target sighting by over thirty times. For example, the Hughes thermogunsight mounted on the M-1 tank is capable of finding targets at 2000 yards, producing a clear target image in complete darkness or through smoke, fog, or rain. The probabilities of hitting a target have increased tenfold since World War II.

The improvement in the killing power of tank-gun ammunition is amazing. New propellants and explosive compounds have made tank rounds many times more destructive as those available in World War II. Moreover, improvements in the understanding of ballistics has led to new types of tank ammunition undreamed of in 1945. For example, the APDS (Armor Piercing Discarding Sabot) is one such round. Weighing forty-one pounds, it leaves the gun muzzle at 5,467 feet per second—over a mile a second—a force more than sufficient for its tungsten core to penetrate 9.5 inches of armor at 6000 yards. After the round burns through the outer armor of an enemy tank in mere milliseconds, the tungsten core fragments sending over 100 shrapnel particles weighing at least an ounce and 600 fragments weighing less than an ounce into the interior compartment of the tank. These fragments ricochet against the tank's interior crew compartment at speeds of 3000 feet per second, sufficient to pierce the bodies of the crew scores of times before spending their velocity.

Another example of the killing capacity of today's tank ammunition is the HEP-T (High Explosive Plastic Tracer) round which works on a different ballistic principle. The HEP-T weighs fifty-two pounds and has a muzzle velocity of 4200 feet per second, carrying a warhead filled with plastic explosive. When the warhead strikes the target, it spreads out in a blob of plastic the size of a dinner plate and is detonated by a fuze. The explosion does not penetrate the armor but leaves a large dent as the explosive force is channeled inward toward the crew compartment. The shock of the explosion is so great that chunks of metal (spall) are blasted away from the interior walls of the tank's crew compartment sending the fragments into the crew's bodies faster than the speed of sound. There are no tanks in the world that can ensure the survivability of their crews when hit with a APDS or HEP-T round. Everyone always dies.

The increased killing power of tanks has increased the need for the infantry to increase its own mobility to survive. In the offensive, infantry has to be mounted in armored vehicles to keep up with the rapid advance of the tanks. The result is the armored personnel carrier (APC). Today, one of every two U.S. infantrymen rides into battle in an APC. The number of armored personnel carriers in the Soviet army is thirty-seven times as great as it was in World War II. War on wheels has arrived.

To be sure, squeezing ten infantrymen into a single APC has its disadvantages. A single antitank round into an APC will kill at least 70 percent of its occupants and wound the remaining 30 percent. Placing so many infantrymen into one target area has increased the probability of multiple kills for tank and missile gunners. Nonetheless, the APC itself has increased the killing power of the infantry many times over since World War II. A single M-113A APC carries thirteen combat troops and mounts a fifty-caliber machine gun and 2000 rounds of ammunition on the vehicle's cupola. It can also mount two M-60 machine guns, each capable of firing a thousand rounds a minute. Its ability to carry ammunition is far greater than a World War II truck. With a complete load, it can carry 3,570 rounds of fifty-caliber ammunition, 8,400 rounds of M-60 ammunition, 5,050 rounds of rifle ammunition, 144 40 mm grenades, four Claymore mines, ten antitank missiles, and their launchers. Such a piece of battlefield machinery simply did not exist in World War II.

The infantry fighting vehicle (IFV) has added yet another dimension to the killing power of the infantry. The American M-3 Bradley is a lightly armored tracked vehicle resembling a large APC. It can carry nine infantrymen into battle. But its real killing power lies in its weaponry. The M-3 mounts either a 25 mm chain gun or the 37 mm Bushmaster automatic cannon. The Bushmaster can fire either armor-piercing or high-explosive ammunition at a rate of almost 1000 rounds a minute. It carries a 7.2 mm machine gun and a dual TOW anti-tank missile launcher with seven missiles. Its turret stabilization system allows it to fire on the move and it has a fully computerized fire-control system with the full complement of imaging sights.

There are many variations of infantry fighting vehicles. By far the most common is to use an APC as a missile-firing antitank platform or as a missile- or gun-firing air defense platform. The APC and its variants have revolutionized warfare, since they place mobility and firepower, including the ability to kill tanks and aircraft, that was nonexistent in World War II in the hands of the infantry. The problem is, of course, is that the other side has similar weaponry with the same capabilities. Once again, technology has increased the intensity and lethality of war.

HELICOPTERS AND STRIKE AIRCRAFT

Nowhere has the impact of military technology been felt more strongly than in the introduction of two major airborne weapons systems, the strike aircraft and the armed helicopter. In World War II, the P-47 ground support airplane could fly 100 miles to its target, stay over the target for less than thirty minutes, and deliver only machine-gun fire and two 250-pound bombs. Today, the A-10 Warthog, specifically designed as a close support and tank killing aircraft, can fly 250 miles to its target, remain over the target area for two hours, and carry over 16,000 pounds of bombs, more than the bomb load of a World War II B-29 Superfortress. In addition, the A-10 carries a 30 mm seven-barreled rotating gun cluster in its nose, which is capable of firing armor and explosive shells each the size of a milk bottle. The gun can fire 4200 rounds per minute. A two-second burst fires 135 rounds into a target. The high-explosive round, thanks to the wonders of modern chemistry, produces an explosive force six times that of a 20 mm shell. Its armor piercing round with its warhead of depleted uranium metal produces fourteen times the kinetic-energy impact of a 20 mm shell and can penetrate any known thickness of tank armor plate. A two-second burst is sufficient to kill a tank several times over.

Another awesome ground-support aircraft is the C-130H Spectre. Originally designed to locate and kill forces hiding in dense jungle, the Spectre truly fulfills the promise of its motto, "death from above." Each Spectre is equipped with four 20 mm Vulcan cannons of six barrels, each capable of firing 6000 rounds per minute. It also carries four 7.62 multibarrel miniguns, which can fire at 10,000 rounds per minute, and a 40 mm Bofors cannon capable of 2000 rounds per minute. As if to add more death to injury, the Spectre also mounts a 105 mm automatic howitzer. The Spectre's purpose is to deliver death from above quickly and silently. Accordingly, all its guns are linked to automatic electronic and infrared detection devices. Its on-board electronics make it capable of "seeing" an enemy hidden in multiple layers of jungle canopy and automatically directing its guns to the target, so that a single pass is often fatal to the enemy below. With all its guns firing at once, the Spectre is capable of reducing all the buildings in a city block to rubble in less than one minute. Captured Vietcong troops who had been through an attack by the Spectre testify that it is an experience they are never likely to forget.

Close air support is, of course, only one role for modern strike aircraft. They are also expected to engage enemy aircraft and destroy them and to intercept enemy forces massing hundreds of miles behind the front. For destroying enemy aircraft, a new generation of air-to-air missiles has revolutionized aerial combat. The AIM-9 Sidewinder, for example, can seek and destroy enemy aircraft up to ten miles away. Its kill-per-engagement record is 92 percent. The A-54 Phoenix missile can be launched as far as 100 miles from its target. On the last ten miles of its flight it is automatically guided by its own homing radar. Its kill-to-engagement record is 90 percent. In short, it is now possible for aircraft to kill each other from distances well beyond the range of sight. Moreover, unlike earlier heat-seeking missiles, modern missiles need not be fired from behind the target. They may approach it with equal lethality from any direction, including head-on.

While missiles have an aura of high tech, it is important to remember the "ordinary" bomb. The problem is, however, that compared to the TNT bombs of World War II, today's bombs are anything but ordinary. A cluster of modern conventional bombs can produce the same explosive effect as low-yield nuclear weapons. Even since Vietnam—where we dropped thirty-six tons of bombs for every square mile of both North and South Vietnam—the increases in the effectiveness of aircraft-delivered bombs have been amazing. Bombs have become more compact and slender, allowing more explosive to be carried by a single plane. Of course, the explosives themselves are many times more powerful than the old TNT filler. They have also become far more accurate, with a number of devices ranging from tail retarding devices to optical and laser guidance systems.

Bombs are also more versatile. They can be used to carry rather ordinary chemical munitions like white phosphorous. Its burns can only be stopped from burning entirely through the body by putting the affected limb under water while a surgeon picks out the pieces of phosphorous. New bombs can also deliver a full range of chemical munitions like mustard and nerve gas. They are cheap and effective. A simple cluster bomb, no larger than an old-fashioned 250-pound bomb, can carry within its casing hundreds of smaller bomblets. Where there had previously been a single explosion, there are now hundreds of smaller explosions vastly increasing the number of shrapnel shards that can slice through a soldier's flesh. A single cluster bomb has the same effect as 600 well-aimed World War II 81 mm mortar rounds impacting at once. Few soldiers can be expected to survive such an attack. If the shrapnel doesn't get them, the concussion will.

The FAM, or Fuel Air Munition, bombs offer a new wrinkle. These bombs carry an explosive liquid—propane, butane, propylene oxide, or something else—which is released in a dense, highly combustible cloud over a battlefield area. When detonated by a delayed fuse carried in the bomb's base, the detonation produces five times the explosive force of an equivalent amount of TNT. Thus a 250-pound FAM can produce the explosive equivalent of a 1200-pound bomb. Three 100-pound FAMs produce a combustible cloud fifty-six feet across by nine feet thick. Upon detonation, the cloud produces an explosive combustive effect greater than a low-yield nuclear weapon. Another bomb, the Daisy Cutter bomb of Vietnam lineage, produces a blast overpressure of 1000 pounds per square inch, a force equivalent to being hit with a baseball bat over every square inch of the body. In Vietnam, Daisy Cutters killed earthworms one hundred yards from the center of the bomb crater.

Battlefield helicopters have revolutionized the mobility of combat forces. Compared to World War II, the mobility of antitank forces mounted on helicopters has increased almost twenty times while the ability to move troop units about the battlefield has increased more than one hundred times. More than any other invention, the helicopter is responsible for the new dimensions of war—the deep and rear battle. Within minutes troops can now be ferried deep into the enemy's rear with their full complement of weaponry. They can also be inserted in the path of advancing enemy forces miles to the front of the line. World War II commanders had no such capacity. Besides the obvious ability of helicopters to ferry troops and carry cargo—a medium-lift helicopter can carry twice the cargo of a World War II "deuce and a half" truck at five times the speed—the most important role of the helicopter is in troop and tank attack.

Attack helicopters can fly close to the ground and surprise tanks and troops. The helicopter provides a much more stable, thus more accurate, missile and gun platform than other aircraft. It can approach within much closer ranges, bring a greater variety of weapons to bear, and do so for much longer periods of time than a fixed-wing strike aircraft. Helicopters such as the A-1 Cobra are equipped with the M-28 chin turret, which can carry two 7.62 miniguns or two 40 mm grenade launchers, which fire 450 grenades per minute over a range of 2000 yards. Each grenade has a lethal radius of ten yards. It can also be fitted with two M-200 stanchon rocket pods each holding nineteen 2.75 inch rockets. In one configuration, the Cobra can carry fifty-four rockets. The 2.75-inch rocket, called "Tiny Tim," has an explosive force equal to that of an 81 mm mortar shell. Those rockets equipped with white phosphorous heads equal the explosive force of the 4.2-inch (107 mm) mortar shell. The linkage of these systems to a full array of electronic sighting and computerized aiming devices, which hold the guns on target no matter what the maneuvering position of the helicopter, enhances their killing power.

In the antitank role helicopters are indeed awesome weapons. A single Cobra can carry eight TOW antitank missiles, which are generally regarded as the best antitank missiles in the world. The TOW's killing range is 4,687 yards. Its shaped explosive charge warhead is capable of piercing any known thickness of tank armor, leaving holes two feet in diameter in the tank's hull. A TOW's optical sight is so good that at 1000 yards, a tank fills the sight screen. Once fired, the missile is guided to its target at a speed of 368 miles an hour.

The AH-64 Apache helicopter is even more deadly as a tank killer. It can carry sixteen TOW missiles or sixteen of the new Hellfire missiles. The Hellfire is a third-generation missile and incorporates a true "fire and forget" homing device. The helicopter aims the missile, fires it, and can then take evasive action with no need to remain on station for three or four seconds to guide the missile to its target. The Apache also mounts nineteen 2.75-inch rockets and a Hughes 30 mm chain gun in the nose. It is also equipped with the full complement of computers and electronic gun sights. Pilots are equipped with a new helmet "killer sight." As the pilot turns to look at a target, the guns automatically follow his head and eye movements. Thus, to see the target is to hit it, and in general to hit the target is to kill it.

The helicopter, more than any other weapon, is responsible for the "swirling tactics" that characterize modern war. The ability of a commander to strike far to his front or deep in his enemy's rear means, of course, that he must be able to counter similar tactics against his forces. Thus, there are no longer any safe areas. Tanks may now be struck hundreds of miles from the fighting zone as they are loaded on railway trains for the journey to the front. Staff headquarters hundreds of miles from the front may be hit. Hospitals, once safely in the rear, along with ports, airfields, communications stations, road junctions, and other strategically important areas are now equally vulnerable. So important has the helicopter become that the Soviets have configured their helicopters with weapons designed to shoot down enemy helicopters on tank-killing missions. The next war may well witness the birth of helicopter-to-helicopter aerial combat.

CHEMICAL WEAPONS

The factor that may influence the modern battlefield most dramatically of all and one for which there are no meaningful ways to determine impact is the use of chemical weapons. Chemical weapons may turn out to be the most deadly means for killing and incapacitating troops in the next war. In the words of one U.S. Army report, "if their use is not inhibited, they could swing the balance in a conventional war."

Chemical weapons were first used on a large scale in World War I on April 22, 1915, at Ypres, Belgium, when the German army released the contents of 5000 canisters of chlorine gas. The victims, two French elite divisions, were taken by surprise, and broke and ran, opening a five-mile gap in the Allied line. After Ypres, chemical munitions were used more and more frequently by all sides. The last year of the war, 1918, saw more chemical weapons used than in the preceding three years. Of approximately 1.3 million gas casualties in World War I, about 92,000 were fatal. No less than 35 percent of all gas casualties, most of them fatalities, were Russian troops, a fact that no doubt accounts for the present Soviet interest in producing and defending against chemical weapons. Those who believe that such weapons are too horrible to be used again ought to remember that the American plan for the invasion of Japan in World War II called for the large-scale use of chemical weapons against civilians to reduce Allied ground casualties. Moreover, the Japanese used chemical weapons frequently against Chinese soldiers and civilians in their attack on China before World War II. Since World War II, chemical weapons have been used in Vietnam, Cambodia, Yemen, the Iran-Iraq War, and Afghanistan. In the minds of most military commanders, chemical weapons are just one more tool of war; their use is expected and planned for.

Today, the Soviet army is fully prepared to fight with chemical weapons. No fewer than 100,000 special troops and units are designed to attack with and defend against chemical weapons. The Soviets have sixteen different chemical delivery systems ranging from aircraft bombs, artillery shells, to chemical grenades and land mines. In addition, most of their battlefield vehicles—unlike U.S. vehicles—are designed to operate in a chemical environment, and soldiers are issued protective suits. What makes the Soviet chemical threat so great is that American chemical capabilities, offensive and defensive, are almost nonexistent. Moreover, chemical weapons are much more effective when used in the offensive, and seizing and maintaining the offensive is the key element in Soviet combat doctrine. The range of chemical weapons staggers the imagination. Such weapons range from simple gas compounds, like mustard gas, to blood and nerve agents for which no real defense exists.

While the use of chemical agents may well kill hundreds of thousands of soldiers—to say nothing of the helpless civilians trapped in or near the fighting with no means of protecting themselves—the major impact of chemical attacks is likely to be psychiatric. And a soldier who is out of action because of psychiatric breakdown is just as useless as a soldier who has been shot. The psychiatric impact of chemical weapons is hard for the average civilian to comprehend. In World War I, for example, a British army study conducted in 1921 found that of the 600,000 Allied gas casualties in World War I, no fewer than 400,000 were psychiatric in origin and self-inflicted. Frightened soldiers would use a small stick to pick up the available residue of mustard gas and apply it on their skin. Once the blisters appeared, they would report to the battalion aid station and get out of the fighting for a short while. In another study done in 1927 the American army found that two of every three men who reported to an aid station complaining of gas symptoms had not even been exposed to a gas attack. Most were suffering the symptoms of chemical exposure, but their cause was psychosomatic.

In a modern war soldiers forced to don chemical protection suits would almost certainly suffer a very high rate of psychiatric collapse within a few hours. Modern chemical suits simply don't work very well. On average, the suit must be changed every ten hours to ensure that chemical residues do not penetrate it. They are made of a rubberized material and are very hot. At 65° a soldier cannot function in a suit for more than three hours. His combat efficiency is reduced at least 50 percent and by as much as 80 percent. One U.S. estimate is that simply putting on the suit reduces the combat effectiveness of troops by 50 percent. Worse, the soldier is encased in a head mask and filter which makes it very difficult to see, as the lenses become fogged. His ability to hear and communicate declines by over 80 percent, and he is subject to rapid heat exhaustion. Nor can he take off the suit to gain relief. Once a chemical alert is sounded, there are few reliable ways to determine what types of chemicals have been used or for how long they will pose a danger. Some agents last six months or longer. Some chemical agents, such as blood and nerve agents, are colorless, odorless, and tasteless, and only a few can be detected by electronic sensors. In many cases the only sure way to determine if the area is safe is to coax a soldier out of his suit and see if he dies.

The soldier is therefore trapped inside his chemical suit psychologically and physically isolated from his comrades. All he can be aware of is the throb of his own pulse, rapid breathing and the smell of his own sweat. To make matters worse, many of the initial signs of chemical poisoning— rapid heartbeat, sweating, and shortness of breath—are exactly like those of normal physiological stress reactions of battle. Isolated from his comrades, the soldier in a chemical suit is forced to deal with his physical symptoms alone. Who can blame him if he misinterprets his symptoms as chemically induced and suffers a psychiatric collapse? If he believes he has been exposed, the soldier is likely to inject himself with atropine, a chemical which, at best, is a poor antidote against chemical attack. The problem is that once he injects himself, the atropine reaction brings on terrible side effects of its own. Common effects of atropine injection are dehydration, incoherency, and mental disorientation, all severe enough to render the soldier useless. The mere suspicion that a unit may have been subjected to a chemical attack is enough, in most cases, to generate a very high rate of psychiatric casualties. In World War I, for example, chemical weapons produced four times as many nonfatal battle casualties as were produced by regular explosive weapons, and most of these were psychiatric.

The ability of fear to debilitate soldiers under chemical conditions cannot be overestimated. In 1985, a battalion of the French Foreign Legion was undergoing a mock chemical attack at its island base in Corsica. This unit had been through this exercise many times before. Usually, a single aircraft would pass low over the troops and drop water vapor, simulating the gas attack. This time, however, the instructors replaced the water vapor with a harmless red powder that the troops had never seen. Once the aircraft released the powder, the seasoned troops of the legion were shaken to the core. The whole battalion, apparently believing that some horrible mistake had been made and that real chemical compounds had been used, simply came apart. Scores of soldiers writhed on the ground manifesting all the symptoms of a genuine chemical attack. Some almost died from their psychologically generated symptoms. The rest either panicked and ran while others froze on the spot expecting to die. While there are no reliable means for predicting the number of physical or psychological casualties that would result from an actual attack, there is widespread agreement that the results would be catastrophic. It is fully expected that the World War I psychiatric casualty rates would be exceeded by several times.

THE POOR BLOODY INFANTRY

Since the sixteenth century the infantry has suffered the greatest number of casualties in any war. Dubbed the "queen of battle" by military commanders, it has always been to those who served in it "the poor bloody infantry." While modern weaponry has increased the infantry's ability to kill by several thousand times since the sixteenth century, it is surely true that the human being has remained essentially the same for at least the last 200,000 years. Certainly we have evolved no mechanisms, biological or psychological, to make us any more able to withstand the killing and maiming effects of weaponry nor is there any evidence that we are any more able to withstand the psychological impact that the horror of war has always had upon soldiers. The weaponry has changed dramatically; the soldiers have remained the same.

The individual infantryman now has at his disposal weapons of much greater destruction than did his predecessors. A single infantryman now possesses the means to shoot down aircraft or kill tanks. But the truth is that the exponential increase in fire power and lethality of other weapons has simply not been matched by either the firepower of the infantry's weapons or, more importantly, the ability to escape the lethal effects of other weapons. What this all adds up to is that the infantry soldier is more vulnerable than ever. The infantry will die in windrows in a modern war much as they have in wars past.

All of this raises the question of casualties. Modern conventional war has become so destructive that neither side has been able to come up with realistic casualty figures as to how many dead, wounded, and psychiatrically broken men would result from even a single day's battle, never mind a long war. U.S. military commanders freely admit that their estimates of

920 men per day per division—approximately an 8 percent loss rate a day—are probably incorrect, since they are based upon computer models that are rooted largely in assumptions drawn from World War II experience.

The one example of two modern conventional armies clashing against one another came in the 1973 Arab-Israeli War. In that war, both sides suffered losses of 50 percent in men and equipment in less than two weeks of fighting. But the 1973 war is not accurately instructive for calculating casualties in a modern conventional conflict. For one thing, the number of forces was nowhere near what it would be in a battle in Central Europe and, equally important, there have been numerous improvements and new weapons since then. A 50 percent loss rate in two weeks can only be regarded as the most optimistic prediction of future conventional war casualties. Even assuming this "best case" scenario, the number of men killed and wounded in a central European battle would approximate 2 million on both sides if the battle lasted only two weeks.

At least the dead will be dead, but what about the wounded? The simple fact is that neither side has sufficient medical resources to deal with the massive numbers of wounded soldiers that will result from a conventional war. For example, the U.S. military has only about half the number of doctors it had in service during the Vietnam War to deal with wounded casualties that will occur at four to five times the rate in much shorter periods of time. There are only 149 anesthesiologists and only 420 surgeons available for wartime requirements. Fewer than 2,000 beds would be available to treat the wounded in Europe, meaning that we would have to evacuate our wounded directly to the United States for treatment. Such a prospect, which is official military doctrine, assumes that the airfields and aircraft from which such evacuations would stage will be available, a doubtful assumption, given the nature of modern war. In every test done on evacuation capability, the United States has found that it simply does not have the aircraft and crews to evacuate large numbers of casualties. Moreover, given the time it takes to evacuate casualties over such long distances, it is expected that 20 percent more soldiers will die needlessly as a result of delayed treatment during the long trip. It seems a foregone conclusion that only the lightly wounded will survive. The rest will die.

Then there are those who will be driven mad by the fighting. In a modern war the chances of becoming a psychiatric casualty are more than twice as great as being killed by enemy fire. And even this standard is drawn from historical experience and cannot be predicted with accuracy in a modern conventional war. A few years ago the U.S. Army attempted to measure just how intense the modern battlefield would be when compared to World War II. The study found that in World War II, heavy combat produced an exposure to enemy "combat pulses"—ground attacks, artillery shelling, aircraft bombing, and so on—at a rate of two to four a day. Today, the enemy as well as allied forces are expected to deliver twelve to fourteen combat pulses a day. Consequently, modern conventional war is likely to be anywhere from four to seven times as intense as World War II combat.

The impact of this level of battle intensity upon the ability of the soldier to retain his sanity is tremendous. If one were able to transport the increases in firepower and lethality of today back to World War II, the number of psychiatric casualties suffered only by the American ground forces in that war would jump from 241,960 to 967,840 at a minimum. But firepower and lethality are not the only factors that increase the probabilities and rates at which soldiers will become debilitated by psychiatric stress. Other factors, paradoxically, are even more important.

Psychiatric stress casualties increase greatly when the soldier feels isolated. Clearly, the need to fight in chemical suits or from within armored personnel carriers where one shot kills all the men on board will increase psychological isolation. Increased physical fatigue strongly affects psychiatric casualty rates. Since the soldier in a modern war will have to fight longer and harder, often cut off from replenishment, psychiatric debilitation rates can be expected to rise even further. The need to fight at night will generate even higher rates as will the need for an almost constant stream of losses and replacements, which will weaken the social cohesion of the combat group, which is the first line of defense against psychiatric breakdown. Finally, the huge increases in indirect fire upon the troops will generate extremely high rates of psychiatric casualties.

Both the intensity and nature of modern conventional war are likely to generate rates of psychiatric casualties never before seen in warfare. Again using a World War II model with constant manpower rates, if the factors associated with modern war had been available at that time, the number of psychiatric casualties would have reached 1 million, an increase of almost five times the actual World War II rate. It is highly probable that the rate of psychiatric casualties in a modern conventional war will account for almost 50 percent of the total manpower loss on both sides. It is, at best, highly questionable whether any army could long sustain such rates and survive.

CONCLUSION

What this brief sketch of modern conventional war should make obvious is that war is no longer a rational response or means to gain political ends. War has become an activity that has surpassed the ability of human beings to endure it. An army sent off to war, even if victorious, will return a bedraggled, maimed mob of mad men. Whatever proportionality between means and ends that may have once existed on the field of battle no longer exists. Even the victors must pass through a slaughterhouse on the way to victory.

War is no longer tolerable to the human mind. We have reached a point where almost everyone exposed to combat will, within a comparatively short time, be killed, wounded, or driven mad. Indeed, the greater threat to the modern soldier is neither being killed nor wounded. It is the threat of being psychiatrically debilitated from mental breakdown. In such circumstances, one can only wonder what meaning such human qualities as courage, endurance, and heroism still have. On a battlefield when large numbers of men are slaughtered for no greater reason than they were in the wrong place at the wrong time, one can only wonder of what worth military expertise and training are. When so many are killed and maimed so quickly, of what value is the notion of personal sacrifice?

What is clear is that most civilians have no idea what they are in for once called to the colors of their country to do battle. Certainly their experiences will far surpass anything they could have remotely imagined. Many of them will be driven mad, and some will never recover. Yet, with all the emphasis on the technology of war, its cost in terms of dollars, and the frequency with which it penetrates our consciousness, the thought of being driven mad by combat never enters most people's minds. How strange, since madness in war has been one of the few constants that have accompanied soldiers from earliest times. And there is every evidence that it will be an even more present companion of those who take the field of battle the next time.

NOTES

1. John Keegan, "The Spectre of Conventional War," *Harper's Magazine* (July 1983), p. 10.

2. All facts, figures, and statistics concerning performance characteristics of the weapons discussed in this chapter are taken from official military manuals or performance data published by the manufacturers of the weapons. Two good sources for this information are FM 100–5, "Operations," U.S. Army publication, 1978, and Tom Gervasi, *America's War Machine* (New York: Grove Press, 1984), which provides an encyclopedic compendium of manufacturers' performance data.

4

Development of Soviet Military Psychiatry

Comprehension of Soviet military psychiatry requires an understanding of its development against the background of Soviet and Russian military history. Like all things Russian, military psychiatry in its present form has been enormously influenced by the experience of the Russian and Soviet armies on the field of battle. The Soviets have shown a marked tendency not to depart radically from the lessons of past wars and, in a number of areas, the Soviets are often considerably behind modern developments because their focus remains on their last battle experience. It is true that armies generally tend to plan for the last war, but this tendency seems particularly characteristic of the Soviet military. Their tendency gradually to adapt the experiences of the past to solving recent problems is evident in their philosophy of equipment design, tactics, strategy, use of the soldier, and many others, including the field of military psychiatry.

1900—1917

Interestingly, the first army to diagnose mental disease as a specific consequence of the stress of modern warfare and to attempt to do something about it was the Russian army during the Russo-Japanese War of 1905. Previously, like the British in the Boer War and the Americans in the Civil War, soldiers were identified as manifesting behavioral problems that affected their ability to fight. But most often their problems were attributed to any number of factors other than the sheer stress of combat. A common practice was to attribute the mental problems of soldiers to cowardice or lack of character, a practice that endured in some Western armies through World War II.

During the Russo-Japanese War, physicians in the Russian Army diagnosed and treated approximately 2000 casualties that they directly attributed to the stress of battle. But the number of soldiers complaining of psychiatric symptoms was so large that they overburdened the medical system and were shipped home and turned over to the Russian Red Cross for institutionalized care. The number of neuropsychiatric casualties reached such proportions that even the home-front resources eventually proved insufficient. The Russian experience in 1905 provided the first example of "evacuation syndrome" in modern times.

The Russians seem to have been the first to place psychiatrists relatively close to the battle front in order to deal with psychiatric breakdown. Most of these psychiatrists, however, came from civilian mental hospitals and had no training in dealing with military psychiatric problems. Psychiatric dispensaries staffed with psychiatrists and other medical personnel were established near the front lines and had their own transport, usually a specially marked ambulance, to deal with stress casualties as distinct from physical casualties.[1] The dispensary staff often included a neurologist, a physician's assistant, and three medics under the direction of a psychiatrist. While most Western armies reached this degree of organization by 1917, the principle of "proximity," stationing psychiatric personnel close to the battle front and treating neuropsychiatric casualties there, was a practical lesson that seems to have been forgotten during the interwar period and did not emerge in practice again until late in World War II. It reappeared in full form in Korea when it was used by the American army and was used again in Vietnam. After the 1973 war in Israel, the Israeli army sent a number of experts to the United States to study American doctrine and practice concerning the problem, and between 1974 and 1983 established a doctrine and structure for treating stress casualties closely based on the American model.[2] On balance, however, the Russian army in 1905 was the first to practice the principle of proximity. Their performance, however, was marginal, since, in fact, not much forward treatment of psychiatric casualties was accomplished.

In the Russo-Japanese War the Russian army established a central psychiatric hospital behind the lines in the city of Harbin, Manchuria. This hospital recorded between forty-three and ninety admissions a day for neuropsychiatric casualties. Of these, only a few could be rapidly treated and sent back to the front. Those who remained in the hospital did so for about fifteen days and were subjected to a variety of treatment therapies. If they did not recover, they were then evacuated to Moscow by train, a trip that often took forty days because only a single railroad track ran from Harbin to Moscow.[3] Evacuees were accompanied by a surgeon and a small staff of assistants, and by the end of the war the Russian Medical Corps had established a number of special trains exclusively for the use of psychiatric patients. These trains had special isolation compartments, restraint rooms, and barred windows.[4]

Although the Russians attempted to treat psychiatric caualties at the front, the rates of successful recovery suggest that the treatment was not very effective. Of the 275 officers admitted to the psychiatric hospital in Harbin during the war, only 54 recovered sufficiently to be sent back to the lines, while 214 were evacuated to Moscow. Of the 1072 enlisted soldiers treated in Harbin, only 51 recovered and were returned to their units, while 983 were evacuated to the rear.[5]

Even in 1905 the Russians began to recognize the problem of secondary gain. They discovered quickly that the further a soldier suffering psychiatric symptoms was evacuated from the front, the less likely he was to recover. Secondary gain is caused by a number of factors. In the Russian view the cause was the perception that stress reactions were often functional for the soldier in that they allowed him to escape the horrors of battle. Once the soldier understood that certain symptoms would allow him to be evacuated out of danger, he began to manifest those symptoms. Moreover, as he was moved farther and farther away from the battle area, his ability and willingness to try to reverse those symptoms became less, so that the farther to the rear he went, the deeper his symptoms became. Secondary gain became a major problem for Western armies in World War I and II.

During the Russo-Japanese War Russian physicians appear to have made significant advances in linking battle stress with certain types of somatic symptoms. An analysis of the diagnoses of hundreds of psychiatric cases during the 1905 war shows that the Russians were already able to diagnose battle stress casualties by modern categories. Russian psychiatrists recorded cases of hysterical excitement, confused states, fugue states, hysterical blindness, surdomutism, local paralysis, and neurasthenia.[6] Interestingly, although they understood that these symptoms were related to battle stress, Russian psychiatrists, drawing on their own German medical educations, tended to define the impact of stress in purely physiological terms. Thus, a wide range of battle-stress symptoms were attributed to traumatic psychosis of organic origins. In the Russo-Japanese War 55.6 percent of the battle stress casualties were attributed directly to traumatic damage to the brain or the nervous system.[7]

By the end of the Russo-Japanese War and certainly by World War I the Russian Army probably had the most practical clinical experience in dealing with stress casualties. To be sure, its treatment methods would be regarded by modern Western standards as somewhat primitive, but for their time they were comparatively advanced. Moreover, the Russo-Japanese War provided physicians in the Russian army with the first practical opportunity to institutionalize clinical treatment methods for stress casualties deduced directly from the organic and physiological premises of Russian biological psychiatry. The mold was set for continuing the physiological approach to the treatment of battle stress that is still used in the Soviet army. Equally important, by defining psychiatric disorders as a disease due to physiological damage, Russian military physicians differed from their contemporaries in the West, who, after 1917, persisted for almost forty years in attributing stress breakdown to cowardice or defects in the soldier's character. Finally, the Russian experience in the Russo-Japanese War established a significant experiential base for institutionalizing the principle of proximity of treatment as a way of dealing with the greater problem of secondary gain.

WORLD WAR I

The experience of the Russian army in dealing with battle stress casualties in World War I remains obscure. It is simply not possible to reconstruct that history in any great detail from available sources in the West or, indeed, even from those available to Soviet scholars themselves because not much literature on the subject of battle psychiatry has survived for reasons that are obvious enough. Most literature dealing with any war-related subject emerges only after the war is over. During wartime, communication is limited for reasons of national security and the obvious obstacles to normal academic or intellectual intercourse. The period following World War I in Russia was marked by events so severe and traumatic that the collection and publication of information on almost any scientific or medical subject was very difficult and, in many cases, impossible. Following the destruction of World War I, in which 11 million Russians died, the entire society was shaken to the core by the Russian Revolution of 1917. Between 1917 and 1920 the Civil War claimed another 4 million lives. Moreover, between 1917 and its reconstitution in 1927 the Russian/Soviet Army virtually ceased to exist as a national entity. Finally, many of the psychiatrists and neurologists came from the upper and bourgeois classes of Russia and hence were killed during the Civil War. Taken together, these events alone would have been enough to ensure that the collection and transfer of information about Russian battle psychiatry would be minimal.

In addition, between 1921 and 1922 Russia suffered a devastating famine, probably the most severe in the history of the country. While exact figures cannot be substantiated, probably more died of starvation during the postwar famine than in both the Civil War and World War I.[8] If so, upwards of 15 million Russians died from hunger and disease in a two-year period.

The emigration of more than 2 million people from Russia, many of them members of the intellectual, academic, and medical elite of the country, further reduces the amount of information available. In 1922 the Soviets embarked upon a disastrous war against Poland, which cost several hundred thousand dead and wounded. In 1928 Josef Stalin began his infamous collectivization plan, in which another 5 to 8 million Russians would eventually lose their lives. In the early 1930s Stalin embarked on the Great Terror, a period of remarkable brutality that eventually claimed 8 million lives. Finally, in 1939 the war against the Finns inflicted more dead and further social disruption.

Thus, between 1917 and 1940, the period in which one would have expected that much of the Russian experience with battle psychiatry in World War I would have finally emerged in print, there is no material available on the subject at all. If one searches the international medical journal *Lancet,* as well as Russian medical journals, from 1914 to 1940, not a single article is found from any source dealing with the subject of Soviet or Russian military psychiatry or the treatment of neuropsychiatric casualties in World War I.

Of course physicians in the Soviet army were thinking about the problems of military psychiatry. In their official histories, always to be regarded with some distrust especially in the area of psychiatry, the Soviets note that between 1918 and 1920 three books a year were published on the general subjects of psychology and psychiatry. Between 1931 and 1940 their official histories list seven books a year published on the subject.[9] Yet, an examination of these works shows clearly that all were highly theoretical in nature and dealt far more with the problem of trying to square Marxist ideology with the clinical approaches of military psychiatry than with actual techniques of the discipline.

Between 1921 and 1940 the Kirov Military Medical Academy in Leningrad continued to do work on the subjects of military psychiatry and psychology, focusing on the area of military teaching and training. These problems were important for the Communist party given the view of the Red Army as a totally new social institution comprised of workers and peasants and based on its own unique psychology of Marxist-Leninism. As with psychiatry and psychology in society as a whole, military psychiatry was affected by the same swings in party positions that impacted upon the discipline and was marked by a continuing attempt to resolve the tension between bourgeois and Marxist approaches to human nature. In the case of military psychology the tension initially resolved itself in the death of the discipline when Stalin simply outlawed it.

The political purges also took a high toll of the old intellectual elite including civilian and military doctors, psychologists, and psychiatrists. After Stalin made it clear in 1936 that he regarded psychology as dangerous to the political consciousness of the citizenry, in the words of a Soviet journal, "a sharp reduction in research in military psychology occurred in practice. Only in military aviation psychology were high rates of research maintained."[10] Only as the purges tapered off and World War II was about to begin did the Party realize that it needed a developed doctrine of military psychiatry and psychology. In January 1941 the People's Commissariat for the Defense of the U.S.S.R. raised the question of the need to develop a military psychology to "create psychological bases for combat and political training."[11] By then it was too late, and World War II broke out a few months later.

Despite the difficulty in obtaining hard data on Soviet psychiatric practice in World War I, it is possible to gain some insight into how the Russian army dealt with the problem by remembering that much of their medical practice during the war strongly paralleled their own experiences in the Russo-Japanese War. In addition, most Russian psychiatric practice was, at base, German psychiatric practice and probably was similar in the military sphere as well. Many Soviet techniques that surfaced in World War II were imitations of techniques used by the German army in World War I. Accordingly, it is highly probable that Russian psychiatric practice in World War I used such basic techniques as electric stimulation of paralyzed limbs, water therapy, rest, and considerable folk medicine derivatives and stimulants.[12] The Germans in World War I used all these techniques, and the Red Army in World War II continued to do so. Beyond such general statements not much can be said in any detail about Russian psychiatric practice in World War I.

WORLD WAR II

Before assessing the Soviet army's ability to deal with battle stress casualties in World War II, it is necessary to establish a baseline against which the data can be analyzed. Soviet secrecy about much of their battle performance in what they call the Great Patriotic War and, since 1950, their effort to write their own version of history complicate this task. There is only one known document that chronicles the activities of the Soviet medical corps in World War II: a 1948 multivolume work entitled *The Experiences of Soviet Medicine in the Great Patriotic War*. One volume deals with the treatment of psychiatric cases.[13] Unfortunately, the work is not available in the West and in recent years has even disappeared from the shelves of Soviet medical libraries. Accordingly, what is presented here regarding Soviet medical performance is based largely on interviews with individuals who served during World War II in the Soviet medical corps.

Western military analysts disagree about exactly how many men the Soviet Union mobilized for military service in World War II and about the number of dead and wounded in that war. T. R. Dupuy in his *Encyclopedia of Military History* states that the Soviets mobilized 25 million, and of that number 7 million were killed and another 14 million wounded.[14] Lt. Col. Robert Glantz of the Strategic Studies Institute of the U.S. Army War College at Carlisle Barracks, Pennsylvania, suggests that Dupuy's figures are too high. He argues that the Soviets mobilized about 20 million men, of whom 5 million were killed and between 8 and 9 million were wounded.[15] Unable to resolve the conflict between the two figures definitively, it seems useful for purposes of this analysis to choose a figure somewhere between the two estimates—22 million—as a baseline. Of this, somewhere in the vicinity of 20 million were eventually put in uniform.

By contrast, the United States conscripted approximately 20 million men for military service. Of these, 14 million passed the initial physical and psychological screening and were eventually pressed into military service. Of these 14 million soldiers, 260,000 were killed and another 480,000 were wounded on all fronts. In terms of military psychiatry, it is interesting to note that of 14 million U.S. soldiers about 504,000 assigned to the U.S. Army suffered psychiatric problems severe enough to be released from military service.[16]

The Soviets apparently had no formal philosophy or standard of selection except for obvious physical impairments that would normally preclude strenuous exercises as well as combat. Their basic philosophy of recruitment was that every Soviet citizen, including women, had to serve in some capacity. There were no nonmedical exemptions. Nor were there any psychological or behavioral models used to screen conscripts as there were in the West. Soldiers were assigned where needed and expected to perform. When they failed, harsh punishments, often death, were imposed. Every citizen age fifty-five or younger who was physically fit was called to military service.

The draft screening procedure centered around a number of local military commissions or commisariats. Medical doctors, usually internists and neurologists, comprised this commission and examined conscripts for general physical health. No psychiatrists served on these examining boards, and no psychiatric tests were administered. Whatever psychiatric screening was done was on an ad hoc basis by neurologists whose physiological orientation permitted them to detect any organic causes that might account for behavioral problems. Besides clear physical disabilities, imbecillia or psychosis so obvious that there was no practical problem in diagnosis resulted in rejection from service. The number of conscripts who were deferred from military service on purely psychiatric grounds was very small indeed.

It is possible to obtain data on the number of Soviet rejections for psychiatric reasons in World War II by interviewing a number of medical doctors and neurologists who served on draft medical commissions during the war; some served as battle surgeons later on. To be sure, the data are not definitive. According to these sources, of the 22 million men who were conscripted only a small number, perhaps no more than 50,000 to 75,000, were exempted from military service for purely psychiatric problems, a rejection rate of less than .25 percent. Even at the extreme the figure would not exceed 1 percent of the total pool examined. By comparison, the United States examined some 18 million men and rejected 5,250,000 or about 29 percent of the total pool for "mental, moral, and physical" reasons. The

United States found 71 percent of its conscript pool fit for military duty, approximately 12,750,000 men. It rejected 970,000 men for neuropsychiatric disorders and other emotional problems. Thus, psychiatric reasons accounted for 18.5 percent of those rejected for military service. As a percentage of the total conscript pool 5.4 percent of those initially screened for military service were rejected for psychiatric disorders.[17] This rejection rate for psychiatric problems was twenty times greater than that in the Soviet Army in World War II.

Given a baseline armed force, the degree to which military units will suffer neuropsychiatric casualties depends first upon a number of factors that are not directly quantifiable: unit cohesion, quality of leadership, replacement system, and others. Yet, three major factors directly related to the rates of psychiatric casualties are the type of battle a unit must fight, its intensity, and its duration. In this regard the Soviets fought almost five long years of war much of it under conditions of disarray and near collapse. Moreover, the intensity of combat and the size and duration of the battles the Soviets fought were, on balance, much greater than those fought by American and British troops with the possible exception of the Normandy invasion and following battle in June and July 1944. The number of physical casualties in the Soviet Army was higher than that of any other combatant, perhaps as high as 8 million dead and another 15 million wounded. For the Soviets, then, World War II was much more intense than for most other combatants with the possible exception of the Germans. On these grounds alone Soviet military units could be expected to have suffered very high numbers of neuropsychiatric casualties.

The number of psychiatric casualties suffered by the Soviet army can also be related to the manner in which they conducted battle. Lt. Col. Robert Glantz of the Strategic Studies Institute at the U.S. Army War College analyzed hundreds of Soviet combat unit histories and diaries and concludes that it was very common for Soviet divisions to enter battle at only 70 percent strength in manpower and equipment. Moreover, common practice was to fight these units down to 25 to 30 percent strength before stopping the attack.[18] Even then Soviet units were often not pulled out of the line. Instead, common practice was to throw another division into the breach, joining the remaining elements of the bloodied unit to the new one and continuing the attack. These practices suggest that the tempo of war was very intense for Soviet units and that Soviet battle doctrine itself probably increased what was an already high level of combat dead, wounded and stress casualties.

The practical challenge of military psychiatry is not so much how to prevent psychiatric breakdown among men engaged in battle. Indeed, there is widespread agreement that while the rates of breakdown may be somewhat controllable, the mechanisms that produce psychiatric breakdown in battle are still far beyond the control of psychiatrists. Some psychiatric casualties are inevitable under the horrors of modern war. The practical task of military psychiatry is to treat as many psychiatric casualties as quickly as possible and return them to their fighting units in order to preserve the manpower strength of the army. By this standard Soviet military psychiatry seems to have done very well during World War II.

Drawing on more than a score of interviews with Soviet combat doctors, including psychiatrists and neurologists, it is possible to arrive at a rough estimate of the number of Soviet soldiers who were diagnosed as suffering from psychiatric problems serious enough to warrant evacuation from their units. These men were lost to Soviet combat units for much if not most of the war. The data suggest that the loss rate due to neuropsychiatric breakdown suffered by the Red Army was certainly under ten per thousand and probably closer to six per thousand. Interestingly, the American Army in World War I suffered about the same rate. During World War II the Soviet army suffered between 96,000 and 100,000 psychiatric casualties that were eventually lost to the fighting units as manpower assets.

A comparison can be made between the Soviet army and the American army in the same war. The American army was apparently less successful in preventing manpower loss as a consequence of psychiatric breakdown. In the American army alone (not counting army air crews, naval or marine casualties) the United States suffered 504,000 separations from military service as a result of psychiatric problems. Of these, 333,000 were true neuropsychiatric cases of psychosis and psychoneurosis. The remaining 171,000 separations from service were due to "behavioral problems" and the "failure to adapt" to military life.[19] Of the 333,000 separations for psychosis and psychoneurosis in combat zones, among those soldiers who saw ground combat duty in Europe, the rate of psychiatric casualty loss was thirty-eight per thousand. This means that the ground combat army suffered approximately 12,616 neuropsychiatric casualties that were severe enough to be removed from the combat pool for the duration of the war. This figure does not include the thousands who broke down in battle, were treated, and eventually returned to their units. During World War II, approximately 40 percent of the soldiers who suffered psychiatric breakdown were successfully returned to their units.[20] American ground forces suffered 234,874 dead and 568,861 wounded. Thus, the ratio of psychiatric casualties to wounded was one to nineteen while the ratio of psychiatric casualties to killed in action was one to forty-three.

What these figures suggest is that while the Soviet army may have suffered higher initial rates of psychiatric casualties (certainly they suffered a higher absolute number of such casualties) than did the American army, once these casualties occurred, the Soviet medical system seems to have been particularly successful in dealing with the problem. At least they minimized the rate of manpower loss to fighting units by treating psychiatric patients and keeping them on the front lines. If the overall rates of return are examined, then it is clear that the loss rate due to psychiatric casualties in the American army was four to six times higher than in the Soviet army. Moreover, the ratio of psychiatric casualties to dead was 2.5 times higher than in the Soviet Army while the rate of psychiatric casualties to wounded was twice as high. In World War II the Soviets were simply able to keep more men fighting more of the time under greater degrees of battle stress than was the American army.

SOVIET COMBAT PSYCHIATRY IN WORLD WAR II

Given the success that the Soviet army had during World War II in sustaining its manpower strength by keeping psychiatric casualty losses to a minimum, it is intriguing to ask just what policies, doctrines, and practices made them succeed so well. One factor that played an important role is the manner in which the Soviets perceived the causes of battle shock and the ways in which they were prepared to deal with it. It is a fact of psychiatric life that expectations tend very much to condition behavior. To the extent that certain physical or psychiatric symptoms are regarded as legitimate, when soldiers are placed in situations of extreme stress, they will tend to manifest these very symptoms. In this sense, then, the behavioral expectations of the military system influence the soldier, who will then tend to realize these expectations as a way of escaping stressful battlefield situations.

The Soviets regarded soldiers who manifested certain battle-shock symptoms as making a very functional adjustment to their environment. Soldiers who wished to escape the horrors of the battlefield were essentially normal, sane people, who were prepared to go to great lengths to escape their environment. The values of the Soviet military subculture framed a set of expectations for both the controllers and the participants in the system. Once the subculture defined the legitimate excuses for avoiding battle, the soldiers were expected to adopt to these standards. Put another way, if a military subculture takes a lenient view of the circumstances that a soldier can use to escape the rigors of the battlefield, then it will probably generate higher rates of psychiatric casualties than those systems that place narrower limits on what is permissible. In the Soviet case, as one might expect of a totalitarian and ideologically motivated military system, the view of battle shock was extremely harsh.

The term for "shock" in the Russian language is *udar,* the same word used for a heart attack, epileptic stroke, or even an electrical shock. Interestingly, there is no clinical term for "battle shock." The Soviets use the term "reaction" for psychological symptoms with no accompanying physical cause. The Russian word for shock delineates a condition that is physiologically caused, has physiological symptoms, and is subject to physiological cure. The Soviet view does not admit to a condition of psychiatric breakdown that is a consequence of purely emotional and psychological factors, for which there is no physiological cause. Even in the diagnosis of schizophrenia and severe psychosis Soviet biological psychiatry places the ultimate cause in some organic disruption of the brain. In World War II the Soviets simply did not regard emotional trauma per se as a legitimate excuse for permitting the soldier to leave the battle. The only legitimate excuse for the soldier suffering from stress was a symptomology that had a clearly discernible physiological cause due to injury.

Combat shock in the Soviet view is something that is organically caused and therefore may be corrected by treating the patient's damaged or disrupted physiology. Those purely emotional or psychic causes that American psychiatrists would regard as expected consequences of battlefield stress the Soviets see as manifest shortcomings in the soldier's character, motivation, or training. The fact that a soldier may be too frightened to move, suffer tremors, have difficulty processing information, be reluctant to fire his weapon, or any number of other symptoms that in the American army would be regarded as significant indicators of battle stress are, in the Soviet army, not taken seriously. They regard such conditions as fear, anxiety, or tremors as normal conditions that develop on the battlefield and place the responsibility for dealing with them and continuing to function squarely upon the soldier.

The Soviets regard a soldier who suffers abnormally high levels of anxiety, fear, or panic either as having a defect in his character or as suffering from problems of improper motivation, morale, and training. Moreover, the Soviets lay the responsibility for failures of morale and motivation not only on the soldier but on the unit commander and, most particularly, upon the political officer. The Soviets refuse to address what in the United States would be regarded as normal symptoms of battle stress as a medical problem. Indeed, except for psychosis, all neurosis among combat soldiers is defined as a nonmedical problem.

Accordingly, in World War II, the Soviets refused to admit that a whole range of psychiatric casualties were in fact psychiatric casualties at all. Instead of treating these casualties in the medical and evacuation chain, they were simply turned over to unit commanders and political officers to be dealt with on a motivational basis. Intriguingly, this seems to have considerably reduced the rate of neuropsychiatric casualties suffered by the Red Army. By refusing to recognize a wide range of neuropsychiatric symptoms as having any validity, the Soviets were able to prevent the evacuation of large numbers of soldiers who manifested these symptoms and to hold them in the battle zone for much longer periods of time.

In World War II Soviet psychiatrists distinguished between what they called "big psychiatry" and "small psychiatry" in attempting to diagnose psychiatric problems. Big psychiatry referred to illnesses that were associated with organic disorders or disruptions of the brain and tended largely to focus upon schizophrenia and the other major psychoses. But psychiatry focused upon behavioral manifestations that could be traced to organic injuries caused largely by some sort of commotion, concussion, or contusion leading to organic brain damage to include neurologic injuries to the spinal cord. Almost all other symptoms manifested by combat soldiers—fear, anxiety, tremors, inability to sleep, partial paralysis, and a range of other symptoms—were regarded as problems of small psychiatry, normally diagnosed as temporary neurosis. Psychiatrists did not deal with problems of small psychiatry at all but left them to unit commanders, political officers, and in more severe cases to neurologists.

In the opinion of many Soviet psychiatrists and other physicians who served in World War II, unit commanders and political officers became excellent clinical diagnosticians. They learned to separate the truly serious cases of psychosis and other problems caused by organic damage from less serious problems. Lt. Col. Robert Glantz of the U.S. Army War College in his study of Soviet units in World War II notes that the role of the political officer in motivating soldiers to fight well has been grossly underestimated and distorted in Western military histories. Glantz points out that the political officer was often the focal point of the unit in sustaining morale and motivation.[21]

Each battalion had such a political officer, who often had a small staff that went into the companies and carried out similar tasks. When soldiers failed to demonstrate the proper motivation and morale, failed to perform correctly, or began to manifest symptoms normally associated with combat stress, Soviet units had someone in place whose task it was to deal immediately with the problem. The presence of the political officer within the unit, together with a comparatively harsh doctrine that strictly defined and limited the symptoms that would qualify as legitimate reasons to evacuate a soldier from the front, led the Soviets to apply two of the basic principles of combat psychiatry, namely expectancy and proximity of treatment. These two principles applied most directly to the range of problems associated with small psychiatry. The result was a low rate of manpower loss from psychiatric problems.

Soviet military psychiatry in World War II used a very strict definition of the "ticket out," the set of symptoms that allowed a soldier to be evacuated from the front lines. The Soviet ticket was defined in nonpsychic, almost purely neurological, terms; it required some physical cause that could be reasonably assessed as causing the soldier's behavioral problem. Not only did the Soviets require that the cause of the problem be organically based, but most often the diagnostic screen also required that the behavioral symptomology be accompanied by a physiological effect such as paralysis, bleeding from the ears or nose, hysteria, or surdomutism. Soldiers who came to the attention of medical personnel without these physiological elements of diagnosis were regarded as shirkers and cowards and were dealt with accordingly.

Given the assumption that a soldier's problems were caused by organic damage accompanied by distinct physical symptoms that could be traced to this damage, Soviet medical personnel, much more than their Western counterparts, assumed that both symptoms and causes could be readily treated. The Soviets assumed from the beginning that the organic causes of psychiatric problems required rapid treatment close to the battlefront. Wherever the soldier with a true psychiatric problem was treated—at division, army, or front level—the task was to treat the physical injury and return the soldier as rapidly as possible to the battlefield. Thus, Soviet combat psychiatry in World War II was premised not only on the principles of proximity and expectancy, but on the third principle of military psychiatry, immediacy of treatment. Equally important, Soviet treatment tended to stress physical methodologies. As a consequence, Soviet psychiatrists could avoid dealing with the soldier's psyche and other emotional problems and could deal directly with his body and brain. This made the provision of treatment close to the front comparatively easy and quick and, in fact, seems to have increased the probability of recovery.

Both medical and command personnel had high expectations that soldiers suffering psychiatric problems would be returned to the battlefront as quickly as possible. When the rate of psychiatric breakdown reached such proportions as to begin to affect whole units, these units were immediately dealt with by special police units and investigators. A high rate of psychiatric casualties in a unit was attributable to a clear failure on the part of the commander and the political officer. Special police units often took severe action against units that did not perform well in battle and, at times, called for the imprisonment of whole units and the execution of their leaders in full view of their men. Harsh as it may seem, the expectation on the part of commanders and Soviet medical personnel that psychiatric cases were not to be taken seriously, were to be dealt with immediately, and if this failed, were to be dealt with harshly, had the desired effect of reducing manpower loss from psychiatric casualty.

The medical system for dealing with psychiatric casualties set a very high and diagnostically precise price for excusing a soldier from battle. Moreover, the Soviet medical evacuation system gave clear priority to the physically wounded and thus mitigated against the evacuation of psychiatric casualties who did not clearly manifest some sign of organic damage. For example, a soldier discovered at the regimental aid station to be suffering from paralysis of the legs would be given a cursory physical examination. If no clear organic cause for his paralysis was found, say a bullet wound or other physiological damage, he would be removed from the medical evacuation chain and put aside at the aid station until the situation quieted down enough for him to be given further attention.

Such medical evacuation system as the Soviets had in World War II was extremely primitive. The initial suspicion with which psychiatric symptoms were met coupled with meagre mechanisms for diagnosing psychiatric casualties with no accompanying physical damage, added to a medical evacuation system that was barely functional, meant that, in practice, fewer psychiatric cases were placed in the evacuation train to begin with. Consequently, most psychiatric casualties remained for longer periods within the battle zone where they were treated by unit commanders, political officers, and regimental surgeons.

As noted earlier, soldiers tend to respond to the expectations and punishments of the military subculture of which they are a part. Soviet soldiers knew unequivocally that without any real physical damage to justify their claim to psychiatric disability their chances of escaping the battlefield were slim while the chances of being severely disciplined or sent to a penal battalion or even shot were considerably greater. The requirement that psychiatric problems be accompanied by some sort of discernible physical symptom—paralysis, surdomutism, or whatever—led soldiers to convert their stress reactions into precisely these symptoms.

Quite simply, the Soviets had a different set of expectations of their soldiers and used a different set of clinical definitions for diagnosing legitimate psychiatric problems than did other armies. By rigorously enforcing these definitions and expectations through harsh battlefield discipline they were able to reduce the manpower loss of their fighting forces. None of this says anything about the ability to prevent initial psychiatric breakdown, which, as already noted, was probably at least as high in its initial occurrence as in other armies in the West. In fact, given the nature, tempo, type, and duration of the battles that the Soviet army had to fight it was probably higher.

The Soviet approach to dealing with neuropsychiatric casualties during World War II was reflected in the structure of medical care and treatment. A basic fact that emerges from an analysis of the Soviet medical structure is the lack of formal psychiatric training for medical personnel below regimental level. Indeed, there were no psychiatrists or psychiatric treatment staff at division level, a condition common in Western armies during World War II, which had existed in some armies since World War I. The Soviet medical structure was primarily directed at the treatment of physiological casualties, and psychiatric casualties were either ignored, given very low priority, or else treated as patients whose behavioral problems stemmed from physiological injuries.

At the army level and at the front, however, there were special hospitals and staff for dealing with psychiatric patients. With very few exceptions, only those patients who were diagnosed as having major psychosis or schizophrenia ever reached these hospitals. The great majority of psychiatric casualties suffered from problems of small psychiatry and simply were never evacuated beyond their division. At the front hospital, located about 100 miles to the rear of the fighting, there was often a complete psychiatric department and a staff of six to eight psychiatrists and neurologists attached to the usual surgical teams. Psychiatric patients were treated by psychiatrists and neurologists. Most of the treatment, however, seems to have been directed by neurologists and focused on the organic damage that was causing the behavioral problem. The front hospital had facilities for about 100 psychiatric patients.

Closer to the fighting was the army-level hospital, located between fifty and seventy-five miles from the battle. This facility had a small psychiatric ward capable of accommodating forty patients, but only some of these beds were actually set aside for psychiatric patients. Two or three doctors made up the psychiatric staff of the army-level hospital. Sometimes army-level hospitals had no psychiatrists at all and relied upon neurologists to treat patients, but usually at least one psychiatrist was in residence. This tendency to mix psychiatrists and neurologists has a long history in Soviet psychiatric practice and is based on the assumption that behavioral aberrations are due essentially to organic disruptions of the brain and nervous system.

At the division level there were no provisions at all for psychiatrists or psychiatric staffs. The division had a medical battalion that provided normal casualty treatment support to the division. Below division there were doctors located at the regimental aid station, which supplemented the division aid station. Many of the doctors at regimental level were neurologists, but most were battle surgeons ranging from trained surgeons to general practitioners. Below the regiment was the battalion aid station staffed by a physician's assistant and a few medics, and at company level one found only the normal complement of company medics. Thus, at division or below the Soviet army made no provision for treating psychiatric casualties. Even when psychiatric casualties reached the division hospital, by and large they were treated by neurologists and other medical doctors. Farther toward the front, there were fewer and fewer medical personnel of any sort. Moreover, no effort was made to incorporate in the training of Soviet medical personnel below division level any knowledge of combat psychiatry. It must be added, however, that with experience most of these people became excellent diagnosticians insofar as they were able to separate problems of big psychiatry from the more normal behavioral problems from which all soldiers under stress suffer.

In some other armies the inability to diagnose psychiatric cases led to the shunting of psychiatric casualties with marginal physical symptoms into the normal medical evacuation chain. As a consequence of either misdiagnosis or ignorance, great numbers of psychiatric casualties who could have easily been retained at the front or within the battle zone were needlessly evacuated from battle. In the Soviet army the opposite happened. Untrained in psychiatric diagnosis, lower-level medical personnel tended to reinforce the system's predominant bias toward regarding certain kinds of behavior as either normal consequences of fear, defects in character, or in other ways that the system itself had defined them. Rather than shunting such patients into the medical evacuation chain, they kept them in the command and administrative chain and diverted them as the system was designed to do to commissars and unit commanders to be dealt with accordingly.

Soviet soldiers and medical personnel understood, however, that there were some categories of psychiatric illness that were so severe that they simply had to be recognized for what they were. In instances of genuine psychosis, soldiers were evacuated rapidly. In these cases the task of the physician's assistants, medics, and battalion surgeons was to diagnose and separate the truly psychotic from those who were suffering from only "normal" combat reactions or problems of small psychiatry. Individuals suffering from normal combat reactions were treated as close to their fighting units as possible. At each stage of the evacuation, depending upon how serious the problem was, psychiatric patients were given lower priority than physical casualties and were shunted aside at battalion, regimental, or division aid stations where they were allowed to rest until they could be examined more thoroughly. Usually, after a few days' rest, even soldiers with the most severe nonpsychotic combat reactions were returned to the fighting. Truly psychotic individuals, on the other hand, were immediately removed from their fighting units and isolated until evacuation was possible. It seems accurate to suggest that by limiting evacuation to those psychiatric cases with extreme and obvious symptoms, the Soviets were able to keep the number of soldiers lost as psychiatric casualties to a minimum. Indeed, during World War I the U.S. Army used a similarly harsh definition for evacuating psychiatric casualties and used much the same evacuation procedure. Interestingly, the rates of manpower loss to psychiatric causes for the U.S. Army in World War I and the Soviet army in World War II were about the same, approximately six to nine per thousand.

One of the ways by which the Soviets were able to reduce the level of battle-shock casualties was by narrowing the diagnostic definition of a neuropsychiatric casualty. Soviet psychiatrists in World War II drew strongly upon their previous experience in physiology and neurology and even more so upon the German psychiatric tradition of locating behavioral problems in the physiological disruption of the brain. Not surprisingly, the treatment of battle shock was a continuation of the biological approach to psychiatry that had been evident in Russia since at least 1860. On the battlefield psychiatrists sustained the belief that behavioral aberration had a physical cause, usually "brain shock," or more clinically, traumatic encephelopathy. This implied some sort of brain damage that interferes with proper functioning of the brain. The basic diagnostic assumption was that soldiers suffering from behavioral problems, psychosis, and even neurosis were suffering from some sort of organic damage to the brain.

Soviet psychiatrists focused upon what they called concussion, commotion, and contusion of the brain usually associated with loss of consciousness as a major cause of overt behavioral symptoms. In more precise terms, Soviet psychiatrists, being first and foremost medical doctors educated in the Germanic tradition of biological psychiatry, attributed behavioral aberrations to some form of bruising of the brain, microbleeding in the interior of the brain, the presence of brain lesions, edema, and microscopic scars caused by trauma or disease. The approach was to attempt to link the soldier's overt behavioral symptoms—paralysis, mutism, blindness, and so on—to the damage that may have been done to certain areas of the brain. It is interesting that this same diagnostic approach was used early in World War I by American, German, French, and British military psychiatrists, who by World War II had largely abandoned it in favor of less strict, less biological, and more psychic and emotional explanations for the symptoms of battle shock.

The requirement that behavioral problems be directly linked to organic damage or disruption simplified diagnosis. Those with damage were moved in the medical chain until they could be treated. Those without damage were usually sent back to the front, sometimes after a period of a few days' rest at a battalion or regimental aid station. In the American army, these same small psychiatry problems were often taken seriously enough to merit treatment and even evacuation. As a consequence, Soviet rates of manpower loss to psychiatric casualties were far less than those in the U.S. army.

Battlefield medical personnel concerned themselves with the organic causes of behavioral aberration and operationally distinguished between neurosis and depression psychosis. Psychiatrists focused upon depression psychosis, soldiers manifesting truly bizarre symptoms and behavior such as curling up into a fetal position or hearing voices or severe conversion syndromes. If one can believe the interviews with Soviet doctors who served in World War II, Soviet soldiers seem to have suffered a very high rate of conversion reactions. Yet, this situation was to be expected, given soldiers' tendency to respond to the expectations and norms of their military subculture and to those precise symptoms that the system defines as acceptable for escaping battle. Since Soviet psychiatrists had defined the "ticket out" of battle as being brain damage that caused overt physiological manifestations, it is not surprising that soldiers began to convert their fears and anxieties into precisely these manifestations. Consequently, such conversion reactions as hysteria, deaf and dumb, surdomutism, partial paralysis, fugue states, and so on—all familiar to Western combat psychiatrists—were common.

Soviet neurologists point out that the rate of conversion reactions became so high in the Soviet army that doctors and other field medical personnel had to develop shorthand tests to determine which conversion reactions were genuine, which symptoms were tied to organic damage and which were shallow enough to qualify as faking. Of course, the Soviets rejected any notion that a soldier could have conversion reactions produced by purely emotional considerations not brought on by physical trauma. Most of the tests or "treatments" that Soviet medical personnel developed were simple and seemed to have worked quite well. Many were drawn from similar treatments used by the German and other Western armies in World War I.

A soldier suffering from a conversion reaction would normally be seen first by a physician's assistant or medic. The first step was to isolate or shunt the patient aside in a designated area of the battalion or regimental aid station. After a time—usually a few hours—medical personnel would check on these patients to determine if their conversion state had abated at all or, as in many cases, if their symptoms had disappeared altogether. If their symptoms had lessened, they would be allowed to remain where they were for a period of up to two days. Usually if a soldier began to come around, he would be assigned some task in the aid station area to keep him busy. Much of the time he was simply allowed to rest for twenty-four or thirty-six hours. In the interim, the aid station's medical personnel continued to deal with their priority mission, the treatment of the wounded and dying. Once the soldier began to recover, he would be sent back to his unit, or his political officer would come for him. If his symptoms did not abate or grew worse, the soldier was evacuated to regiment.

Once a patient suffering severe conversion symptoms reached regiment, the search for the organic damage responsible for his behavior began. If the doctor suspected that there was no organic cause for the patient's behavior, the soldier would be shunted aside again at the regimental aid station and allowed to rest for a few hours or even a few days in order to give the symptoms time to abate. If he began to come around, he would, as at the battalion level, be given some task to perform. Interestingly, a number of Soviet battle surgeons confirm that much of the manpower in the division's medical company—litter bearers, cooks, orderlies, and so on—was comprised of soldiers who were being held at division while their psychiatric symptoms cleared up. Normally, a recovering psychiatric patient could function quite well in this role as long as he was kept safe from the direct risks of battle.

After a day or two, the soldier was examined by the regimental surgeon in order to find the organic cause of his symptoms. Like military psychiatrists in other armies, these surgeons quickly learned that despite Soviet psychiatric theory, soldiers were quite capable of showing symptoms of organic damage when there was no such damage present. For these cases Soviet medical field personnel administered a number of "treatments" designed to determine the nature of the patient's illness and to produce counter stimuli that might bring him around.

One of the most commonly used techniques was the Kaufmann Method invented by French psychiatrists and used by the German army in World

War I. It was a specific treatment for dealing with patients suffering from surdomutism. The object of the treatment was to force the patient to speak as a way of breaking the syndrome. Electrodes were placed on the patient's throat and moderately intense and painful electrical current was administered. The object was to shock the brain, as in electro-convulsive therapy that was also used in other cases, into acting normally again. From the patient's perspective it often seemed that the choice came down to sustaining his symptoms by enduring a considerable amount of pain or abandoning his symptoms as a way of ridding himself of the pain. This method was also used to treat patients suffering from partial paralysis.

Another method for dealing with conversion reactions was to place a rubberized mask over the patient's face and gradually induce a feeling of suffocation. This technique was used to treat soldiers suffering from fugue states, inability to speak, and paralysis. The premise behind the test was that only those whose conditions were traceable to organic injury would be able to tolerate the suffocation until they lost consciousness. A variation of the technique was to wrap a rag around the patient's face and pour water on it to simulate the feeling of drowning in the hope that he would respond. Still another test was to poke the paralyzed limbs of the soldier with needles in order to produce enough pain to get him to respond with movement. Soldiers in fugue states were often tested by the simple device of making a sudden loud noise and watching for physiological reactions, which would prove that the state was not induced by true organic damage. These tests were used extensively by medical personnel at all levels of the medical treatment system but seem to have been used most commonly by doctors at the army and division levels. Soviet psychiatrists and doctors report that in a large number of cases, especially after the soldier had a few days of rest away from the fighting, these treatments were successful.

Only the most severe combat reactions or truly psychotic patients were evacuated out of combat. The screening methods for shunting psychiatric patients aside, holding them at the lower-level aid stations, and returning them to their units after short periods of rest worked well in dealing with most of the small psychiatry problems. Even when faced with genuine psychiatric problems, the tendency was not to evacuate a patient beyond division if it could be avoided. Doctors and commanders feared that once a patient was evacuated for purely psychiatric reasons, other soldiers would be encouraged to develop similar symptoms. Every effort was made to find some assignment for the soldier so that he could continue to serve. Even rest was normally accomplished within the general zone of fighting. By keeping soldiers in some useful job, no matter how minor, the Soviets were able to get some use out of even broken manpower. Moreover, a soldier assigned to some useful task in the rear area was more likely to recover eventually from his psychiatric disability.

As in any army, under conditions of heavy combat the system of casualty treatment and evacuation broke down, and the Soviet army reacted differently in its treatment of psychiatric casualties than did most Western armies. In the West, for example, when heavy casualties overburdened the medical system, soldiers with symptoms of psychiatric breakdown were very often placed into the medical chain and evacuated to the rear rather than being detained and treated at the front. This practice further over-burdened the entire evacuation and treatment system. The Soviets reacted differently. When casualties became heavy, those suffering from psychiatric problems were treated even more harshly. In general, if a soldier could walk and had no obvious physical wound, he was immediately turned back to the fighting. Moreover, special military police units conducted regular patrols through the medical aid stations gathering up stragglers or soldiers who were not wounded and forcing them back into the line. As a consequence, when physical casualties increased, the number of psychiatric evacuations actually decreased, exactly the opposite of what happened in most Western armies.

During World War II the only soldiers who received serious treatment from psychiatrists where those that were evacuated back to army-level hospitals. Those treated at the front were, as noted, treated perfunctorily or, in many cases, not at all and returned quickly to the fighting. Those patients that were evacuated to army or front level were suffering from genuine psychosis or severe conversion reactions; others were simply so deranged that they could not function. Almost all, with some exceptions among the psychotics, manifested some physiological symptoms accompanying whatever battle trauma they had suffered. In other cases diagnoses indicated cases of deep reactive psychosis. Because the screening procedure operated so effectively at the lower levels, if not very humanely, only the most severe cases of battle shock were finally evacuated.

The treatments administered at army- and front-level hospitals were essentially the same as those used by the French and Germans in World War I to treat similar cases. A number of treatments had been used by the American and British armies in that war as well. A psychiatric casualty sent to an army-level hospital had a normal stay of two weeks for "mild" cases, three weeks for moderate cases, and up to six weeks for the most severe cases. Those who recovered in this time were sent back to the front. For the most part the Soviets did not make great effort to return recovered soldiers to their units. They realized that their practice of fighting units down to the nub would result in very high casualties to combat units. Thus, they probably did not see much value in attempting to return soldiers to units that in many cases had been decimated or destroyed while the patient was recovering in the hospital. In some instances, Soviet front commanders actually forbade the practice of sending men back to their units.

Walter Dunn points out that the Soviets did not use a unit replacement system during the war as did the Germans and British but instead adopted an individual replacement system built around replacement depots, which strongly resembled the system used by the United States.[22] Soldiers recovering from wounds or combat shock were gathered up by special police units and taken to replacement depots where new units were formed or from which individuals in small groups were sent to units already committed or preparing to go into battle. The special police units would regularly visit the hospitals at the army and front level, especially the psychiatric hospital wards, in order to ensure that every soldier capable of returning to the fighting did so. Whatever else one may think of the system's lack of humanity and compassion, it worked very well in reducing manpower loss. When it is recalled that almost every soldier in the Soviet army who wasn't killed was wounded at least once, this ability to recover the wounded and return them to battle looms large as a factor in the victory of the Soviet army.

Interviews with Soviet neurologists, psychiatrists, and surgeons who worked at army-level hospitals suggest that the Soviets were able to return well over 80 percent of the cases held in psychiatric wards, a figure twice as high as the 40 percent returned by the American army. Moreover, it must be remembered that the task was made somewhat more difficult by the fact that only the most severe cases of psychiatric debilitation reached the rear in the first place and that the absolute numbers of psychiatric casualties of all types at all levels of the medical structure were certainly much greater than in Western armies.

Diagnostically, the Soviets reported a number of severe conversion reactions also witnessed by Western armies in World War I including severe hysteria, surdomutism, paralysis, blindness, and others. They also encountered severe depression psychosis sometimes accompanied by memory loss, schizophasia, severe tremors and convulsions, and inability to control body functions. Because the Soviet "ticket out" was defined in physiological terms, most of the symptomology emerged in these terms. They also found that the highest rates of psychiatric casualties were found among infantrymen, and the armored corps comprised the second largest category.[23] Soviet psychiatrists did not find this unusual, since infantrymen are often subjected to artillery bombardments, which caused contusions and concussions. Armor troops were often banged around inside their machines and lost consciousness. At army-level hospitals soldiers who did not recover after six weeks were sent rearward to the front-level hospitals where the same time schedule for recovery used at the army-level hospital obtained. Generally, very few psychiatric casualties recovered at the front level, and most were placed into the civilian public health system (such as it was) where they were normally discharged from the military.

A significant part of the treatment of neuropsychiatric casualties at army- and front-level hospitals involved the use of drugs. Perhaps the term "drugs" is inadequate if by drugs one means relatively sophisticated chemical agents that can be used to treat specific brain disorders with some precision. More correctly, Soviet psychiatrists relied upon a range of plant and animal derivatives that fell more in the category of folk medicines. To be sure, authentic drugs such as chloryl hydrate and barbiturates were also used, but it is important to bear in mind that during World War II no army had sophisticated drugs for use in the treatment of psychiatric problems. In the Soviet case, this development was even more retarded by the terrible disruptions that the Soviet Union had suffered almost without respite since 1914.

With this caveat, one can still point to a range of folk medicines, usually plant derivatives, that Soviet psychiatrists found helpful in dealing with battle-shock cases. Given that Soviet psychiatric doctrine assumed a physiological cause for psychiatric disruption, the use of chemical compounds to treat the damage to the brain made good sense.

A common treatment, also found in the West, required the administration of chloryl hydrate to induce long periods of sleep as part of general rest therapy. Early in the war Soviet psychiatrists, like many psychiatrists in other armies, learned that even the most severe manifestations of combat shock, including reactive psychosis, would often respond well to a period of concentrated sleep. To induce sleep, chloryl hydrate drops were frequently used. The results were often dramatic and rapid.

Another treatment involved the use of what Soviet physicians called "brom" or bromide, also used in the United States at the same time. It took the form of either natrium bromide or sodium bromide administered intravenously. It had the effect of calming the patient down and putting him into a shallow sedative state. It was also widely used to build up body fluids and to treat brain concussions, contusions, and seizures. Bromide use was discontinued in the United States when it was found that it often caused brain damage.

Other herbal medicine compounds that Soviet psychiatrists used were valeriana or valadium, ginseng, powdered reindeer horn, goldroot, and mandarin root, all of which were sedatives or stimulants of one sort or another. The Soviets made extensive use of aloe, which they used in liquid form and administered intravenously. In the United States aloe has recently been used in suntan lotion and for the treatment of insect bites and minor burns. The Soviets found it very useful in treating a range of traumatic brain injuries and preventing the formation of scar tissue in the brain after concussions and contusions. Intriguingly, doctors report that an excellent treatment for preventing and treating small brain lesions was something called "fibs," a natural compound made from some sort of special mud, refined to a liquid, and injected subcutaneously.

Two other treatments that Soviet psychiatrists used very effectively were magnesium and calcium chloride administered intravenously (IV). Magnesium IV's were used as a sedative that also was useful in combating brain edema. Its value lay in the ability to control the dosage for long periods of time, inducing a sedative effect on the patient without disrupting too much of the body's chemistry. Calcium chloride was used as a general stimulant. Administered in IV form, it gradually raised the excitation level of the patient without inducing shock. This treatment was used extensively in dealing with stupor, fugue states, neurasthenia, or patients who could not be brought back to full consciousness.

Two treatments used extensively in the United States, narcohypnosis and abreaction, were used only rarely in the Soviet military. Soviet psychiatrists report that they felt that these techniques usually took too long to work when they worked at all. They also found that patients tended to resist them. The Soviets did use regular hypnosis from time to time, often coupled with various tricks such as telling a patient to eat onions while under hypnosis. But in general they did not see such techniques as particularly valuable and used them to determine if the patient was so deeply psychotic that normal short-term therapy would not work.

After treatment at the army- and front-level hospitals, those who did not recover (about 20 percent) were shipped farther to the rear, taken out of the military evacuation chain, and seconded to the civilian district health hospitals. Here they were separated into two types of cases, those who were severely psychotic and not expected to recover and those who were only moderately psychotic. The former were shipped to mental wards where they were quickly forgotten. The latter were sent to chronic care hospitals. The military operated a small number of special hospitals after the war to treat specific disabilities, but such hospitals were few. In all of northwest Russia there was only one hospital, located on an island near Leningrad called Valaam. The building complex on the island formerly housed a monastery but was converted into a military hospital. This hospital had a special psychiatric section probably of fewer than one hundred beds. In the normal course of things, severe psychiatric cases were discharged into the public health system, which itself was in shambles. Interviews with Soviet citizens report that after the war it was not uncommon to see clearly mentally ill soldiers roaming the streets of cities and villages in considerable numbers allowed to make their way in society as best they could.

Those soldiers who after the war claimed disability pensions for psychiatric problems that could not be clearly traced to physical injuries were most commonly denied any pensions or help. In order for a Soviet soldier to qualify for any type of war-connected disability, he had to have a complete medical record justifying his condition. Psychiatric cases had to have a certificate signed by a psychiatrist that the patient's condition was due to some brain or neurological injury incurred in battle. If no organic damage could be demonstrated and the soldier was neurotic or even profoundly neurotic, he would simply be denied any pension. Those who went to the public health service to obtain these certificates often had to face a battery of painful tests to confirm the diagnosis. In many instances, the tests were designed to discourage the applicant.

CONCLUSION

After World War II Soviet military psychiatry remained essentially the same as it had been during the war. In 1967 it received a renewed emphasis from the military interested in matching Western research and advances. Immediately after the war Soviet military medical personnel conducted a thorough review of their medical experiences during the war and published it in a multivolume work. A complete volume was prepared on the subject of military psychiatry. By 1967 Soviet military psychiatrists seem to have realized that some of the problems of small psychiatry that they had encountered probably needed more study, especially in light of the Soviet military's desire to evolve a doctrine of preventing combat shock in the new environment of the nuclear battlefield. After the war several psychiatrists and, after 1967 some psychologists, received grants from the military to study the problems of small psychiatry as they relate to battle stress.

When the Soviet army changed its battle doctrine after 1967 and began to plan for a war in a nuclear environment in which the level of shock casualties would be enormous, the interest in preventing and treating battle shock increased again. Nonetheless, as of this writing, most of these efforts have been conducted by psychologists more than psychiatrists and have been confined essentially to research settings. What few applications there are have been directed at pilots, submariners, astronauts, and other highly skilled technicians in an effort to control fear and anxiety and prevent degradation of performance. The experiences in ground combat forces of World War II have conveyed the message to the military psychiatric establishment that their mechanisms of diagnosis and treatment worked adequately. They have, of course, tried to keep abreast of more modern methods of treatment, especially the revolution in psycho-pharmacology that began in France in the 1950s and have attempted to incorporate some of these developments in their own treatment methodologies.

On balance, the Soviets regard their experience with military psychiatry in World War II as superior to the Western experience in dealing with the same problem. The Soviets continue to believe that a strict definition of what constitutes an acceptable level of traumatic stress can itself be very useful in preventing large numbers of psychiatric casualties by the simple expedient of refusing to recognize a number of symptoms that in Western armies would result in the loss of the soldier to his fighting unit. As in World War II, this doctrine is still strongly enforced by unit commanders, political officers, and a medical establishment that refuses to recognize psychiatric debilitation, except at the extremes, that is not clearly tied to physical injury. Interestingly, the Soviet system of treating psychiatric casualties is based on the same practical principles of proximity, immediacy, and expectancy that underpin Western military psychiatry. The Soviets regard their experience in dealing with psychiatric breakdown as largely a success, and upon this success they have since continued to build and develop their approach to combat psychiatry.

NOTES

1. R. L. Richards, "Mental and Nervous Disease in the Russo-Japanese War," *The Military Surgeon,* Vol. 26 (1910), p. 179.

2. Richard A. Gabriel, "Stress in Battle: Coping On The Spot," *Army Magazine* (December 1982), pp. 36–42. Further information was obtained in an interview with Dr. David Marlowe, chairman of the Department of Military Psychiatry, Army Institute of Research, Walter Reed Hospital, Washington, D.C.

3. Richards, "Mental and Nervous Disease," p. 180.

4. Ibid.

5. Ibid., p. 185.

6. Ibid., pp. 186–187.

7. Ibid., p. 185.

8. My thanks to John Windhausen, professor of Russian history at St. Anselm College for his help in assembling information on the Russian famine.

9. Josef Brozek, "Fifty Years of Soviet Psychology: An Historical Perspective," *Soviet Psychology,* Vol. 3, No. 1 (Fall 1968), pp. 48–57.

10. Ibid. p. 52.

11. Ibid.

12. A number of Soviet psychiatrists interviewed for this project report using these techniques in World War II. They also indicated that such techniques were presented in their medical school lectures as being derived from Russian battle experience in World War I.

13. This document was brought to my attention by a graduate of the Kirov Military Medical Academy. An academy professor helped with the research for the work. After two years of searching, this writer's best guess as to its location is a medical library in East Germany.

14. T. R. Dupuy, *The Encyclopedia of Military History* (New York: Harper & Row, 1970), p. 1198.

15. Interview with Lt. Col. Robert Glantz, U.S. Army War College, Carlisle Barracks, Pennsylvania, July 23, 1984.

16. Eli Ginsburg, *The Lost Divisions* (New York: Columbia University Press, 1959), p. 93.

17. Ibid., p. 35.

18. Glantz interview, July 23, 1984.

19. Ginsburg, "Stress in Battle," p. 61.

20. Estimates provided by David Marlow and Col. Mike Camp of the Department of Military Psychiatry at the Army Institute of Research, Walter Reed Hospital.

21. Interview with Col. Robert Glantz of the Strategic Studies Institute, U.S. Army War College.

22. Walter S. Dunn, Jr., "People Policies in Combat," *Parameters*, Vol. 14, No. 1 (Spring 1984), pp. 49–59.

23. This information comes from interviews with a number of Soviet psychiatrists and battle surgeons who served in World War II.

5

Soviet Battlefield Psychiatry

This chapter examines the structure and practice of modern Soviet battle psychiatry. The analysis centers around the tasks performed by military psychiatrists in Western armies and their counterpart functions performed by Soviet military psychiatrists.

Among the more common tasks of military psychiatrists in Western armies is screening conscripts for military service. During World War II, the United States military developed relatively extensive screening mechanisms for sorting out those conscripts whose ability to withstand the stress of combat was questionable. The standard for both psychiatric and physical fitness was the same, namely that all soldiers who entered military service were expected to be "fit for combat." At least until 1944, almost no thought was given to selecting conscripts who were not fit to withstand battle but who could be used in other, noncombat assignments. As a consequence, psychiatric screening eliminated a great deal of manpower that could otherwise have been put to good use in support, supply, and administrative roles. This was not the case for the Soviet army in World War II, and it is not the case now.

Of the approximately 22 million conscripts examined for military service by the Soviets in World War II fewer than 100,000 were rejected for purely psychiatric reasons. Perhaps no more than 250,000 conscripts were rejected for physical reasons. Thus, less than 1 percent of all Soviet conscripts were rejected for military service for all reasons combined. In a practical sense, the Soviet army impressed almost every conscript it examined.

The role of the Soviet military psychiatrist in draft screening today is much smaller than in the West and, in many cases, practically nonexistent. The civilian public health system is structurally parallel to the military district and commissariat system used for conscription, and Soviet draft boards (draft commissariats) are provided with lists of all patients undergoing psychiatric care in their military districts. If a conscript has been diagnosed by the civilian health clinic as having a history of psychiatric illness, the conscript usually is not even called by the military for examination. Those with marginal or recent histories of mental disturbances will usually be called and examined by the usual team of military doctors comprised of internists and neurologists. Sometimes the psychiatrists take extra time to determine if a conscript is faking his symptoms. Soldiers without any mental history are given perfunctory neurologic examinations similar to those given to American conscripts. Psychiatrists administer no battery of psychiatric tests to conscripts, nor does there appear to be any systematic use of psychiatric questionnaires. In general, if the conscript has not established a convincing history of mental illness prior to being called for military service, the military will make every effort to ensure that he serves.

Every civilian health district within the Soviet Union has a neuropsychiatric dispensary, which keeps records on all patients within the district with psychotic or severe neurotic mental health problems. The structure of the mental health clinics was established in the mid-1920s. In the mid-1970s the Ministry of Mental Health and the Institute of Forensic Psychiatry established a project to computerize all information on every patient in the country who had been treated within the public health system with special emphasis on psychiatric conditions. There is now a centralized computer file kept on all psychiatric patients. Interestingly, the basic diagnostic categories used by the Soviets to categorize the data are those used by ICD-9, the commonly recognized international diagnostic manual widely used in the West.

In 1980, the Institute for Forensic Psychiatry conducted a study of the military's psychiatric screening procedures as well as the basic psychiatric applications of the national public health system. They discovered two interesting facts. First, on a nationwide basis the number of diagnosed cases of schizophrenia in each mental health district tended to vary directly with the number of psychiatrists who were present within each mental health district. Second, in their study of draft rejections for psychiatric reasons the institute found that the highest rates of draft rejections for psychiatric reasons were in the Baltic republics of Latvia, Estonia, and Lithuania.[1] The highest rate was in Lithuania, where the rejection rate was eight times higher than for any other Soviet republic. The most common diagnostic reason for these rejections was oligophrenia which, in the Soviet lexicon, may be generally translated as mental retardation or "dull-wittedness." It is useful to recall that in World War I one of the most common causes of rejection in the American army was a similar condition, then defined as "imbecillia."

With regard to draft avoidance or duty assignments based on psychiatric disability, Soviet military authorities assume as a matter of course that a sizable number of people will attempt to fake mental or physical problems as a way of escaping the rigors of military service. As in any army, Soviet conscripts have evolved a number of tricks to escape military service. But the stress that Soviet examiners place on physiological disability as opposed to psychiatric disability as the legitimate way of escaping military service has made the task of the reluctant conscript very difficult. Such ruses as placing pencil lead under one's tongue to produce a fever or taking drugs or binging on sugar in order to produce physical symptoms of illness are not uncommon, although they do appear to be far less effective in eliminating the conscript from military service than in some countries in the West.

In order to deal with the inventiveness of conscripts, Soviet doctors often segregate soldiers who manifest specific symptoms that appear to be false or self-induced. A common response is for Soviet doctors to treat the symptoms in such a way as to make the complaints worse. In one instance, for example, a number of soldiers who were complaining of diarrhea were given stool softeners for three days, the theory being that if they were faking to begin with, the discomfort of having to defecate all the time was worse than submitting to their military duties. On balance, however, the level of medical complaints and attempts to avoid service has not been a significant problem for the Soviet army since 1967 when the Soviets established a nationwide system of premilitary training and physical screening.

One of the factors that has reduced the problem of draft and duty avoidance has been the harsh view taken by medical examiners of psychiatric problems. A range of problems that might qualify an individual for rejection in Western armies are simply not acceptable in the Soviet army. Such problems as mild neurosis, anxiety, night sweats, or bedwetting are seen as a lack of character or defective personality, which the conscript has a responsibility to overcome. They are not viewed as legitimate psychiatric problems.

With the establishment of DOSAAF in 1967, the already low rate of exemption for psychiatric reasons dropped even further. Unlike Western youth, a Soviet conscript reports to his military commissariat for draft examination with a long and detailed history of not only medical but also social and educational aspects. All Soviet youth ages sixteen and seventeen are enrolled in the DOSAAF system where they undergo military training and physical conditioning. Moreover, extensive records are kept on their behavior and attitudes. This file precedes the conscript to the draft commissariat even before he is called to military service. Therefore, it is almost impossible for a conscript with a record of normal behavior to fake a psychiatric problem in order to avoid military service. Even those individuals with a history of psychiatric problems often have difficulty convincing draft examiners that the problems are severe enough to merit exemption.

The Soviets can reduce psychiatric exemptions from military service by the simple practice of distinguishing between those individuals who will be able to serve in combat units and those who can perform noncombat duties. On the basis of the conscript's record and performance in premilitary training some effort is also made to select those who may be better suited for more complex and technical military assignments. These individuals also receive somewhat more extensive psychiatric screening, especially for such assignments as police units, missile units, or submarines. The Soviets seem to have grasped the fact that military manpower can be conserved by conscripting individuals with physical or even minor psychiatric problems and using them to good effect in noncombat duties. In addition, the Soviets maintain a large number of construction battalions, to which almost anyone who meets even minimal standards can be assigned. As a consequence of these practices the role of the military psychiatrist in draft screening is considerably less than in the West. American intelligence estimates suggest that 92 percent of all conscripts called to military service eventually serve.[2] The Soviets feel that too large a role for the military psychiatrist would probably result, as in the Western experience, in too great a rate of exemption from military service for psychiatric reasons.

SOVIET COMBAT MEDICAL DOCTRINE

Soviet combat medical doctrine was shaped by the experiences of World War I and II, where the medical structure had to deal with tremendous casualties. In the first six months of World War II the Soviets lost 2.4 million men killed and wounded. Moreover, the Soviets never really had the capacity to treat such a great number of casualties effectively. Consequently they have drawn three lessons from their medical experience in World War II, all of which remain central to their medical combat doctrine today.

The first is that war produces tremendous numbers of casualties, and a medical system must be designed to deal with this fact. The Soviets feel that the stress of war will make itself felt most clearly on the number of physical casualties incurred, which can be saved through medical treatment. As in World War II, the Soviet medical corps neither intends nor is designed to treat psychiatric casualties seriously. The Soviets expect to endure great numbers of physical casualties especially if the war is fought within a nuclear context. Dealing with large numbers of casualties has received renewed emphasis since 1967 when changes in Soviet battle doctrine forced them to examine seriously the impact of nuclear weapons on casualty rates.

A second characteristic of the modern Soviet medical evacuation system also emerged during World War II. The Soviets have totally and completely integrated the entire civilian public health system into the military medical structure, so that most serious casualties can be expected to be treated at front-, and army-, or district-level hospitals. They have no intention of going to war without first mobilizing the entire civilian medical establishment and conscripting between 8000 and 10,000 doctors for military service.

Finally, Soviet medical doctrine clearly emphasizes the evacuation of casualties to rear areas for treatment rather than treating them at the front. Defense Intelligence Agency studies on Soviet combat medical treatment make it clear that the emphasis is on treating the soldier in the unit only to the extent needed to keep him alive, so that he can be evacuated to the rear rather than holding him at regiment or battalion and reintegrating him into his unit.[3] One reason for this practice is that the Soviets do not use a unit replacement system as do some Western armies. No real attempt is made to return wounded soldiers to their original units.

Like the Americans, the Soviets replace individuals rather than units. Recovered wounded in the American army did not normally return to their units but were sent to replacement depots (not to be confused with the replacement battalions of the German army) where they were individually sent to various units as the need arose. However, the Soviets have made one important change in this practice. Soviet combat doctrine requires that units be fought down to 30 to 40 percent strength before being replaced. Rather than refilling a unit with individual replacements, the Soviets plan to commit another unit to battle in its place, linking the replaced unit with the replacing unit, passing command to the new unit, and continuing the assault. This means that a unit's membership and even command structure keeps changing as the battle rages. As a consequence, the Soviets intend to evacuate their wounded and have them recover at army, front or district hospitals; they will then be reassembled at replacement depots. At these depots whole new units will be formed and then thrown into the battle, so that there is no real possibility that Soviet soldiers will be returned to their original units.

Soviet historical experience has been reinforced by modern developments, especially the likelihood of fighting on a nuclear battlefield and by the Soviet belief that the next major war will generate tremendous numbers of casualties from chemical and biological agents. Thus, the Soviet medical corps is configured first and foremost to deal with mass casualties by getting them out of the way and not allowing them to hinder units' ability to continue the offensive. This, in turn, is further supported by Soviet doctrine which requires a high tempo of battle in a continuous offensive to break the will of the enemy. Since the Soviets also believe that a war in the West will be relatively short, perhaps lasting no more than ninety days, they hope to be able to gain victory quickly by getting the most out of their troops over a short period of time. There will be plenty of time, in the Soviet view, to treat the wounded and save what can be saved after their combat forces have defeated the enemy.

Some idea of the relatively low priority the Soviets place on treating the wounded as opposed to evacuating them is gained by noting that medical supplies are given the lowest priority in the logistics train.[4] Unlike Western armies, the Soviet army has few organic vehicles in the division that are dedicated to medical evacuation and almost none that are dedicated to providing medical treatment. While the Soviets are making some effort to use helicopters for medical evacuation, these efforts are minimal and conditioned by the Soviet belief that the unarmed helicopter will be terribly vulnerable to hostile fire in a modern war. Accordingly, evacuation of the wounded to regimental and division collection points will be carried out not by organic vehicles dedicated to the task, but by empty supply carriers. Trucks and APCs will move to the front delivering POL and ammunition. On the way back to the rear resupply points they will stop at regimental and divisional clearing stations to pick up the wounded and remove those tagged for evacuation. The Soviets are not going to spend a great deal of time and effort treating casualties at the lower combat echelons. They will try to evacuate those they can to the rear as the tempo of battle permits. The major exception to this rule seems to be in the treatment of psychiatric casualties.

The lack of concern given to the treatment as opposed to the evacuation of casualties is reflected in the medical treatment structure. Soviet units have medical stations at company, battalion, regiment, and division organized in much the same fashion as in Western armies. However, in training military medical personnel the emphasis is placed upon their role in conducting the administrative task of moving casualties to the rear far more than upon treating them at the front. At regiment and division, the chief medical officer functions almost entirely in an administrative capacity rather than in a medical one. It is only above division, at the army or front level, that the wounded soldier receives any serious medical treatment. All other medical stations are seen as essentially through-put rather than treatment stations.

Given the Western experience in dealing with psychiatric casualties, it is interesting to consider the impact of Soviet medical evacuation policies on psychiatric casualties. It must be remembered that the Soviets intend to use the same diagnostic and screening mechanisms for dealing with psychiatric casualties that they used in World War II. Large numbers (by Western standards) of neuro-psychiatric casualties will not be allowed in the medical evacuation chain at all but will be handled in administrative or command channels by the unit commanders or the political officers. In the modern Soviet army there is a political officer assigned to every company, whereas in World War II there was one assigned to each battalion. One can reasonably expect that the screening of psychiatric casualties will be somewhat more thorough than it was in World War II. For the most part, Soviet psychiatric casualties will be detained and treated in command channels or allowed to build up at the various medical clearing points, where they receive the lowest priority for evacuation.

True neuro-psychiatric casualties will be shunted into the normal medical evacuation chain and moved to the rear. Those soldiers which manifest concussion, contusion, or some other kind of physiological problem associated with their mental disturbance will be moved at least to division level and in many cases farther rearward. They will be given a period at the army-level hospital of about two weeks to recover in a neuro-psychiatric ward. If they recover, they will be assigned to a replacement depot for further service. Given what we know about battle-shock treatment in the West, this practice may result in a greater number of deep neurosis casualties who might otherwise be turned around quickly. On the other hand, this may be balanced by the fact that if the Soviets can sustain in the patient the belief that his problem is basically physiological in origin, once the physical aspects of the problem are addressed, recovery may be fairly rapid.

If Western models are correct, between 40 and 50 percent of soldiers exposed to battle in a modern war can be expected to suffer some sort of neuro-psychiatric problem. The Soviet models offer different estimates. Their research, in which they calculate the shock effect of battle by using examples of natural disasters such as earthquakes, natural gas explosions, large fires, and so on, suggests that even in a nuclear battle zone the Soviets do not expect any more than 10 percent of the casualties to result from genuine neuro-psychiatric reasons.[5] With no way of treating neuro-psychiatric casualties in lower-echelon holding areas on the grounds that casualties without physiological symptoms are not genuine psychiatric casualties at all, the Soviet medical support system may find itself terribly overburdened with great numbers of neuro-psychiatric casualties. Yet, if their filtration systems, namely the command channels, political officers, and harsh clinical diagnostic definitions of what constitutes a mental casualty, operate as effectively as they did in World War II, then the number of psychiatric casualties who are evacuated back to division may well be lower than in Western armies.

The propensity to evacuate soldiers to the rear for medical treatment seems to have led the Soviets to use drug therapies at the lower levels of the medical treatment system to stabilize shock casualties and then move them to the rear. No one can reasonably foresee to what extent this will lead to a degree of misdiagnosis so that they may end up placing neuro-psychiatric patients in the medical chain when they otherwise could be treated much more rapidly and effectively at the front. The emphasis on drug therapies to counter the physiological effects of nuclear shock and battle stress may create serious problems for the medical service by evacuating casualties that simply should not be evacuated.

These circumstances raise the question of the quality of medical personnel who will conduct the diagnostic screening of psychiatric casualties. In general, the quality of military medical personnel whose task it is to sort out genuine neuro-psychiatric casualties from the others is weak. The Soviet emphasis on the physiological basis of mental problems has led military medical diagnosticians to look for and emphasize those casualties that respond to physiological treatment and who manifest obvious symptoms. This suggests to a number of Soviet military psychiatrists that these people may not be very well trained in the practical problems of recognizing and diagnosing neuro-psychiatric casualties. This could lead to a number of additional problems.

First, it could result in soldiers who are suffering from true psychiatric problems that could be dealt with by lower level medical personnel being turned over to the political officers and unit commanders without first receiving any kind of significant treatment. Second, it could result in an inability to make a correct diagnosis or to screen large numbers of psychiatric casualties which would evacuate individuals who otherwise could be treated very effectively and more rapidly at the lower-echelon levels. The fact is that the Soviet medical service has all but abandoned the responsibility for dealing with all but the most severe neuro-psychiatric symptomologies. Only those symptomologies that are clearly accompanied by organic disruption can be adequately dealt with within the medical system. What this suggests is that soldiers with psychiatric problems unaccompanied by physical damage may easily be misdiagnosed.

The quality of medical training given to Soviet military medical personnel who are responsible for adequately recognizing and dealing with psychiatric casualties is a real problem indeed. Even in Western armies, for example, in the Israeli Defense Force (IDF), the problem makes itself felt. Although the IDF generally provides excellent quality doctors, psychiatrists, and psychologists in its field units for the precise purpose of diagnostic screening and treatment of psychiatric casualties, during the 1982 war in Lebanon almost one half of the IDF's psychiatric casualty evacuations were misdiagnosed and needlessly evacuated to the rear.

The Soviets seem to be far more concerned with evacuating the normal physically damaged casualties than in treating them at the front. They are very concerned about being able to stabilize and evacuate patients who are in shock, that is biological shock. Those soldiers who suffer psychological reactions to physical damage will be evacuated and treated in the same manner as any other physical casualty. Those who manifest psychiatric symptoms in the absence of physical damage will either be ignored, shunted aside in local holding areas, or turned over to commanders and political officers.

Once a casualty reaches division, he will be reexamined and a determination made whether to retain him at the division hospital or move him farther to the rear. Regardless of what level the casualty is retained, after two or three weeks it can be expected that special police units will make regular rounds of military hospitals and treatment sites selecting soldiers who have sufficiently recovered from their wounds to be sent to replacement depots. There they will be assigned to new units and recommitted to battle. However else the Soviets handle the problem of evacuation of psychiatric casualties, they intend to make the doctrine of expectancy operate whether at the lower levels where the soldier is turned over to the political officer or the unit commander or at the higher levels where the soldier will eventually be sent to a replacement depot. The point is to convince the Soviet soldier that a psychiatric disturbance is, in itself, not a legitimate cause for escaping one's military responsibilities. Even genuine psychiatric casualties are expected to return to the fight. Those who refuse will simply be forced to return.

PSYCHIATRIC CASUALTY SERVICING STRUCTURE

At front level the Soviet army maintains a complete psychiatric hospital with a director for psychiatric care and a special section for dealing with neuro-psychiatric casualties. In addition, every military district has its own district hospital in which all medical specialities are available including psychiatric care. The staff of the district hospital includes three or four neurologists and about the same number of psychiatrists. The Leningrad Military District Hospital, for example, has five neurologists and four psychiatrists on its staff. They normally care for inpatients while perhaps two other doctors will care for military outpatients. The focus at both the front and the district hospital is on neurologists, who in general are regarded as more valuable than psychiatrists. They can diagnose and treat the physical causes of brain disorders, which are seen to be the root cause of psychiatric problems. The Soviets see the neurologist as less specialized and probably more likely to look for physical damage as the cause of behavior than would a psychiatrist.

At the army level there is a small psychiatric ward capable of accommodating up to forty beds. By and large the treatment schedule calls for the psychiatric patient to remain at army level for two weeks while undergoing treatment for minor psychiatric problems, three weeks if his problem is more serious, and no longer than six weeks if he has a truly serious problem. At the end of six weeks the patient will either be sent to a replacement depot or turned over to the civilian psychiatric establishment for further treatment. Such a discharge is normally accompanied by the assessment that the soldier can no longer be of any functional military use even in noncombat assignments.

At division level there is the normal complement of battle surgeons and doctors, but usually there are no psychiatrists or psychiatric wards. The division is seen as a combat fighting unit and is staffed mostly with medical surgical personnel who can deal with the common casualties of war. There is no equivalent in the Soviet army of the division-level psychiatrist as found in many Western armies. Equally important, there is no support staff of psychologists, social workers, or counselors, which have become commonplace in Western armies. The problems usually handled by this staff are, in the Soviet army, dealt with by the unit commander, his executive officer, or the political officer.

At the regimental level there is the normal medical staff comprised of a regimental surgeon and sometimes a neurologist, but again there are no psychiatrists or psychologists. The problems of small psychiatry that surface here are dealt with by the unit commander or the political officer. The same is true at battalion level except that there is no doctor present. Medical treatment at battalion is handled by the battalion *feldsher,* a trained physician's assistant. The role of medical personnel below division in treating psychiatric casualties is to select the truly serious neuro-psychiatric cases from the less serious ones. The first level at which a genuine neuro-psychiatric casualty can be treated seriously is at army level. In the main, however, most instances of psychiatric disability are treated functionally at the lower level by short periods of rest and returned to the line because of the harsh clinical definitions of psychiatric disability that are used to screen cases.

The training of medics, *feldshers,* and even doctors in psychiatric triage is almost nonexistent and is in any case well below that found in Western armies. The Soviets do not prepare for treating neuro-psychiatric and neurotic reactions as much as they prepare for treating the physically damaged. There seems to be a belief that to train lower-echelon medical personnel too well in psychiatric triage might result in an increase in psychiatric casualties as severe diagnostic definitions are eroded. There are no psychiatric assistants like those found in the American army to help deal with psychiatric casualties. Although there are independent medical detachments that come under the authority of the medical department of the chief of the army front that can be sent to divisions to help with medical problems, none of these special teams deal with psychiatric problems. There are no special psychiatric teams similar to those used by the American army in Vietnam. If one examines the Soviet medical structure up to army level, the fact is that there are no organic staffs to deal with truly neuro-psychiatric cases as a special problem area.

Conversations with Soviet psychiatrists and battle surgeons suggest that the Soviet military is acutely aware that the presence of certain kinds of physicians within easy access of the troops tends to cause the troops to use the physicians' medical specialty as a way of avoiding duty or battle. The Soviets also believe that the Western experience with psychiatric casualties in World War II, especially the American experience, was caused in large part by the presence of psychiatric diagnosticians and a lax set of diagnostic categories deployed too close to the troops. Soviet medical authorities readily admit that it is probably not a good idea to "go too close" to the battle with psychiatrists or even neurologists because their mere presence tends to increase the number of soldiers that are diagnosed as psychiatric casualties. As a consequence, the Soviets have no intention of making psychiatric services readily available to the troops in a combat zone.

The political officer is a unique resource in the Soviet army. Originally instituted to ensure the political loyalty of military commanders, the political officer has long since acquired more relevant functions. The Soviet army is the only Western army that has an officer and small staff within combat units who are directly responsible for ensuring the morale, motivation, and fighting spirit of the soldier. In this sense, the political officer is an important adjunct to the commander. The Soviet commissar, although often denigrated in Western military literature, was often held in high esteem by soldiers in World War II. Combat histories of the Soviet army clearly show that it was often the political officer who was the most motivated and most talented soldier in the unit. Although a considerable number of political hacks served as political officers, by and large this has changed since the war's end. The Political Academy, which was founded prior to World War II, has been upgraded considerably, and most of the political officers today are college graduates who have also taken courses in psychology if not psychiatry to aid them in their primary function of maintaining morale and motivation. During World War II the political officer was found only at battalion level or above. Today he is found at the company level as well and, at some point in the future, it is likely that they will be assigned to platoons as well.

The soldiers nickname the political officer "the priest," but they do not usually seek him out as a confidant or a counselor in the Western sense. He is charged with knowing what is going on among the troops in a unit, and in practice there is usually little that escapes his attention. While the soldier is unlikely to come to him, he will probably seek out the problem soldier if only to remind him of his responsibilities. In this sense, he can function as the first line of defense in locating and dealing with any kind of psychological problem among the soldiers. Again, however, he deals with these problems as a member of the command staff and not as a medical practitioner. However, the personal participation of the political officer in battle and his presence on the front line greatly increase his stature and authority in dealing with psychiatric problems. Soviet psychiatrists note that these conditions often make him more effective than trained psychiatrists who give advice safely from the rear areas.

Perhaps as a consequence of the lack of psychological services in the Soviet army coupled with a harsh regimen of military life, there seem to be very high rates of behavioral problems among the soldiery. There are, for example, very high rates of assaults upon sergeants and even officers by common soldiers. The "caste system" within Soviet military units undoubtedly produces a great deal of stress on the soldier. Soldiers usually live in cramped conditions, cooped up on their military bases, subject to harsh discipline, the wrath of exploitative sergeants, and poor and monotonous diets. Even the brief respite from military life in the form of a pass is usually not for overnight. Sojourns off the base are carefully controlled and usually accompanied by an officer or sergeant. There are few diversions and even fewer ways to relieve stress. Access to women is almost nonexistent. There is a considerable amount of alcohol consumption, although research on the subject tends to suggest that the amount of drinking is actually less than that normally found in the society at large. The social system of the military produces much greater stress upon the Soviet soldier than soldiers must endure in Western armies. An American soldier, for example, would regard the conditions of Soviet military life as the equivalent of being in a prison. This stress frequently boils over into assaults on noncommissioned officers (NCOs) and even officers and manifests itself more seriously in high rates of suicide and suicide attempts.

When Soviet soldiers were asked, "Did you ever hear stories about people committing suicide in other units?" 84.1 percent of the survey respondents indicated that they had indeed heard such reports while in military service. At least 48.7 percent of the respondents reported that someone in their unit had attempted to commit suicide.[6] This rate of suicide attempts must be interpreted in light of the fact that many suicide attempts are really attempts to get a release from military service. Nonetheless, from almost any perspective the stress of Soviet military life tends to produce a very high rate of problems that most armies of the West would regard as psychiatric, requiring attention from either a psychiatrist, psychologist, or at least a counselor. In the Soviet army such facilities are simply not available.

A soldier who is suffering from a psychiatric problem or tries to commit suicide will almost always be sent to prison. He may, however, be held in jail only for a short time until a team of psychiatrists from the army- or front-level hospital can interview him and diagnose his problem. Even this examination requires a request from his commanding officer, who, in making the request, is admitting that he cannot handle the problem. Therefore, they are likely to send for a psychiatrist to examine a problem soldier only after the commander and the political officer have repeatedly tried to deal with the problem themselves. If an examination reveals that the problem is essentially behavioral rather than some sort of physiological condition, the soldier is usually turned back to his commander for punishment or simply retained in prison. If, on the other hand, the soldier is truly mentally ill, he will usually be sent back to a rear-area military hospital for treatment. If his problem can be cured or at least ameliorated, he will then be returned to his unit to complete his military service, and the time spent in the hospital will often not be counted toward his military enlistment. In short, it is "bad time" that must be made up.

If the soldier is diagnosed as having a genuinely serious problem that cannot be dealt with by the military medical system, he will be turned over to the public health system and discharged from the service. It is important to note that the rate of discharge for psychiatric problems in the Soviet army in peacetime is very low. The Soviet authorities clearly do not want to set a precedent of allowing individuals out of military service for this reason. Accordingly, soldiers with psychiatric problems not clearly stemming from organic causes are dealt with very severely, and every effort is made to keep the soldier in military service even if he cannot be a useful member. It is, in the Soviet view, far more important to send the message to other soldiers that psychiatric debilitation will not be rewarded with release from military service than it is to ensure that the soldier receives adequate medical treatment to deal with his problem.

PSYCHIATRIC TREATMENT

In their treatment of psychiatric patients the Soviets have historically stressed therapies based in biological theory. This approach has been characteristic of Russian psychiatry since before the turn of the century, and it still is today. With the partial rehabilitation of Soviet psychology as a separate discipline since the mid-1960s, there has been a rise in other treatment methodologies, what the Soviets generically call "socio-rehabilitative therapies." By 1981 Soviet textbooks on the subject were calling each approach—the socio-rehabilitative and the biological—"equally important." Nonetheless, in most therapeutic environments it is the medical doctor, usually a neurologist or a psychiatrist, not the psychologist, who remains the predominant figure and who generally oversees treatment. In those few situations where psychologists are allowed to administer therapies, they are often formally informed that by law a medical doctor, often a neurologist, must be present or oversee the treatment. Nonbiological therapies are, in any case, regarded with suspicion and have yet to establish their validity in the eyes of the psychiatric establishment.

Basic biological therapies have been evident in Soviet military psychiatry at least since 1905 and have their parallel in the West. The most common include somatic therapy, physical therapy, active therapy, narcotic sleep therapy, insulin comatose therapy, medical convulsive therapy, and electroconvulsive therapy. With the rise of what the Soviets call the "pharmacological era of psychiatry," which they date from the French research into psychotropic drugs in the 1950s, many of these basic "biological shock" therapies have been replaced with those based on drug applications. Soviet

psychiatrists apparently think very highly of drug intervention therapies
and suggest that the use of psychopharmacological agents

has spread the boundaries of therapeutic action, changed the appearance of psychiatric hospitals and revealed new possibilities for social labor readaptation with
the return of patients to society and labor activity. Because of the simplicity of use,
speed and impact on the psychological disorders and the comparative safety of
these substances, the volume of psychiatric aid has considerably increased and extended the possibilities of extra-hospital treatment.[7]

By the early 1970s, the drug revolution in the Soviet Union had taken
full hold, and there is no doubt that it has become a major feature in the
treatment of psychiatric problems. A list of major drugs used in Soviet
psychiatric practice with the conditions for which they are prescribed appears in Table 3.

While the Soviets cite their own contributions to the development of
psychopharmacological agents, many of these claims are overstated. For
the most part the commonly used drugs in the Soviet Union are still im-
ported from abroad, and most of the major advances in their discovery
were first made abroad most notably in France, Germany, Hungary, and
the United States. A number of drugs have simply been copied and given
other names.

Although there has been an increase in the use of drug-related therapeutic techniques, control over therapies for treating combat shock or other
mental problems in the military still resides with psychiatrists and neurologists. The concept of drug therapy has actually strengthened the idea of
the organic origin of mental aberration and recommends itself as an excellent treatment therapy to psychiatrists, since drugs work directly upon the
physiological functions of the brain. Thus, "drugs address the brain and
have points of application in the specific material structure of the brain
and produce complex neurotrophic effects."[8] Among military psychiatrists, the basic diagnostic assumption remains that combat shock or any
other mental aberration suffered by a soldier under fire is organic in origin
and must be treated as such.

Soviet psychotherapy still seems to have a suspicious reputation acquired during the Stalinist days. The Soviets have not been practicing clinical psychotherapy very long, only since the mid-1970s, and consequently
many of their treatment therapies still have major problems of acceptabil-
ity. They also have some difficulty in establishing the connection between
therapies and success rates because they lack sufficient data bases to make
statistical comparisons. One can get some sense of just how carefully controlled psychotherapy as practiced by Soviet psychologists is by noting that
there is still a public law in effect that guides the use of psychotherapies.
This law, first promulgated by the People's Commissariat of Public Health,

Table 3.
Drugs Used by Soviet Military Psychiatrists in Treatment of Neurosis and
Psychosis

For Psychosis	
Antipsychotics	
Sedatives:	(aminazine, propazin, Levopromazine, chlorprotixine, reserpine, leponex)
Selectives:	(triftazin, meterazine, haloperidol, carbiidn, pimozide)
Generals:	(mazheptyl, trisedyl)
Mood elevators:	(thyoridazine, perphenazine, Frenlon, fluorophenazine, fluspiridine, primozide, eglonyl)
Antidepressants	
Sedatives:	(amitriptylene, surmontyl, azaphine, fluoracisin, prothiaden, oxylidine, pyrazidol)
Thymoanaleptics:	(imizine, pertofran, anafranil, Notriptyline)
Stimulants:	(iprazide, nuredal, benazide, transamine, nitazepam)
For Reactive States/Neurosis	
Tranquilizers	
Sedatives:	(meprobamate, amizyl, chlordiazepoxide, oxazepam, Nitrazepam, phenazepam, mebicar)
Stimulators	
Minor mood elevators:	(trioxazin, diazepam, medazepam)
Psychostimulants:	(pervitin, meridil, piridrol, syndocarb, centrophinoxine, pyriditol)

Source: G. Avrutskiy and A.A. Neduva, Treatment of the Mentally Ill
        (Moscow: Medit sina, 1981), p. 56

requires that psychotherapy must be conducted at all times in the presence
of a psychiatrist or a physician. This decree, incredibly, was originally issued in 1926 and is still regarded in Soviet textbooks as the main guideline
for the use of psychotherapy in clinical situations.

Soviet psychiatrists rely heavily upon drug therapies to deal with problems resulting from battle stress as well as from other kinds of trauma, in
line with the Soviet belief that there is nothing unique about the stresses
of battle per se. Much Soviet research on the subject tends to reinforce the
belief that many symptoms of stress encountered on the battlefield can be
found as readily in other disasters such as plane crashes, large fires, tor-
nadoes, earthquakes, and the like that civilians suffer. There is, then, no
large gap in the treatments offered to soldiers suffering from combat psychosis and those provided to civilians suffering from psychosis induced by
other factors.

In their treatment of stress, the Soviets have continuously made use of folk and herbal medicines, and a number of these compounds are still in use today. Such natural tranquilizers and stimulants as valeriana, pantacrene, leonuria, ginseng, leuzeue, and eleuterococus continue to be used although clearly to a lesser extent than twenty years ago. Some others, such as chloryl hydrate and cardiac bromide, are still used widely as are calcium and magnesium IVs. Soviet psychiatrists see these natural compounds as having some advantages over alternative chemical compounds. Often they can be taken orally in droplet form. Furthermore, they do not overstimulate the soldier and usually do not bring on exhaustion. In addition, natural stimulants are more easily dissipated by the body's system than are most synthetic compounds. On the battlefield, *sanitors* and *feldshers* carry medical kits that contain pills, liquids, and even injections of these natural compounds along with the basic drugs for treating stress reactions. Although natural compounds are still much in evidence, the fact remains that the basic thrust of Soviet military psychiatry in developing treatments for stress reactions remains focused in its attempts to develop synthetic drugs. Psychopharmacology is rapidly coming of age in the Soviet Union, and its developments tend to parallel those in the West.

The Soviets are trying to adopt essentially Western diagnostic criteria for treatment of syndromes specifically related to battle stress. As noted earlier, the use of ICD-9 has been enforced by the Ministry of Health on the public health system in an effort to standardize diagnostic criteria. In general, the Soviets tend to use many of the same major diagnostic categories for defining battle shock—related problems as they use in dealing with shock reactions resulting from other causes. In dealing with battle-shock reactions Soviet military psychiatry uses diagnostic categories that emphasize reactive states. They further subcategorize reactive states into acute shock reactions, depressive reactions, and reactive delirious psychosis. Other diagnostic categories related to battle shock include neurosis, neurasthenia, hysterical neurosis, and hysterical psychosis. A diagnostic category that is not used very much in the West but that has a long history of use in the Soviet military addresses those symptomatic psychoses resulting from infectious diseases. A relatively complete list of diagnostic categories, including a list of those frequently used in the West but not used by Soviet psychiatrists, is presented in Tables 4 and 5. It is interesting to examine how the Soviets functionally define these diagnostic categories and what specific treatments are recommended for each.

Soviet military psychiatry sees reactive states as being caused by short-term traumatic impacts upon the soldier. Trauma, in the Soviet lexicon, refers exclusively to physical injury. It is not used, as in the United States, to denote a nonphysical impact that might produce psychological reactions. The onset of a reactive state is very rapid and hence clearly distin-

Table 4.
Symptom Indicators Used by Soviet Military Psychiatrists to Diagnose Battle
Neurosis and Psychosis

For Neurosis:	For Psychosis:
Irritability	Depression
Fatigue	Melancholia
Nervousness	Abulia
Insomnia	Apathy
Anxiety	Stupor
Phobia	Agitation
Low suppressed mood	Compulsion
Hypochondria	Delusion
Iatrogenia	Hallucination
Obsession	Denial of disease
	Depersonalization
	Extreme anxiety

Table 5.
Common Terms Used in Western Military Psychiatry Not Used by Soviet Military
Psychiatrists

Post-traumatic stress disorder
Anxiety disorder
Battleshock syndrome
Neurotic depression

SOURCE: Richard Gabriel, _Soviet Military Psychiatry_.
Westport: Greenwood Press, 1986) p. 144

guished from the effects of long-term battle fatigue. Reactive states can set in within hours or even minutes of exposure to trauma. In the Soviet view psychotic reactions are directly related to the nature and intensity of the traumatic event and are not seen as a mechanism for triggering deeper psychological problems. In addition, the reversibility of a psychotic reaction is in direct proportion to the degree and impact of the initial trauma, a view that fits very well with the traditional notion that trauma acts primarily to disrupt the physiology of the brain by disordering the conditioned reflexes of the second signal system.

The Soviets maintain that their view of trauma-induced psychosis as being caused by a disruption of brain function is very realistic, and they define reactive states as having certain characteristics. They see the reactive state as a functional response to stress, which serves a purpose for the soldier, namely allowing him to escape from battle or to close off some horror he may have witnessed. Accordingly, the Soviets understand the problem of secondary gain. They understand that a soldier "gains" or profits from remaining in his reactive state, and as way of approaching treatment, they make every effort to demonstrate to the soldier either through traumatic therapy or threats of punishment that this gain will not be tolerated.

A second characteristic of reactive states is their reversibility and temporary nature, a view directly deductible from their assumption that the brain learns by conditioned response. The objective of treatment is to recondition the brain or shock it back into its normal pattern of operation. Once the trauma abates and the brain returns to working normally, the reactive state should dissipate. In short, if brain patterns have been disordered by trauma, the removal of the trauma—or the infliction of a stronger stimuli—ought to result in breaking the psychosis. There is simply no question of psychosis lingering in the absence of trauma in the sense that it results from deeper psychological problems that the trauma happened to bring to the surface. A third characteristic is that the Soviets regard the problem of reactive states as essentially nonpsychogenic, that is, reactive states do not result from longstanding psychological problems. Instead, they are a specific and temporary response to traumatic conditions that the organism has suffered. The removal of the soldier from these conditions is often sufficient, in the Soviet view, to reverse the syndrome.

Soviet military psychiatrists clinically distinguish three types of affective battle reactions: acute affective shock, depressive pyschogenic shock, and reactive delirious psychosis. In acute affective shock, the onset of the reactive state is very rapid and takes many forms, including paralysis, blindness, and surdomutism. Sometimes, though rarely, will acute reactions produce a psychogenic stupor. In general, the Soviets place stupor in the category of depressive reactions. To treat acute reactive shock, the Soviets immediately isolate the individual from the traumatic event and move him from the risk zone. They also try to insulate him from other members of his unit in order to prevent any contagion (although, interestingly, the contagion effect is denied any validity in Soviet psychiatric theory). If necessary, the soldier is immobilized with restraints. Drugs are administered immediately to stabilize the patient. Frequently heavy impact doses, as much as 100 to 150 milligrams, are given by injection on the spot until the sedative takes hold. The drugs of choice to treat acute affective shock are

Phenazapen, Phenazepam, Ilenium, Siduzin, and Amitriptylene, all of which are very strong tranquilizers. After the patient has been sedated, other tranquilizing doses are administered to sustain the sedated condition. These less powerful but sustaining compounds include Aminazine, Tisercin, and Chloprothixene. These drugs are also administered in relatively high doses until the patient has recovered.

The Soviets find that the most common manifestation of reactive psychosis is what they call *depressive reactions*. Here they recommend an intense therapy using Amitriptylene, an antidepressant. Again the practice is to administer heavy initial doses to prevent deepening the depression. They distinguish between types of depression and prescribe different degrees of drug doses to deal with them. In general, however, a true psychotic depression is usually treated with very high doses of Ampriptylene, Melipramine, and Pyrazadol. Shallow depression seems to respond fairly well to high doses of Azaphen.

Soviets call reactive delirious psychosis, a very severe reactive depression accompanied by strong physiological symptoms, a "tightened reactive state." It is characterized by such extreme symptoms as delirium of pursuit, auditory hallucinations, surdomutism, and a complete disassociation from reality. In treating this condition the Soviets have made use of neurolyptics such as Triftazin, Perheneazine, and Trisedil. The Soviets recognize the validity of a number of psycho-traumatizing situations encountered in battle. These situations can cause extreme psychomotor excitation in the soldier, which may last for several hours. The symptoms include sensory delirium, false perceptions, and strong affective fear. Soviet psychiatrists suggest that strong and immediate treatment be rendered to deal with these symptoms before the syndrome can gain a strong hold on the individual. Their experience suggests that the rapidity of treatment is fundamental to reversing the reaction. Reactive delirious psychosis is treated like cases of acute shock, and the therapy of choice is to administer strong neurolytics with sedative effects. Some more commonly prescribed drugs used in these cases include Aminizene, Levopromozene, Chrlophophysine, and Tryphotizine, all given in high doses intramuscularly.

In specific cases of extreme psychomotor excitation resulting from trauma the use of Aminezene and Levopromozine at twenty-five to fifty milligrams a day by injection is recommended. Also used is a 2 percent solution of Dimedrol, a 25 percent solution of Magnesium Sulphate or a solution of Barbamyl in combination with a 10 percent solution of Glucanated Calcium and 10 percent Calcium Chloride administered intravenously. In the treatment of hysterical stupor the use of psychomotor stimulants is prescribed, using Syndocarb at thirty to forty milligrams a day accompanied by a mild tranquilizer.

Soviet military psychiatrists stress that reactive psychosis is strongly associated with battle stress. Though they are aware that there are other kinds of reactions to battle shock, the primary emphasis seems to be on dealing with reactive psychosis, and the reason is clear enough. If one takes the view that the soldier's behavior is totally a function of the organic operations of the brain and that any disruption of brain functions will produce physiological symptoms (and vice versa), then the focus on the strong physiological symptoms that accompany reactive psychosis is logical. For Soviet military psychiatrists, reactive psychosis has become a kind of "bottom line." Here the soldier will most commonly manifest the kinds of problems that will have the greatest effect on the combat unit. More important, reactive psychosis is accompanied by clear physiological disruptions and symptomology, which facilitates diagnosis by a psychiatrist rather than a battle surgeon. Thus, Soviets tend to emphasize reactive states in their treatment of battle stress. With this combination of a physiological and a psychiatric problem Soviet psychiatrists can most clearly deal, given their biological assumptions about the roots of human behavior.

Soviet psychiatrists are not trained to deal with psychiatric problems that have no clear accompanying physiological symptoms. In the West, such problems may be regarded as being rooted purely in the emotions. In the Soviet view, they are not recognized as legitimate psychiatric problems at all but as problems of "small psychiatry." But in reactive psychosis one finds the precise kind of case for which the Soviet psychiatrist is well trained to deal, namely a psychiatric disturbance caused by a physiological trauma that manifests itself in external symptoms which can be dealt with directly usually through drug therapy that affects the organic operations of the brain. It is hardly surprising, therefore, that Soviet military psychiatrists seem to concentrate on dealing with reactive psychosis as the most important form of neuro-psychiatric breakdown that they will have to deal with in future wars.

While Soviet military psychiatrists are quite capable of recognizing a wide range of other battle-shock reactions, they do not seem to spend a great deal of time and effort treating them. For example, they see neurosis as a consequence of fear and anxiety. They are likely to regard it as a minor problem and treat it with short-term tranquilizer therapy. Often, except when the neurosis is deep and debilitating, they will define the condition as small psychiatry to be handled appropriately outside medical channels. In treating neurosis, vegeostabilizers are used to break down the physiological disruptions in the organism, which are the cause of fear and anxiety. Soviet psychiatrists seem to take neurasthenia only slightly more seriously. Neurasthenia takes the form of weakness, exhaustion, increased reduction of mental and physical efficiency, transitions of mood, and an inability to focus and process information. These symptoms are regarded as hypostenic as opposed to hyperstenic forms of neurasthenia. The major treatment recommended is tranquilizer therapy to break the organic reaction patterns (what the Soviets call vegetative disruption autonomic nervous system patterns). The hyperstenic forms of neurasthenia (an interesting diagnosis in itself) are characterized by an extreme form of excitation. Once again, tranquilizing drugs are recommended, including Meprobamate, Emisile, Elinium, Trapazine, and Phenazecom. In its hypostenic forms, neurasthenia is treated with antidepressant drugs and stimulants including Trioxizine, Sougexin, and the psychostimulants Sindocarb and Sindophine. The Soviets emphasize that, as with other battle stress—related problems, the treatment of neurasthenia should begin as quickly as possible. They emphasize that the possibility of psychological dependence on drugs should also be monitored.

Soviet psychiatrists seem to have achieved some success in the treatment of asthenic states through the use of a new class of drugs called "nootropes." While not much has been published in Soviet literature about this new class of drugs, it is believed that they work basically by affecting the metabolism of the cells of the brain. Examples are Iminalon and Ancebol. Not much information about the efficacy of these drugs or their chemical composition is available, but one Soviet pharmacologist noted that they were invented in Japan as GABA derivatives and are in fact widely used in Europe where they are manufactured under license.

Soviet military psychiatrists also recognize three other categories of battle-shock reactions: hysterical neurosis, hysteria, and pyschasthenia. Hysterical neurosis is characterized by short-term, reversible, and pyschogenically nonpsychotic disorders. Examples of this condition are temporary mutism, asthasia, abasia, hysterical fits, and weeping. The specific conditions that separate hysterical neurosis from reactive psychosis are unclear except that one distinguishing factor seems to be the rapidity with which the patient responds to treatment. Thus, initial treatments for dealing with hysterical neurosis are the traditional ones (used in World War I by almost all armies) of slapping or shaking the soldier, shouting, causing pain, emersion in cold water, or any other means of causing a shock to the patient in order to bring him out of his condition. There are, of course, more modern treatments, which follow if the syndrome cannot be broken in the traditional manner. These treatments require injections of drugs such as Elinium and Phynazepam.

Two other categories of battle shock are hysteria and psychasthenia. Hysteria is defined as affective instability expressed in behavior and is generally characterized by the same symptoms as hysterical neurosis although not as deeply. The treatment of choice is either shock or tranquilizers. Psychasthenia is characterized by an alarming overanxiousness and uncertainty about one's ability and surroundings usually accompanied by lowered moods. The use of psychostimulators is indicated in the treatment of this condition.

In addition the Soviets have identified a type of psychiatric disruption that is organically based and seems almost absent from American literature. This is the type of psychiatric, often psychotic, reaction to poisoning or infectious disease. It is called exogenic symptomatic psychosis and, in the Soviet view, is clearly based in the disrupted physiology of the patient. Soviet military psychiatrists identify five basic types of symptomatic psychosis: delirium, epileptic excitation, twilight states, confusion, and hallucinations. Given that armies throughout history have almost always suffered more casualties from disease than from enemy fire, the focus on mental aberrations caused by disease processes probably has a long history in Soviet military medicine. Moreover, it is the kind of problem that would find a ready audience within Soviet psychiatry given its biological assumptions about human behavior. Since organic patterns may be disrupted not only by battle shock but by disease, fever, and viruses, the Soviet military psychiatrist is comfortable in dealing with the psychiatric effects of infectious diseases.

One is struck in reading Soviet military medical literature by the emphasis it places upon the treatment of mental disruptions caused by the external environment. The impact of such hostile climates of extreme heat and cold on the ability of the soldier to maintain the mental strength to continue the battle have been closely studied. This is a direction of study that is only moderately evident in American military psychiatry and, where it appears, is not reflected in the research of psychiatrists as much as in the work of battle surgeons. In the Soviet case, one again encounters the tendency to join the medical doctor and the psychiatrist at the point of common origin, where the physiological disruption of the brain produces behavioral aberrations.

CONCLUSION

Although it is clear that the Soviet theory and practice of battlefield psychiatry is strongly rooted in both Marxist dogma regarding the materialist neurophysiology of man and Soviet combat experience in World War II, the fact is that Soviet practice in military psychiatry remains far more a prisoner of dogma than a practical art based in experience. The result is that when compared to the armies of the West, particularly the American and Israeli armies, Soviet battlefield psychiatry is neither well articulated in its casualty servicing structure or willing to face the practical realities that a future conventional war will present. The conclusion seems warranted that when compared to the state of affairs in the U.S. Army, the Soviets are not nearly as well prepared to deal with the levels of psychiatric casualties projected for a future war as they could be if only they could free themselves from the self-imposed imprisonment of Marxist-Leninist dogma.

NOTES

1. Information about this study was provided by Soviet medical personnel now living in the West whom I interviewed. These individuals had either taken part in the study itself or had read it while in the Soviet Union.

2. This estimate is provided by Defense Intelligence Agency analysts who specialize in studying the personnel policies of the Soviet army.

3. *Medical Support of the Soviet Ground Forces* (Washington, D.C.: Defense Intelligence Agency Report, March 1979), p. 8.

4. Ibid., p. 4.

5. These estimates were provided by Soviet military psychiatrists in personal interviews.

6. Richard A. Gabriel, *The Mind of the Soviet Fighting Man* (Westport, Conn.: Greenwood Press, 1984), pp. 43–45.

7. G. Avrutskiy and A. A. Neduva, *Treatment of the Mentally Ill* (Moscow: Meditsina, 1981), p. 6.

8. Ibid. p. 26.

6

Development of American Military Psychiatry

PSYCHIATRY AND WAR

Psychiatry, in one form or another, is as old as human beings. In its most basic form it emerged at the precise moment one human being attempted to help another deal with personal anguish. People have always faced many of the personal tragedies—death of a child, loss of a spouse, fear of the unknown, and an awareness of one's own mortality—that modern people face, and there is every reason to believe that they suffered from the same pain and anguish in dealing with these problems that we do. Moreover, early human understanding of the environment and human behavior was so inexact that people resorted to religion to deal with fears and ignorance. The first shamans earned their keep within primitive societies by providing explanations and rituals that enabled people to deal with their environment and personal anguish. Early people, no less than we, dealt with forces that they could not understand or control and attempted to come to grips with their vulnerability in much the same way we do, by trying to bring some order to their universe. Those who could interpret and explain that universe in whatever terms were the precursors of our psychiatrists.

Psychiatry is a different discipline from psychology although the differences are becoming increasingly narrow. Psychiatrists have historically been defined as "healers of the mind" while psychologists are defined as "those who studied the mind." This distinction, based in the difference between medical doctors who treated mental illness and scholars who studied it, has become less useful in the modern era, especially in military psychiatry, as psychologists have carved out a significant role as clinicians treating those suffering from emotional problems. Traditionally, psychiatry was closely tied to the general practice of medicine and the discipline of psychiatry has its roots in attempts to link human behavior to the physiology of the brain. With the recognition that human beings often suffer from purely emotional problems that have no physiological explanation, clinical psychology has also come into its own. Most of those who deal with the problem of battle stress in the military establishments of the world are psychologists, not psychiatrists. Both have become "healers of the mind."

Psychiatry had its beginnings in people's attempt to explain the causes of strange behavior in others, behavior that they initially attributed to forces outside the afflicted individual. Whether the problem was death, disease, cowardice in battle, or debilitating fear in war or on the hunt, its causes were attributable to larger forces that humans could not control. Accordingly, the earliest explanations for mental illness—as recorded in ancient Babylon in 2750 B.C.—were attributed to the anger of powerful deities that people had angered by their immoral behavior. Since people cannot live in a world in which they feel they are totally helpless, early psychiatrists attributed madness—and even defeat in battle—to faults in a man's character. Both Egyptian and Hebraic concepts of mental illness (and even physical illness) were rooted in the notion of individual sin. Not until the rise of Greek medicine was it possible for ancient psychiatrists to break away from these notions that sin caused madness. The Greeks were the first to bring to the study of medicine and the physiology of the brain the systematic use of reason joined with empirical observation that led to the conclusion that madness was caused by physical and emotional forces within the individual and not by diabolical outside forces.

Modern psychiatry has its roots in the Greek empirical method of medical observation. Greek physicians studied the brain in detail. At the same time, however, they based their medicine on a view of human nature that permitted the development of the first theory of personality. This idea, first put forth by Plato, attributed mental problems to purely emotional causes. Thus, the Greeks were the first to develop the dualism that still characterizes psychiatry. One view saw human behavior as rooted in the physiology of the brain, a view evident today in the study of brain chemistry. A second view rooted human behavior in the mind, which produced its own reality—perceptions, emotions, and so on—quite apart from the physiology of the brain. This view is evident in modern-day Freudian psychiatry. The tension between these two perspectives drove the development of psychiatry through the ages.

Psychiatric thought from the time of the Greeks to the fall of Rome was characterized by a predominant emphasis on physiological explanations for mental illness. This *biological psychiatry* was eclipsed by more irrational explanations for madness beginning in the Dark Ages (between the fifth and twelfth centuries). Much of what passed for psychiatry in this period was essentially doctrinally formed and enforced by a single universal Catholic church. By the thirteenth century it had degenerated to the point where mental illness was viewed as the product of demonical possession brought on by the sins of the sufferer. The most common explanation for madness was possession caused by witchcraft, in which the sufferer willingly allowed himself to be possessed by demons and other spirits of the devil. Because the possessed person had willingly brought about his own evil condition, the only appropriate treatments was torture, recantation, and burning at the stake.

The Renaissance saw the reemergence of the traditional Greek notion of human behavior based in the physiology of the brain. The anatomical studies of men like Leonardo da Vinci helped propel a rapidly developing discipline of medical investigation. Established religions resisted this return to more empirical methods of medical investigation at every turn, and throughout the Renaissance medical investigators were often executed for heresy.

The Enlightenment of the seventeenth century, with its emphasis on scientific investigation of all aspects of human existence, gradually moved psychiatry away from purely emotional explanations for mental illness. By the eighteenth and early nineteenth centuries, medical science had developed to the point where knowledge of the brain seemed to offer the promise of dealing with mental illness through an understanding of the operations of its physiology.

The eighteenth and ninteenth centuries saw the full development of this view into the discipline of biological psychiatry. On the battlefields of the Civil War, Crimean War, Franco-Prussian War, and the Russo-Japanese War of 1905, biological psychiatry gained and maintained the predominant position in explaining human behavior. Attending physicians at each of these wars saw them as a great opportunity to learn more about the brain and its influence on human behavior. While the predominant effect of these wars on the study of medicine was the birth of the field of neurology, they also produced the first military psychiatrists. Biological psychiatry would maintain its dominant position in the discipline until the 1930s when Sigmund Freud offered an alternative explanation for human behavior based primarily upon the emotions. At present, psychiatry in general, and military psychiatry in particular, is again divided over alternative ways of explaining and dealing with mental phenomena. Psychiatrists often hold to the biological view and psychologists to the Freudian view.

Military psychiatry is a recent development, dating only from the Civil War where neurologists made a systematic attempt to link damage to the brain to emotional behavior. In a strict sense, however, military psychiatry did not emerge as a separate discipline until the Russo-Japanese War of 1905. While psychiatry over the centuries reflected two different views of human behavior and mental illness, the military establishments of the West from the time of the Greeks until World War I proceeded to develop almost totally ignorant of the debate. For military commanders the problem of dealing with fear in battle had a more pressing urgency and was dealt with in more direct ways.

Military perceptions of why men collapse in battle were formed more than 2000 years ago in the military experiences of classical Greece (450 B.C.). The Greeks believed that performance in battle was a function of the character of the soldier. Greek military literature emphasized the connection between the moral character and military training and heroism in battle. Heroes were men who controlled their fears; cowards succumbed to them; that was the only relevant criterion for assessing soldierly performance. So strongly did the Greeks hold this view that for almost 400 years they resisted the adoption of superior military technologies, with which they were quite familiar because of their wars with the Persians, on the grounds that to adopt weapons of greater range and lethality would destroy the distinction between heroes and cowards. After all, if a hail of arrows from Persian bows could kill at a distance of 200 yards thus eliminating hand-to-hand combat, then war had become too indiscriminate, killing heroes and cowards alike by mere chance. In order to sustain the view that moral character distinguished the good soldier, the Greeks refused to change their tactics or adopt the new "immoral" weaponry of their enemies. The fact that these weapons were more effective mattered not one whit.

The conviction that the soldier's character was the most important element in deciding performance under fire persisted for centuries. In World War I French soldiers were expected to overcome the German's technological advantages by sheer force of courage and will. French *élan* was expected to be the crucial difference. The result was that thousands of soldiers went over the tops of their trenches and walked slowly to their deaths into the teeth of enemy machine guns and artillery. Any sane calculation of war at that time would have concluded that the technology of war—the objective circumstances of the battlefield—had become more important than heroism or courage in gaining victory. Yet, the myth persisted with devastating effects. On July 1, 1916, the British army launched the Battle of the Somme. In less than four hours, 52,000 Englishmen had been killed or wounded. Many of their officers went over the top carrying only swagger sticks. And still they went, wave after wave, to meet their inevitable deaths. The myth of moral character as the dominant factor in a soldier's performance is no less alive today than it was in 1916, and it is no less false.

If there were no military psychiatrists before the Civil War, it is nonetheless true that earlier armies had sought to deal with the major problem of breakdown in battle in ways that are familiar to modern military psychiatrists. If mental collapse was a function of poor moral character, the task of military commanders was to prevent it. Armies adopted a number of measures to reduce manpower losses from battle shock.

The obvious way of reducing battle shock was to emphasize programs to instill moral character. Greek and Roman generals sought to toughen their armies by strict regimens of military discipline and hardship. Spartan soldiers from boyhood were not given enough to eat, nor were they allowed to wear sandals. They were trained to endure physical hardship and thus develop the will to overcome it. Another method was to use the soldier's sense of self-respect to overcome fear. Greek and Roman armies made great efforts to form military units comprised of men from the same town or city. The Greeks even made it a practice to station homosexuals and their lovers in the same units. These policies increased the social cohesion of the fighting group, and similar techniques were used right through World War I and II. In World War I the British always tried to raise regiments on a county basis, as did the Canadians, Germans, and French. Some were even raised from single occupations like miners and longshoremen. Throughout World War II, German regiments were still being drawn from the same city or town.

A common method of controlling a soldier's fear was to convince him that the costs of behaving improperly were always greater and far more certain than any possible gains from behaving improperly. Harsh discipline, including whippings, starvation, and the threat of execution became commonplace solutions among the armies of the seventeenth and eighteenth centuries. A commonly stated truism said that men must fear their officers more than death from the enemy, an injunction of Prussia's Frederick the Great, the father of the German army. As late as the 1870s the American army used tattooing and branding as punishment for cowardice. In World War I, French units that refused to fire on the German trenches were subject to artillery bombardments from their own guns. After the mutiny among the French on the Western front in 1917, men of the rebellious divisions that refused to attack were selected at random and publicly executed. British, French, and Canadian armies in World War I stationed battle police just to the rear of the front lines with instructions to shoot soldiers who turned away from the fight.

Other solutions to the problem were found in religious faith and ritual. Medieval commanders never went into battle until they had heard Mass and communion was delivered to their troops. Priests have always been in attendance at battles, usually urging the soldiers to fight harder "for God and country." In the Vietnam War, Terrence Cardinal Cooke stood on the flight deck of an American aircraft carrier blessing the pilots as they took off on bombing runs against targets in North Vietnam. Going to religious service before battle remain commonplace ritualistic defenses against fear even in the modern soldier. Muslim soldiers in Iran commonly attend a final religious service at which they are given a small plastic key to open the doors of paradise after they die in battle. And the impact of ritualistic practices should not be underestimated especially in a world that has been treated to a number of attacks by terrorists who have demonstrated their willingess to die in the service of a cause.

For at least 1000 years armies have used chemical means to steel the will of their soldiers against fear. The Vikings of the ninth century routinely used chemical stimulants made from deer urine. British soldiers to this day are entitled by military regulation to a stiff jigger of rum before going into battle. On the field of Waterloo in 1815, rum made the difference for a number of heavily engaged British units. In the Philippine Insurrection at the turn of the century, the Mauro Indians took drugs prior to battle as did a number of southwestern American Indian tribes. American soldiers in Vietnam stiffened their courage with marijuana or "skin-popping" diluted heroin or opium. Soviet soldiers in World War II were routinely given drugs made from herbal compounds to calm their nerves. While modern armies may be exploring more sophisticated chemical means to control fear, drugs have long historical precedent.

What these attempts to prevent battle stress have in common is the fact that they have not succeeded very well simply because a soldier's character has very little to do with his ability to endure the stress of battle. While some men collapse sooner than others, the critical variables are the objective conditions of battle to which the soldier is exposed. Despite the best efforts of military establishments to stem manpower loss from battle shock, the fact is that armies have always suffered great reductions in combat power as soldiers become debilitated through fear either to the point where they collapse and have to be evacuated or, more commonly, to the point where they are so frightened that they cannot function. At the Battle of Gettysburg, for example, hundreds of rifles were found with several balls and charges stuffed into their muzzles. Their owners were so frightened that they continued to load the rifles and simply forgot to pull the trigger after each load. Moreover, as the killing power of weaponry increases, the number of soldiers who will certainly suffer battle-shock symptoms is increasing at an alarming rate.

AMERICAN MILITARY PSYCHIATRY IN THE CIVIL WAR

The Civil War was the most destructive war in American history, killing and wounding more men than any other before or since. Psychiatry was still in its infancy. Although some psychiatrists recognized that men could become debilitated for purely emotional reasons, the major thrust of the discipline was the study of brain physiology and the attempt to link disruptions of that physiology to behavioral disorders. Within the United States there were fewer than a dozen mental hospitals and none for patients who developed mental disorders in war or military life. Care of the mentally ill rested in the hands of a handful of superintendants of these mental asylums, and the movement for humane treatment of the mentally ill, which had begun in France fifty years before, was just beginning to take root in the United States. Within the military itself, there were no psychiatrists at all, and the military continued to take the traditional view that soldiers who broke down in battle were cowards or had a "weak" character. American military psychiatry by 1860 had not come very far since the Revolution and was, in many ways, considerably behind the development of the discipline in Europe.

It is easy to forget just how primitive battlefield medicine was in the Civil War. Operations were performed without anesthesia, surgeons rarely if ever washed before examining open wounds, and infection was regarded as a normal and beneficial part of the healing process. It was a war of medical horrors. At the Battle of Gettysburg Union Army surgeons collapsed from exhaustion because they had to amputate so many limbs— most of them while the patient remained conscious! In this context, the lack of trained psychiatrists to deal with emotional and behavioral problems becomes a minor problem.

The Civil War, the progenitor of modern war, saw the first use of new and horribly destructive weapons on a previously unimagined scale. On the battlefields of Antietam, Gettysburg, and Chancellorsville troops made their first headlong frontal assaults against repeating rifles and pistols whose rates of fire caused thousands of casualties. The Civil War saw masses of men attacking frontally against massed rifled artillery guns whose repertoire of caliber and shot caused horrible casualties. The use of the delayed timed artillery fuse, which allowed artillery rounds to burst above the heads of advancing soldiers, increased the number of head wounds dramatically. The lack of any protective headgear also contributed to the number of head and neurological injuries. The introduction of telescopic rifles complete with spiral barreled rifling greatly increased the accuracy of massed rifle fire. The Gatling gun, a somewhat primitive but nonetheless effective machine gun made its appearance with devastating impact. The technology of war was making the battlefield much more lethal than it had ever been before and the predictable result was an increase in the number of dead, wounded, and psychiatric casualties. The Civil War marked the first step on the road to truly modern war.

Almost immediately medical officers had to deal with the problem of psychiatric casualties. Since the War Department had rejected the offer of a group of superintendents of insane asylums to treat the problem on the battlefields, treatment fell to surgeons. The experience that these surgeons gained with psychiatric cases led to the birth in the United States of the field of neurology and hardened even further the tendency of medical practitioners of the day to regard the cause of mental problems among soldiers as damaged physiology of the brain. Nonetheless, even these neurologists had to admit that there was a range of disorders that afflicted soldiers but had no sound physiological explanation. By 1863, at their urging, the first military hospital in the United States devoted to the treatment of psychiatric casualties was founded.

The most common psychiatric condition with which medical officers had to deal was nostalgia, a cluster of symptoms resulting from emotional and physical fatigue that made it impossible for the soldier to continue fighting. They also began to encounter a range of symptoms that mimicked different diseases but lacked any sound physical cause. Thus, for every hundred soldiers discharged for "nervous disease," 28.3 manifested a condition that mimicked epilepsy and 20.8 a condition that mimicked paralysis.[1] Today we know that these symptoms are conversion reactions produced by strong affective fear. No less than 6 percent of all medical discharges were for "general insanity" brought on by the war.

Psychiatric symptoms became so common that field commanders, with the support of medical doctors, pleaded with the War Department to provide some form of recruit screening to eliminate the soldiers susceptible to psychiatric breakdown. In 1863, the Union Army instituted the world's first psychiatric screening program of recruits. It didn't help any more than it did in World War I, and the number of psychiatric cases continued to increase.

It must be remembered that only a handful of physicians in the country had any experience in dealing with psychiatric patients whose conditions were brought on by emotional turbulence. For the most part they were superintendents of civilian mental asylums, and none saw service during the war. Accordingly, military physicians were usually at a loss to deal with cases of "insanity." In the first three years of the war soldiers who became "insane" were mustered out on the spot. This solution was particularly cruel, although it had long historical precedent in the armies of Europe. Insane soldiers in the Union and Confederate armies were often escorted to the main gate of a military camp and turned loose. Others were put on trains with no supervision, the name of a hometown or state pinned to their tunics. Others were left to wander until they died from exposure or starvation. By 1863, the number of insane or shocked soldiers wandering around the country was so great that there was a public outcry. In that year the military finally forbade the discharge of insane soldiers. Instead, they were sent to the newly established military hospital for the insane.

While statistical records are incomplete, by the end of the Civil War almost 6000 soldiers had been discharged from the Union Army alone for the psychiatric condition of nostalgia. The number suffering from "epilepsy" and hysterical paralysis was probably twice as large while the number discharged for insanity also reached several thousand. It is fair to assume that the Confederate totals would be similar, although there are no surviving data. Although the problem of psychiatric breakdown reached major proportions by war's end, not a single article or book on the subject was published once the war was over. The military psychiatric hospital was closed, and the government made no effort to deal with the psychiatrically wounded by involving the doctors who treated mental illness in the civilian community. The problem was conveniently forgotten, and except for the advances in neurology, battle shock and psychiatric debilitation were no longer of concern to the military. This failure to learn from experience would return to haunt the American army when it took the field in World War I.

WORLD WAR I

The outbreak of World War I immediately produced large numbers of psychiatric casualties within Allied armies. Within Allied armies, military psychiatry was almost unknown as a functioning discipline and, more important, few Allied physicians knew or recalled the Russian experience with psychiatric casualties only ten years earlier. As a consequence, the medical establishments of the West thought they were dealing with an entirely new phenomenon in which "the present war is the first in which the functional nervous diseases (shell-shock) have constituted a major medico-military problem."[2] It was believed that most psychiatric cases were the consequence of new weapons, particularly large-caliber artillery. Mental debilitation was widely believed to be caused by the concussive effects of shelling which disrupted the physiology of the brain. Emotionally rooted explanations—such as fear and anxiety—were regarded as highly conjectural and were never granted wide acceptance.

For the first two years of the war French and British armies simply evacuated psychiatric cases deeply to the rear. British casualties were transported to medical hospitals in England itself with the predictable result that few recovered completely and almost none were returned to the fighting. In France, the early practice of evacuating psychiatric casualties to civilian hospitals deep in the country had to be abandoned by 1917 when political opposition to the war made this practice difficult. It tended to feed wartime opposition further. By 1917 both French and British armies were making great efforts to treat psychiatric cases close to the front with the hope of eventually returning the cured to the fighting.

Americans regarded the stories that filtered back about new types of mental diseases afflicting soldiers in other armies as a medical curiosity. The American army had no structure for treating psychiatric casualties at all and very few psychiatrists in its ranks. Its only experience with psychiatric casualties had come ten years before when American soldiers stationed with Gen. John J. Pershing on the Mexican border were shown to be suffering a rate of mental illness three times higher than the entire state of New York.[3] Not until 1917, just before the American entry into World War I, did the War Department begin to take an interest in psychiatric casualties.

At the urging of a coalition of civilian mental health professionals organized under the name of the National Committee for Mental Hygiene, a committee was established to consult with the surgeon general to establish a structure for dealing with psychiatric problems in the military forces. Dr. Thomas Salmon, a member of the committee, visited England to learn firsthand how the British and French were dealing with the problem. His recommendations became the basis for establishing an American corps of psychiatrists to deal with psychiatric casualties. In short order American soldiers were fighting in France, and the number of psychiatric casualties grew to significant proportions.

The American military began to train doctors and supporting staff in military psychiatry. By war's end, the U.S. military had 693 psychiatrists in service with 263 stationed overseas.[4] Psychiatric staffs were organized in each division and small psychiatric hospitals capable of handling thirty patients at a time were set up near the front lines. Larger hospitals were established farther to the rear but still within a reasonable distance. The Americans were following established Russian and German practice in attempting forward treatment of psychiatric casualties.

An important part of the practical treatment of psychiatric casualties eventually became known as the principle of expectancy. Psychiatric patients were to be treated as close to the front as possible. In principle, all casualties were screened at a clearing station near the lines to determine who could be treated near the front and who was to be shipped to rear-area hospitals. Whether near the front or in the rear, medical personnel conveyed to the soldier the idea that as soon as he recovered, he would be expected to return to his unit. Being separated from his unit, he was told, was detrimental to the soldier and to his comrades who wanted him back. In World War II, the principle of expectancy was found to be a most important element in preventing a patient from developing secondary gain.

American military psychiatrists found that most psychiatric casualties were not suffering from physiological damage to the brain. Emotion, not brain damage, was the most frequent cause of the full range of psychiatric symptoms. They also found that many symptoms would cure themselves simply with a few days of rest, food, and respite from battle. The American army never made as extensive use as other armies of such therapies as hypnosis and electroshock. And the success rate was fairly good; about 40 percent of psychiatric casualties were returned to the fighting where, of course, many of them became psychiatric casualties again.

While the American strategy for dealing with the problem worked fairly well, by the time American troops became engaged in the war in large numbers, the nature of the war had changed. Trench warfare had given way to a renewed war of movement and maneuver. This meant that psychiatric treatment facilities were never able to retain their position close to the front as the armies moved rapidly forward in one offensive after another. Therefore, the medical service never succeeded in stopping large numbers of psychiatric casualties from being evacuated in normal medical channels to points deeply in the rear. The need to remove the wounded from the front lines simply meant that many psychiatric casualties were evacuated along with surgical casualties, effectively by-passing the psychiatric clearing stations.

By war's end, the American psychiatric medical structure had only limited experience in dealing with the practical problems of holding and returning psychiatric casualties to the front. Worse, the American army began to draw the wrong lessons from its experiences. Although it knew that most psychiatric casualties were not caused by damage to the brain, it continued to believe that men collapsed in battle primarily because they were of weak character. The solution, therefore, was to reduce the number of conscripts with a predisposition to collapse from entering the military forces in the first place. The fact that most psychiatric practitioners who had served during World War I had drawn their experience from civilian hospitals where they treated the insane, and because a number of symptoms exhibited by soldiers under fire paralleled the symptoms manifested by their civilian patients, they, too, subscribed to the wrong lesson.[5]

The lesson learned should have been that all men are subject to psychiatric collapse simply as sane men reacting to insane circumstances. The principal lesson drawn, however, was that soldiers had to be rigorously screened for predisposition to breakdown. When these "unfit" were eliminated, it was reasonably expected that the problem would largely disappear. It was the wrong conclusion. While the army did benefit from its establishment of permanent psychiatric hospitals within its medical structure and the presence in each division of a psychiatrist, for the most part the lessons of forward treatment and expectancy were lost in the effort to develop exact psychiatric tests that draft boards could use to eliminate those with a predisposition to collapse. The idea that psychiatric collapse is the reaction of even sane men when placed under great enough stress was given no credence. World War II would finally teach the American military just how wrong it had been.

WORLD WAR II

Given the lessons that the American army drew from World War I, it is not surprising that the main effort to reduce psychiatric casualties in World War II was focused on screening draftees in order to weed out those thought to be predisposed to psychiatric collapse. The army used the best available psychiatric tests and rejected no fewer than 1.6 million for military service, a rejection rate of 18.5 percent, nearly seven times higher than in World War I.[6] If the assumption that some men are more disposed to collapse in battle than others was correct, then the American army should not have suffered serious problems of psychiatric casualties, since it had already screened out those most disposed to breakdown. In fact, the rate at which soldiers in World War II were admitted to psychiatric hospitals was double the World War I rate, and separations from service for mental and emotional reasons increased almost seven times over the rate for World War I. Psychiatric casualties constituted the single largest category of disability discharges in World War II.[7]

Because the American military put so much faith in screening out the unfit, it made little provision for dealing with psychiatric casualties in the first two years of the war. In general, through 1943 there were no divisional psychiatric facilities of any worth in the field, and the common practice was to evacuate all psychiatric casualties far to the rear. The result was a medical disaster.

In the early days of the Tunisian and Sicilian campaigns (1943) the rates of psychiatric casualties were staggering. Some divisions had rates of 1200 to 1500 men per thousand per year. Whole battalions became debilitated because of stress-related problems. On average, 35 percent of all nonfatal casualties during this period were psychiatric. Worse, because they could not be treated near the front, they were evacuated ninety or more miles to the rear to theater or corps level. The result was that no more than 3 percent of these evacuations ever returned to combat. A report published in 1944 records that nearly all the men in rifle battalions not otherwise disabled by wounds became psychiatric casualties in the North African theater.[8]

By 1944, it was apparent to military medical authorities that every soldier exposed to combat was subject to psychiatric collapse. In the Volturno, Rapido, and Cassino actions, medical personnel began to notice that even old combat veterans, many of whom had received decorations for bravery, were beginning to collapse under the stress (Old Soldier's Syndrome). What finally drove home the point was that the Air Force was suffering high rates of psychiatric debilitation among its air crews. These men had been specially selected for their intelligence and stability and had been given long periods of stress training while becoming pilots.

By late 1943, the military began to recognize that psychiatric breakdown was too common a phenomenon to be regarded as abnormal. The diagnostic name for psychiatric collapse was changed from "psychoneurosis" to "exhaustion," a change indicating that there was nothing particularly shameful about collapsing under the stress of battle.

Having realized that it had made a mistake in believing that recruit screening would make the problem of psychiatric casualties largely disappear, the army now found itself unprepared in doctrine and resources to deal with a growing problem that threatened its combat power. There were acute shortages of psychiatrists army-wide, and the shortage of psychiatrists for division-level service never was truly solved by war's end. Worse, the training of psychiatric assistants and line medics was almost non-existent. By 1944 the military had succeeded in reestablishing a World War I hierarchical structure for treatment with facilities at division, army, and theater levels. Because these facilities were never fully staffed until late in the war, they never functioned as well as in World War I. More important, the ability of the system to function well depended heavily upon the medics and physician's assistants stationed at company and battalion aid stations. Since these personnel often had no training in screening psychiatric casualties, the system persisted for months in evacuating casualties that could easily have been held at battalion or division and returned to the fighting. Nonetheless, in the last days of the war, the system began to function fairly well just as the prospect of victory began to reduce the number of psychiatric casualties in the ranks. Return rates of soldiers suffering psychiatric casualties began to rise but never equaled the return rates of World War I.

After the war the military medical departments began to collect and analyze the data relevant to their experience with psychiatric casualties. It was finally determined that psychiatric breakdown was not the result of a predisposition to collapse. Rather, it was at last accepted that battle stress would break all soldiers exposed to it long enough, a fact buttressed by the finding that over time there was no difference in the rate of psychiatric breakdown between new and veteran soldiers.[9] In 1948 Roy Swank and Walter Marchand, two civilian psychiatrists, detailed for the first time the dynamics of psychiatric collapse, pointing out that after thirty-five days of sustained combat no less than 98 percent of combat soldiers manifested adverse psychiatric symptoms.[10] The principles of forward treatment and expectancy, which had first emerged in World War I, became official military doctrine, and psychiatrists were permanently assigned to division medical facilities. In its training doctrines, however, the belief persisted that trained soldiers could be made to withstand the horrors of the battlefield for long periods. The military had not yet realized that war itself was changing radically.

KOREA AND VIETNAM

The outbreak of war in Korea in June 1950 found the military relatively well prepared to deal with psychiatric casualties. For the first two months of the war as American units were repeatedly defeated and driven back to the Pusan perimeter, psychiatric casualties skyrocketed to rates two and three times higher than had been observed during World War II. Once the front had stabilized, however, the military was able to position its psychiatric casualty teams in the country and put into practice the lessons it had learned in both world wars. For the first time American troops had trained psychiatric practitioners close to the battlefront who were able to deal with psychiatric casualties. Although throughout the war the rate of psychiatric casualties was, on average, only slightly less than it had been in World War II, the severity of the reactions were generally fewer, and more psychiatric casualties were returned to the fighting than had been possible in World War II.

World War II had shown that a major element in preventing battle shock was rooted in the strong peer attachments that members of combat groups formed with one another. Unit cohesion was regarded as the primary mechanism for keeping soldiers under stress functioning for acceptable periods of time. It provided a support for the normal propensity of a sane man not to want to be alone during times of stress and supported the strong need to appear courageous or at least not fearful in the eyes of one's comrades. Despite all this, psychiatric casualty rates continued to be high as the nature of war became more destructive and lethal.

As important as unit cohesion was now seen to be, during the Korean War the military established a policy of individual replacement and rotation out of the combat zone rather than replacing and rotating whole units. As a consequence, once a soldier neared the end of his nine-month tour, he began to suffer from "short timer's syndrome," a condition in which fear tended to be exaggerated and his combat performance declined. Often psychiatric symptoms would set in as the soldier was nearing the end of his tour of duty. Moreover, individual rotation and replacement made sustaining group cohesion more difficult. The soldier's attachment to his peers quickly shifted from his platoon to his buddy. Often when a buddy was killed, the survivor felt alone and would himself become a psychiatric casualty. The military had learned the importance of group dynamics and attachments in sustaining sanity under stress but failed to sustain groups in place for long periods of time.

Once the war settled down into a stalemate, there was still the need to maintain large, fully armed forces constantly on the alert. Although clashes were few and far between, the soldier still found himself in a hostile environment deprived of many of the comforts of home. During periods of prolonged noncombat stress, psychiatric casualties began to occur once again at rates not appreciably lower than they had been during combat. All the symptoms of nostalgia first diagnosed among European armies in the sixteenth century and found among Civil War soldiers began to appear again with the result that significant numbers of soldiers became psychiatric casualties. Furthermore, nostalgic casualties often showed up in secondary reactions such as frostbite, alcohol abuse, constant complaints of lower back pain and general malaise. The experience of four centuries of soldiers under noncombat stress was repeating itself. Today, large combat forces still remain on the Korean peninsula although they have not seen combat action in over twenty years. Nonetheless, secondary symptoms of stress remain. In 1985, the combat force of 14,000 men stationed in Korea reported no less than 12,000 cases of venereal disease among its soldiers.

During the ten years of the Vietnam conflict the number of psychiatric cases evacuated out of country was the lowest in any war in which America has participated in this century. While there is no doubt that some of this was due to the presence of psychiatric teams to treat the problem in country, there are other more important reasons for the low rate of evacuations. First, by any standard Vietnam was not much of a combat war. There were few large-scale engagements with the enemy, and even these were of comparatively short duration, almost never lasting more than a few days. Second, the enemy possessed few weapons capable of inflicting heavy casualties. The Vietcong had little artillery and no capacity for air attack, weapons that historically have produced large numbers of psychiatric casualties. Third, the Vietnam War was one of base camps. Typically, small American units would foray forth for a few days in search of the enemy, who usually refused to do battle. After a few days in the bush, American units would return to base camps, where they were safe and surrounded by many of the comforts of home. Fourth, most combat actions were ambushes, which, although terrifying for their participants, almost never lasted more than a minute or two at most. There was, in short, no prolonged combat stress for most American soldiers. Fifth, the American army was so "tail heavy"—that is, had so many support troops in rear areas—that at the peak of American engagement in that war, 565,000 troops could muster only 88,000 combat soldiers to do actual battle with the enemy. For most American soldiers in Vietnam, contact with the enemy was rare indeed. Finally, the short, one-year tour of duty in country, combined with a number of other devices, relieved tension. Among these was the ready availability of prostitutes, bars, alcohol, music, phone calls home, and drugs.

During the periods of greatest combat action, most notably the Tet Offensive of 1968 and the few set-piece battles that it produced (Huy, Saigon, Ban Me Thuet, and others), the rate of psychiatric casualties approached Korean and World War II proportions. Most psychiatric casualties were nostalgia, now termed "disorders of loneliness." As the war drew to a close, the number of medical evacuations for these disorders skyrocketed. To be sure, many soldiers, far more than in any other war, carried away with them a number of psychiatric symptoms that did not come to the attention of military medical authorities in country but which, nonetheless, produced severe symptoms after the soldier had returned to the United States. While the figures are unclear, estimates of soldiers suffering from post-traumatic stress disorder range from 500,000 to 1,500,000. If these figures are correct, Vietnam produced more psychiatric casualties than any other American war.

Even a brief analysis of military psychiatry through the ages makes it plain that war tends to produce very large numbers of soldiers who suffer psychiatric collapse as a consequence of its horror. Moreover, for large numbers of soldiers, just being in a military environment in some foreign land, even if there is no fighting or if there is only a remote threat of combat, the strain is too much for them to take. While their symptoms are not usually as dramatic as those found in soldiers exposed to direct combat, they are no less debilitating to the individual soldier and of no less concern to the commander who is trying to maintain the fighting strength of his unit.

Moreover, it is clear that despite any number of attempts to prevent and deal with psychiatric casualties, the traditional methods so far attempted do not work very well. Even among those soldiers treated successfully, their return to the line is likely to mean that they will once again become psychiatric casualties. There seems no escape for most men.

All this suggests that psychiatric collapse in battle is the reaction of sane and normal men forced to adjust to insane and abnormal circumstances. Soldiers will continue to suffer psychiatric breakdown regardless of what military psychiatrists attempt to do about it. The causes of psychiatric collapse, it is worth repeating, have little to do with the soldier's character or predisposition to weakness. Psychiatric breakdown is an inevitable by-product of war, as inevitable as the dead, the wounded, and the maimed. Far more important in understanding battle shock are the objective conditions of the battlefield that men must face. By any reasonable standard of comparison, until now those conditions have been mild compared to what the soldier must confront in modern war. That is why the traditional ways of dealing with the problem will no longer work.

Modern conventional war has become so lethal and so intense that only the already insane can endure it. As studies of World War II psychiatric casualties revealed, only those soldiers who were already aggressive psychopathic personalities before entering combat could remain mentally unbroken after thirty-five days of exposure to battle. The rest, sane men at the start, simply were driven to psychiatric collapse. The technology of modern war has reached a point where it will generate millions of psychiatric casualties while, at the same time, engendering conditions that make treating these casualties almost impossible within the battle zone. Modern war will render useless the traditional means of dealing with the psychiatrically broken. The next war will confront man with the unsolvable problem of devising a solution to a problem of his own making.

War will require continuous combat, increasing the degree of fatigue on the soldier to heretofore unknown levels. Physical fatigue, especially the lack of sleep, will increase the number of psychiatric casualties enormously. Other factors—high rates of indirect fire, night fighting, lack of food, constant stress, large numbers of casualties, and others—will ensure that the number of psychiatric casualties, along with physical casualties, will reach disastrous proportions. And sheer numbers will overburden the medical structure to the point of collapse.

The ability to treat psychiatric casualties will all but disappear. In the first place there will be no safe areas in which to treat soldiers debilitated by mental collapse. The modern technology of war has made such locations functionally obsolete. To take only one example, the ability of modern armies to locate aggregations of troops by their "infrared signatures" given off by groups of soldiers and their supporting equipment (trucks, generators, radios) makes forward-area facilities of any sort highly vulnerable from weapons ranging from rocket-assisted, laser-guided artillery to attack helicopters. It will be next to impossible to maintain even the geographic stability of medical stations near the front as both sides require that the front be kept in constant motion while they engage in a continuous series of meeting engagements. When everyone is on the offensive, no one, especially medical treatment stations, can remain in place for risk of being destroyed.

Medical facilities deep in the rear will be equally at risk as both sides try to engage in the "deep battle" for the precise purpose of destroying the other side's supporting infrastructure. Each side will count heavily on deep battle to paralyze its adversary. Moreover, in many instances, frontline strong points will be deliberately by-passed by attacking forces who can inflict far more damage on the enemy's ability to continue the battle by disrupting his rear and can do so with far fewer losses than if frontline strong points are engaged. The merging of frontline and rear-area offensive and defensive forces into a giant swirling movement of destruction and death will make it impossible for psychiatric treatment facilities to position themselves to treat significant numbers of casualties. Worse, a psychiatric casualty who is lucky enough to find himself evacuated to the rear might well find himself in a combat situation more intense than that which he left at the front line. Alternatively, he may simply be killed along with the rest of the wounded huddled around a medical service point. Quite simply, there will no longer be any place for a casualty to be safe. Even the wounded are now at great risk.

Even if it were possible to stabilize psychiatric and medical treatment stations in safe areas in the rear, they would be too far to the rear to treat the psychiatrically broken successfully. Treatment must be close to the battle. If it is not, experience has shown that evacuation far to the rear tends to deepen and fixate the patient's symptoms, greatly reducing his chances of recovering quickly enough to be returned to the battle. Thus, evacuating soldiers in itself generates psychiatric casualties. Worse, once soldiers come to understand that medical evacuation is possible—indeed the only remote hope of dealing with psychiatric casualties—more and more soldiers will collapse. Any number of armies, from the Russians in 1905 to the Israelis in 1982, have witnessed the effect of the "evacuation syndrome" in the increasing rate of psychiatric breakdown.

Even if we assumed that some way could be found to stabilize and protect frontline medical treatment stations, the time required to restore the physiological and emotional needs of the soldier will be too long to make the return of the soldier to his unit practical. Many cases of psychiatric collapse respond quite rapidly to simple sleep, rest, and food. At the minimum, even these rudimentary therapies require twenty-four to forty-eight hours to work successfully. No one in his right mind would or could remain stationary on the modern battlefield for this length of time. Anyone who does can fully expect to be annihilated. The need to move the patient at frequent intervals mitigates against rapid recovery.

Much is made in the practice of treating psychiatric casualties of returning the soldier to his unit once he has recovered. The reason is that the soldier may have spent weeks or months with his comrades, and his return strengthens the cohesion of the group. Furthermore, because he is no stranger to his comrades, his return facilitates the soldier's recovery. Experience in World War II and Korea shows clearly that soldiers who were not returned to their units were at greater risk of becoming psychiatric casualties again in a very short time.

In modern war, it is highly likely that it will be impossible to return wounded or mentally fatigued men to their units. In the first place, the unit is likely to have quickly moved on. The mobility of the modern battlefield makes rapid movement the key to survival. A psychiatric casualty out of action for twenty-four hours would have little chance of finding his unit let alone catching up with it. Moreover, there may simply be no point in finding one's old unit. It may have been decimated. During World War II, the Soviets made no attempt to return wounded soldiers to their units for the simple reason that units engaged in battle often ceased to exist during the time it took a casualty to recover and return. Men in these units were replaced at such a rapid rate that a returning soldier was likely to find few of his old comrades alive. Instead, the Soviet army collected casualties from aid stations and formed entirely new units, which they then committed to battle. As expected, the number of soldiers who broke down again was very high. Even in a war as short as the Israeli invasion of Lebanon in 1982 IDF medical personnel found it very difficult to return casualties to their own units. In most instances, recovered casualties couldn't find their units because they were moving so fast or the combat situation made it impossible to reach them.

It must be kept in mind that psychiatric casualties do not occur in a medical vacuum. Rather, they are part of the normal "casualty stream" comprised of thousands of surgical casualties, those who are physically wounded. While neither the Soviets nor the Americans have been able to predict with any accuracy the level of casualties that will result from a conventional war, it can safely be assumed to reach over 100,000 within days of the outbreak of battle. The stream of casualties will reach enormous proportions, easily overwhelming the ability of each side's medical services to deal with it. This will force medical personnel to use triage, practices developed for mass casualty disaster situations.

Triage requires the separating of casualties into categories of seriousness in order to provide treatment first to those who have the best chance of survival. The most seriously wounded and incapacitated will be treated last and often not treated at all. In triage situations physical casualties have priority of treatment and first claim on all medical resources even though, paradoxically, psychiatric casualties are most likely to be able to return to action with minimal treatment. The Soviet army found itself in this situation in which one must cruelly choose what casualties to treat many times during World War II. It always resolved the situation in favor of physical casualties.

Under these conditions, psychiatric casualties will build up around the few stable medical servicing points, but there will be few medical personnel to care for them. As has already been pointed out, the medical structures of each side do not have enough manpower to deal with even the level of surgical casualties of World War II, let alone with psychiatric casualties. In the Soviet army, for example, there are no psychiatrists or psychiatric assistants below army level. While the American army intends to station psychiatrists and a complement of psychiatric assistants in every division, there are today only 213 psychiatrists in the entire army, and most of them are not stationed with combat divisions. In other words, there are fewer psychiatrists than there were with U.S. forces in Europe during World War I.

These circumstances evoke a vision of thousands of psychiatric casualties clustered around the few surviving medical stations with no one to treat them. Groups of exhausted, blind, mute, and dazed men will be left unattended to roam about the battle area. Most of these men will have collapsed because they could not stand the horror at the front, only to be transported back to a living hell in which the screams of the wounded and the sight of the dead and dying may be even more upsetting to an already disturbed mind. If the medical station is attacked, hundreds of psychiatric casualties, too stunned to defend themselves, will be killed. If the medical station is warned of an impending attack, it will have to move rapidly and leave the mentally broken to shift for themselves. The vision of thousands of broken and helpless soldiers wandering aimlessly around the battlefield and in the rear areas is enough to give any soldier nightmares.

CONCLUSION

American military medical professionals admit that the conditions that will prevail on the modern conventional battlefield will render armies virtually unable to deal even moderately well with the large numbers of broken soldiers, which they expect to result from high-intensity combat. Certainly the more traditional methods of dealing with them, which were not all that successful in previous wars, will not work. Modern war makes it likely that there will be no refuge in which to treat psychiatric casualties, few if any therapists to treat them, no time for adequate rest and recuperation, and no real possibility that the soldier will be able to return to his unit. What there will be are thousands of mentally shattered men left to wander about in the battle zone until they too are killed or maimed. Whatever glory there may once have been to war has rapidly disappeared if, indeed, it ever existed at all.

NOTES

1. Albert Deutsche, "Military Psychiatry in the Civil War: 1861–1865," in *One Hundred Years of American Psychiatry* (New York: Columbia University Press, 1944), p. 377.

2. Edward A. Strecker, "Military Psychiatry in World War I: 1917–1918," in *One Hundred Years of American Psychiatry* (New York: Columbia University Press, 1944), p. 386.

3. Lawrence Ingraham and Frederick Manning, "American Military Psychiatry," in Richard A. Gabriel, *Military Psychiatry: A Comparative Perspective* (Westport, Conn: Greenwood Press, 1986), p. 61.

4. Strecker, "Military Psychiatry in World War I," p. 388.

5. Ingraham and Manning, "American Military Psychiatry," pp. 61–63.

6. Ibid., p. 67.

7. Ibid.

8. Ibid., p. 75.

9. Lawrence Ingraham and Frederic Manning, "Psychiatric Battle Casualties: The Missing Column in a War Without Replacements," *Military Review* (August 1980), p. 24.

10. Roy Swank and Walter Marchand, "Combat Neuroses: Development of Combat Exhaustion," *Archives of Neurology and Psychiatry* (1946), p. 244.

7

American Battlefield Psychiatry

The military medical structure for dealing with psychiatric casualties in the U.S. Army is the most sophisticated, best articulated, and most advanced among all armies of the world. However, this judgment must be balanced by the fact that many of the structures for dealing with psychiatric problems that are described in this chapter are, while having been already approved for implementation, still largely in the planning stages. Moreover, the American army remains far short of its projected goals in terms of being able to provide the necessary trained medical manpower that will enable the planned doctrines to work effectively. Whether the U.S. military will be able to follow through on its plans for building a comprehensive medical structure for dealing with psychiatric casualties before it goes to war again remains at this time a very open question.

The medical doctrines for treating psychiatric casualties are strongly rooted in the American army's own combat experience and in the practical experience that other armies of the world, most notably the Israeli army, have undergone since 1973. Probably nowhere else does one encounter the willingness of a modern army to study the experiences of other armies systematically more than in the way the American army has in dealing with psychiatric casualties. In particular, American military physicians have established a close working relationship with the military establishment of Israel, which has provided a laboratory to test American medical doctrine and practice in dealing with psychiatric casualties. Where those doctrines have been improved by Israeli battle experience the American military has been quick to note the advantages of such changes and to begin to adopt those that seem beneficial, given the U.S. Army's size, force mix, structure, and different types of missions.

The high level of close cooperation between the IDF and the American army in dealing with the problem of psychiatric casualties began almost immediately after the 1973 Arab-Israeli War. Until then the IDF had experienced few difficulties in dealing with psychiatric casualties. Most of its wars were short, and the Israelis were always on the offensive; few Israeli soldiers succumbed to battle stress. As in other armies since time immemorial, psychiatric collapse was viewed as idiosyncratic, probably due to innate character features of the soldier's personality and, in any case, not a great problem for the overall fighting ability of IDF forces. The near disaster of the 1973 war changed all that.

For the first time a number of Israeli combat units almost met disaster on the battlefield as a consequence of manpower loss brought on by psychiatric collapse. As the war entered its second week of intense fighting, the Israelis encountered great difficulty in curing psychiatric casualties and returning them to their fighting units. More than 3000 IDF soldiers and officers succumbed to battle shock, threatening the army's ability to continue the fight. After the war, large numbers of these remained incapacitated for months or years, and many others were never able to return to military service. The Israelis had experienced the horror of modern conventional war, and the reaction of their soldiers to the horror threatened to undermine the ability of the IDF to guarantee the security of the State of Israel.

Immediately following the 1973 war the IDF established a separate unit of the medical department to investigate and solve the problem of psychiatric casualties. One new unit was called the IDF Behavioral Research Unit. Some idea of the importance with which the Israelis viewed the problem can be gained from the fact that the new unit came directly under the office of the IDF chief of staff and reported directly to him, bypassing normal command channels. The highest levels of the military establishment were concerned about the problem of psychiatric casualties and expected something to be done to solve it. On the medical treatment side the Israelis were quick to establish field units for dealing with psychiatric casualties. In 1973–1975, the initial model that the Israelis used for treating psychiatric casualties on the battlefield was based on the American experience in World War II and Korea.

Because the Israelis had no experience with the problem of psychiatric casualties, they turned to their American allies for help. Research and information exchanges were quickly established with the American military medical community. The result of these contacts was the establishment in the IDF of U.S. doctrines and structures—most notably the establishment of the division psychiatrist and his staff—for dealing with psychiatric casualties.

The close working relationship between United States and IDF medical personnel charged with dealing with psychiatric casualties has continued for fifteen years with both sides making the most of it. The IDF transplanted a number of U.S. doctrines, practices, and structures directly into its own medical corps and combat units. But as the Israelis were exposed to frequent combat and other small-scale wars, they gradually altered these basic structures to match their own experience with psychiatric battle casualties. In a few areas they invented new doctrines, structures, and techniques, which the American Army found to be useful and which are being adopted by U.S. forces.

It is difficult (and beyond the scope of this work) to attempt to trace the flow of intellectual influence in developing techniques for treating psychiatric casualties between the IDF and the U.S. military. Yet clearly a number of Israeli innovations for dealing with the problem have been adopted by the U.S. military.[1] These include:

1. The wider use of counseling personnel to deal with a range of soldiers' stress and adjustment problems that affect battle performance but are not necessarily caused by exposure to combat itself. Thus the U.S. Army now has psychiatric and psychological counselors and supporting staffs in place down to the division level to deal with such problems as alcoholism, drug use, family separation and fragmentation, adjustment to military life, and others.

2. The increased emphasis on preventing psychiatric collapse by the constant monitoring and development of unit cohesion among military units. While the idea that unit cohesion is the first line of defense against battle stress is an old one, the Israelis were the first to develop testing mechanisms for measuring cohesion and to provide an empirical data base for ensuring the reliability of the instrument itself. In this regard the American military is establishing a number of programs in its military units to strengthen the human bonds that are the first line of defense against psychiatric collapse under fire.

3. The use of mobile psychiatric treatment teams from higher headquarters (division and corps), which can deploy forward with the combat brigades, regiments, and battalions to augment the psychiatric resources normally available to these fighting units. This has given real meaning to the doctrines of immediacy and proximity in treating psychiatric casualties within the battle zone. It is now official U.S. doctrine to have corps medical assets seconded to the fighting divisions and brigades although the organization and staffing of these assets is still in the early stages of development.

4. The establishment of reconditioning units close to the lines where psychiatric casualties can be treated within a military environment—as opposed to the traditional hospital setting—in order to speed their recovery and return to the combat units. The staffing of such reconditioning centers will be a basic task of the Combat Stress Control company located at the corps level of American fighting units. At present, however, only six such teams exist at varying states of readiness, and most of them are located in Reserve units.

While a number of other minor though important innovations and practices of the IDF have been adopted by the American military, one should not draw the conclusion that the United States has adopted Israeli practice in toto. Quite the contrary. However, one of the reasons why the IDF has been so successful in developing techniques for dealing with psychiatric casualties is simply that it has had much more combat experience over the last ten years with its regular line units than has the American army. On the other hand, the ability and willingness of the U.S. military to take cognizance of this experience and to tailor relevant Israeli innovations to its own size, force mix, and missions must be counted among the most important success stories of the American army in the last twenty years. The result has been to make the American army the most prepared of all military forces in the West to prevent and deal with psychiatric casualties in the next war. These developments stand in marked contrast to the Soviet army, which has maintained its doctrines and practices for dealing with psychiatric casualties almost unchanged since World War I.

U.S. MILITARY PSYCHIATRY DOCTRINE

The Soviets, it will be recalled, base their military psychiatry upon a materialist view of the human psyche, in which all behavioral operations of the soldier are traceable to the physiology of the brain. Accordingly, in the Soviet view a soldier undergoing psychiatric collapse is suffering from some damage to or malfunction in his brain or nervous system brought on by physical trauma or shock. In Soviet military practice the first step in diagnosing battle shock is to determine which part of the soldier's brain or nervous system has been physiologically damaged. Then treatments are targeted at remedying the damage. Soviet military psychiatrists do allow for cases of battle shock for which there is no apparent physical cause but are likely to attribute such cases to "defective character" or outright cowardice.

In American military psychiatry the psychology of the soldier is seen to be far more complex and not nearly as strongly rooted in physiology, although American physicians would readily admit that there are cases in which physical injury does produce psychiatric disturbances. By and large American military medicine abandoned the biological view of battle shock after World War I when its studies, along with those of the French and British, showed that large numbers of shocked soldiers had suffered no discernible physiological injuries. Ever since then American doctrine has tried to establish a middle ground between the physiological elements of stress and those that are more psychological. By the end of World War II the U.S. military had abandoned the view that soldiers were disposed by their character and upbringing to psychiatric breakdown, a view that contributed heavily to the large number of psychiatric casualties that the U.S. Army suffered in World War II.

American military psychiatrists maintain that almost no one is immune to psychiatric collapse in battle if one is exposed to enough stress over time. Except for a small number of soldiers, about 2 percent in World War II, psychiatric collapse is inevitable if the stressors of battle are strong and persistent enough. One military expert on the subject has suggested that psychiatric collapse in battle is in fact "the reaction of a sane man to insane circumstances."[2] This view of psychiatric collapse is based on findings that suggest that under prolonged conditions of stress the normal survival mechanisms of the body—heart rate, respiration, sweating, adrenal secretions, and so on—can become fixed at very high rates, which are quite beyond the control of the soldier. These intense and prolonged physiological reactions interact with the chemical operations of the brain affecting the psychology of the soldier. Even if he doesn't suffer a purely psychological collapse, sooner or later—usually with thirty days of exposure to sustained combat—the soldier's physiology itself will collapse, precipitating psychiatric symptoms. Quite simply, there is no such thing as "getting used" to combat; sooner or later everyone collapses unless preventive measures or treatment is administered.

Given that American military psychiatrists subscribe to a wider definition of the nature and causes of battle shock, they have been much more disposed to examine the phenomenon in greater detail and to draw conclusions based in empirical data than have the Soviets, who still base almost all of their approach to military psychiatry in Marxist theory and nomological biological psychiatry. One result is that American military psychiatrists have been much more sensitive as to labeling psychiatric casualties. Its own experience has demonstrated quite convincingly that using the wrong labels for psychiatric casualties has a very deleterious effect on the chances for recovery. It also affects the length of time necessary to effect a recovery. This "iatrogenic effect" has, in past wars, actually served to deepen the casualty's symptoms, making them harder to reverse, and created expectations within the mind of the casualty that he act like a "patient," a condition from which he "gains" considerably. In the later days of World War I, this fact was important enough to lead American battlefield psychiatrists to be reluctant to diagnose a patient's condition in any specific terms. Instead, the designation "NYD/N" was widely used, meaning for "Not Yet Diagnosed/Neuropsychiatric". By conforming to the expected role as a patient, the soldier escapes returning to the fighting. His expected role may deepen considerably, thus making it very difficult to reverse and prolonging treatment to the point where he fails to return at all.

The American army began World War II by labeling psychiatric casualties as suffering from "psychoneurosis," a term that had strong connotations of defective character and mental illness in the mind of the soldier. Since it was a term that civilian physicians used to describe mentally ill patients, it created the impression that it was due to defective character traits such as cowardice. Certainly the term implied that the condition of psychiatric collapse was due to some defect in the soldier's personality rather than to the objective factors produced by the stressors of the battle-field. Soldiers diagnosed as suffering from psychoneurosis quickly began to "live their roles" and suffered additional problems of low self-esteem that often made recovery difficult and in some cases impossible.

By 1943 military psychiatrists became cognizant of the iatrogenic effect of the psychoneurosis label and introduced a new term to describe the psychiatric casualty—combat exhaustion. The implications of this label were that the soldier had simply seen too much combat and, although he had acquitted himself well, he was simply exhausted. The term "exhaustion" strongly implied its physical analogy—physical exhaustion—which suggested that everyone had limits no matter how brave. Indeed, this condition began to appear among seasoned veterans who, prior to collapse, had fought bravely and well. The idea that every man has his breaking point went a long way toward removing negative connotations of the soldier's character and made it somewhat easier for the psychiatric casualty to retain his self-image. Moreover, since psychiatric collapse was defined as being due in large extent to external as opposed to internal factors, it made it easier for the broken soldier to recover once the external stressors had been removed.

By Korea and the Vietnam War American military psychiatrists had adopted the terms "battle fatigue" and "combat exhaustion" together to describe the range of psychiatric symptoms that emerged among combat soldiers. The positive effect of this label was that it implied that the soldier was even less responsible for his condition than before. This new definition was accompanied by the establishment of programs within the military that communicated to the soldier that he, like all normal men, was subject to mental collapse if the objective conditions of the battlefield were strong and persistent enough. Military psychiatrists began to take increased cognizance of the physical elements that contributed to psychiatric collapse, such as hunger, thirst, lack of sleep, isolation from comrades, and so on. By 1982, the formula used to express the dynamics of psychiatric collapse was:

$$\text{BATTLE FATIGUE} = f\,(\text{Intensity} \times \text{Duration of Stress}) = \text{Individual's Preparation}$$

This perspective made it possible to remove some of the more onerous implications and consequences of psychiatric collapse while at the same time clearly recognizing that there were things the military could do and the soldier could learn to prevent or slow the onset of psychiatric symptoms. This made it imperative that the military identify those stressors that contributed to collapse and that military organizations take concrete steps to minimize the impact of these stressors upon the soldier. Programs designed to train the soldier properly, to increase cohesion, to ensure that the soldier received as much sleep as possible, to require two-man foxholes as a way of warding off a sense of isolation, to make every effort to return a stress casualty to his unit, and a number of other programs now established in the American military are designed specifically to prevent or treat the onset of psychiatric collapse and thus retain the fighting ability of combat units. In this sense, U.S. military psychiatry is among the most successful examples in the West of integrating theory and practice within a combat army.

The progress achieved in conceptualizing the nature of psychiatric collapse made it possible for the U.S. military to devise more precise indicators of battle stress in order to determine when it would most likely occur. This development was very important, since in past wars men suffering from normal combat stress reactions were often misdiagnosed and needlessly evacuated to the rear when they could more easily have been treated nearer the front and returned more quickly to the fighting effort. If one expects to prevent and treat psychiatric casualties successfully, an absolute requirement is a clear clinical picture of the symptoms of the condition. A failure to delineate clearly in both theory and practice "normal" from "abnormal" reactions will result in the needless evacuation of many casualties, which can quickly result in heavy manpower losses to combat units.

Table 6 lists those symptoms that the American army defines as "mild" combat stress reactions. While they go beyond the "normal" stress reactions found among civilian populations under stress, these "mild" reactions are recognized as symptoms quite normally associated with the stress produced by combat. In general, soldiers suffering these reactions are expected to continue to perform with rudimentary treatment within their units on the line or only slightly behind the line.Treatment for mild cases of battle fatigue is accomplished in the soldier's own unit or in its nonmedical combat service support facilities. Medical personnel will provide only "outpatient" or "sick call" support. Mild cases of battle fatigue are comparatively easy to reverse, and U.S. Army estimates suggest that 60 to 85 percent of these casualties can be restored to full combat effectiveness within one to four days provided they are kept close to their units and not mistakenly evacuated in the normal medical chain. The basic rule for dealing with soldiers manifesting these symptoms is to determine to what extent the symptoms are having an effect on the ability of the soldier to perform his military function. For the most part soldiers are expected to perform in spite of the presence of these symptoms. Medical personnel dealing with mild combat reactions understand that the mere presence of the symptoms is insufficient to remove a soldier from the fighting. Rather, the key element is the effect the symptoms are having upon the soldier's overt behavior.

A unit engaged in heavy combat can expect, by official estimates, to generate 120 battle-fatigue casualties per division per day. Since this estimate is based upon what the U.S. military admits are incomplete computer

Table 6.
Mild Battle Fatigue Symptoms

```
Thousand-yard stare

Tension, startle, response, tremor

Physical complaints

    Musculoskeletal
    Cardiovascular
    Gastrointestinal
    Genitourinary

Extreme irritability

Inertia, indecision, indifference, inattention

Insomnia, terror dreams
```

Source: "Mental Health Resources In The Combat Zone,"
Lecture presented by faculty of US Army Academy
Of Health Sciences, San Antonio, Texas, August,
29, 1985.

models rooted in assumptions about World War II levels of combat intensity, its validity is doubtful. In all probability, the proportion of psychiatric casualties will be much higher, especially if the number of dead and wounded in a particular unit increases. Of the 120 estimated psychiatric casualties, 60 percent will manifest severe levels of battle fatigue and will have to stay in a medical treatment facility for periods of one to four days. Two thirds of these cases are predicted to be able to return to their units. However, 15 to 40 percent of moderate to severe battle-fatigue casualties will fail to improve in four days and will require another one to three weeks of "reconditioning" before being able to return to duty. This "reconditioning" must take place in a stable environment farther to the rear. Of casualties sent to reconditioning centers, 5 to 10 percent will fail to recover, will have to be evacuated, and will be permanently lost to the fighting effort although every effort will be made to salvage some personnel at this stage for use in service and support duties. While these levels of psychiatric debilitation are severe enough, it is worth repeating that in all probability the estimates will prove to be too low by as much as 100 to 200 percent.[3] Table 7 lists the symptoms of moderate to severe battle fatigue used by military diagnosticians.

In truth, psychiatric collapse, except at the extremes, is difficult to diagnose, especially when a unit is heavily engaged in combat. There are a number of conditions that field diagnosticians may easily mistake for psychiatric collapse. Since a major problem that all armies face in dealing with psychiatric casualties is needless evacuation of soldiers resulting from misdiagnosis, it is very important for field diagnosticians to be aware of a number of conditions that often appear to be psychiatric symptoms when in fact they are not. Table 8 provides a list of what the military calls "battle fatigue equivalents" which often appear to be psychiatric symptoms.

American military psychiatrists have developed a number of basic principles that they use to guide the employment of medical resources to treat psychiatric casualties. The first set of principles is known by the acronym PIE, which stands for Proximity, Immediacy, and Expectancy. Originally developed by the Russians in their treatment of psychiatric casualties in the Russo-Japanese War of 1905 and later confirmed by the experience of Allied armies in World War I and II, they form the basic operational principles for dealing with psychiatric casualties in all modern armies. They have already been explained in detail in Chapter 6.

Table 7.
Moderate/Severe Battle Fatigue Symptoms

Depression (motor retardation, crying, survivor
    guilt)

Anxiety reactions (gross tremor, extreme startle)

Memory loss (amnesias, complete or partial fugue,
    flight reactions)

Conversion reactions

    Sensory loss of function--eyes, ears, touch

    Motor loss--paralysis, abnormal tics

    Speech loss--stuttering, mute, unclear speech

    Mimic injuries--laser, NBC

    Disorganization--outbursts, panic, freeze, stupor,
        hallucinations

Source: "Mental Health Resources In The Combat Zone"

Table 8.
Symptoms Mistaken for Battle Fatigue

Environmental illnesses (heat stroke, hypothermia)

Blunt trauma injury (concussion, sensory motor symptoms)

Substance abuse (alcohol, narcotics, amphetamines,
                hallucigenic drugs)

Anticholinergic delerium (atropine poisoning)

Anticholinesterases (low dose nerve gas)

Endemic psychiatric and personality disorders

Source: "Mental Health Resources In The Combat Zone"

A second set of treatment principles in the U.S. Army goes by the acronym IMPRESS and represent a refinement of the PIE principles. The first IMPRESS principle is immediate treatment. Past experience has shown that the more rapidly a stressed soldier receives treatment, the less likely are the symptoms to deepen and the greater his chances of recovery. All modern armies attempt to deliver treatment as quickly as possible, although in actual combat this is very difficult. The second principle requires that medical treatment personnel "maintain a military atmosphere" in treating psychiatric casualties. The soldier must not be treated as a "patient," a condition that can provoke in the soldier's mind a dependent role and lead to a deepening of symptoms. Even when the soldier has become a psychiatric casualty, he is not called "patient" but "soldier." Casualties are not "admitted" to a hospital but are "held for treatment" as "outpatients" or "reassigned" for "temporary duty" to a treatment facility. Their medical personnel are not called doctors, nurses, or therapists, but by their military titles as "commanders," "sergeants," or "supervisors." This operational principle reflects the Israeli experience with battle-stress casualties. They found that a soldier who is retained for treatment in a "military" environment" tends to retain his role as soldier rather than assuming a dependent role as patient. This, in turn, tends to facilitate recovery. The U.S. military makes every effort to ensure that its treatment of psychiatric casualties takes place within a "normal military environment."

Proximity of treatment is another principle underlying American battle psychiatry and requires that the diagnosis and treatment of psychiatric casualties take place as close to the battle line as possible. Ideally, it can be done within the soldier's unit, although in practice this is often difficult. A soldier's loyalty to his comrades is the strongest factor in his recovery, but such loyalty rapidly fades with time and distance from the unit. Loyalty is replaced by a deep-seated guilt that he has let his comrades down and that they will think poorly of him. Moreover, experience in past wars has shown that when a soldier is evacuated from his unit, a tendency toward secondary gain becomes evident and will retard his recovery. Thus, every effort is made to maintain a soldier's ties to his unit. In the IDF when a recovered soldier is about to be sent back to his unit, it is common practice to have one or two of his buddies come to the treatment facility and accompany him.

IMPRESS requires that a soldier suffering from battle shock be given adequate rest and replenishment as part of his treatment. In most cases, a day's sleep, good food, water, and a new uniform have very positive effects in aiding the recovery of mild to moderate cases of battle fatigue. Accordingly, as we shall see, American medical units targeted at treating psychiatric casualties have the capability of feeding large numbers of psychiatric patients. Once again, however, this treatment is deliberately kept simple and austere and takes place in a non-patient-care setting within the tactical military environment, for it is aimed at restoring the soldier's physical condition and confidence.

Expectancy is truly a key principle in the successful treatment of psychiatric casualties. After all, the soldier succumbed to stress in the first place because he could not deal with the horrors of combat. It is absolutely imperative, in the American view, that soldiers not get the idea that their collapse will allow them to be removed from the fight. Indeed, as happened in the Russian army in 1905, if the soldier begins to perceive that battle fatigue will succeed in removing him from the fight, the number of such cases will rise exponentially. Thus, a soldier must understand that after he recovers, he will be expected to return to combat duty and that one of the major ways in which he can regain his self-respect and confidence is precisely by returning to his unit where his comrades have continued the fight in his absence.

The last two IMPRESS principles require that on-the-spot treatment be kept "short and simple" and that it be supervised by medical personnel. Often such simple therapeutic techniques as counseling, perspective, ventilation, and minimal use of tranquilizers and sedatives can work wonders, especially if the soldier is suffering, as most are, from mild to moderate symptoms. The requirement that trained medical personnel supervise the treatment of psychiatric casualties is designed to prevent misdiagnosis, which leads to the needless evacuation of a soldier and the loss of a combat asset to the fighting unit. Accordingly, one of the major tasks of psychiatrically trained medical personnel is to act as "evacuation interruptors" to prevent needless evacuation of soldiers. In the 1983 Israeli–PLO war in Lebanon, the IDF learned to its chagrin that two thirds of its psychiatric casualties were needlessly evacuated. The result was the institution of a new rule for air evacuation. Unless a soldier manifested a physical wound, he was not to be evacuated until first examined by psychiatric personnel within the combat unit. In the U. S. military, medical personnel attempt to screen casualties early in the treatment process and to make differential diagnoses as soon and as far forward as possible in order to avoid needless evacuation.

Overlying both the PIE and IMPRESS principles is the larger concern with preventing psychiatric casualties. While all men have their breaking point, the American army attempts to prevent psychiatric casualties by a number of programs to enhance unit cohesion, foster realistic training, and provide for the soldiers' physical and social needs and those of their families. Experience has shown that the first line of defense against psychiatric collapse is the strong bond of cohesion among men in combat units. In World War II, for example, it was demonstrated that elite units had lower levels of psychiatric casualties than regular units. The Israelis have proven beyond doubt that cohesion increases when men have confidence in themselves and their leaders, especially officers. While cohesion is critically important, it seems true that in a full-scale conventional war it will be difficult to maintain once the shooting starts. Units can be expected to sustain heavy casualty rates, resulting in rapid turnover in personnel as a constant replacement stream is needed to sustain fighting strength. Under these conditions, soldiers will rapidly become strangers to one another, especially as their officers and NCOs are replaced. Such severe conditions will inevitably erode the cohesion of units, and the army will have to rely upon its organized medical structure for dealing with psychiatric casualties to maintain the fighting strength of combat units.

PSYCHIATRIC CASUALTY SERVICING STRUCTURE

Perhaps the most important variable in the equation of successfully treating psychiatric casualties is the degree to which an army is prepared to establish and staff institutional structures that are directly charged with dealing with the problem. In this regard, the American army is planning to set in place the most sophisticated organizational structure in the world for dealing with psychiatric casualties. Moreover, the structure is well thought out and seems, above all, to be a practical solution to preventing manpower loss through psychiatric collapse. Only the Israeli army rivals the American army in structure and personnel staffing, but its task is made somewhat easier by the fact that it is a smaller military force with fewer missions.

While all combat medics at the company and battalion level receive some training in recognizing, screening, and treating psychiatric casualties, the reality is that these personnel can deal only with mild to moderate stress cases. To be sure a company or battalion medic can be quite effective in preventing the needless evacuation of stress casualties, but treatment of those functionally debilitated by stress is more commonly achieved at brigade level. Every separate brigade in the American army will have a mental health section within its medical treatment company that is organic to the brigade. The mental health section has a behavioral science NCO and two behavioral science specialists. No officers are assigned to the mental health section. The basic missions of these personnel are to perform triage on psychiatric casualties with a primary emphasis on removing from the psychiatric casualty stream those soldiers who can be held and treated at brigade; they also decide which cases are severe enough to be sent back to rear areas for more complete treatment. In short, they act as "evacuation interruptors." Brigade mental health personnel are charged with providing counseling and basic restoration treatment to those moderate psychiatric cases that can be held at the brigade level. The brigade mental health section has the capability to hold and treat casualties as long as forty-eight hours. If the soldier does not respond in that time, he is shipped farther to the rear.

However, the U.S. military plans that in case of heavy combat, brigade mental health sections would be augmented with additional personnel in order to increase the capability to deal with psychiatric casualties. The brigade's medical treatment company will be augmented by sections of the division-level medical battalion's forward support medical company. This unit will send a holding squad forward into the brigade. Each squad has two patient-care specialist NCOs and two combat field medical specialists. When augmented, a brigade mental health section will be able to provide tents, cots, and meals for up to forty battle-fatigue cases and minimally wounded. In addition, the corps-level Combat Stress Control company can also augment brigade resources with additional resources.

The psychiatric care resources of an American division are adequate to meet most contingencies. Each division has within it a Division Mental Health Section, which may be located within the treatment platoon of the main medical company (in armor, mechanized infantry, or motorized divisions) or, as often happens, in the headquarters section of the medical battalion's headquarters and support company (for light infantry, airborne, and air assault divisions). The Division Mental Health section has three officers: a psychiatrist, a social work officer, and a clinical psychologist. In addition, there are six or seven behavioral science specialists at the NCO rank. Under some circumstances, personnel from this section can be sent forward to augment the treatment capabilities of the brigade.

The officers of the Division Mental Health section maintain and operate a central neuropsychiatric screening facility in the division rear within the medical support company. Once again, however, they may deploy forward into the brigade if circumstances warrant. Usually, if a behavioral science specialist is sent forward to brigade from division, he will act as the Combat Stress Control coordinator in the brigade, coordinating all mental health facilities with division. The primary missions of the Division Mental Health section are to provide (1) preventive consultation with the commander to ensure conditions that contribute to prevention of psychiatric collapse, and (2) expert levels of diagnosis and triage to psychiatric casualties, and training and evaluation of the medical service personnel in the division. In general, the division mental health officers are not charged with direct patient care except when casualty flow loads are light. These offices are basically "evacuation interruptors" and screeners. Actual sustained treatment of psychiatric casualties under normal circumstances is provided by the Combat Stress Control company located at the corps level, which sends sections of its direct support platoon into the division to increase its capabilities to deal with heavy psychiatric casualty loads.

Among the most innovative and effective institutional responses to the problem of dealing with psychiatric casualties is the establishment at corps level of the Combat Stress Control (CSC) company. It is the main source of additional supply of mental health resources to the division and the brigade. The mission of the CSC is to provide a coordinate program of mental health support to corps units and to send teams forward into the division, brigade, and regiments to supplement mental health personnel organic to these smaller units.

The Combat Stress Control company has five separate missions. The first is consultation. It provides advice and assistance to commanders and staff of supported units (1) to monitor, control, and reduce the stressors that result from a unit's deployment and combat roles; (2) to conduct programs that prevent soldiers from becoming battle-fatigue casualties and other types of psychiatric patients; and (3) to screen soldiers who are mentally unsuitable for military duty. In short, its mission is to take all appropriate steps to prevent the soldier from becoming a psychiatric casualty.

The second mission of the CSC is reconstitution of combat units that have been withdrawn into reserve or to receive replacements. The goal is to ensure that the soldiers in these battered units receive sufficient rest, food, and other replenishment and that the strong bonds of cohesion among battle-weary troops are rebuilt and new members of the unit sufficiently integrated into the combat team. This of necessity involves the treatment of some battle-fatigued soldiers, so that they can be returned to combat duty. This role is a main innovation in the American army with the CSC's other missions having some historical precedent going back to World War II.

Another mission of the CSC is restoration of battle-fatigued soldiers by treatment of up to four days at or near forward-area medical facilities.

Generally, this restoration involves rest, physical replenishment, and other activities such as counseling designed to restore the soldier's confidence in himself. The CSC can treat an estimated maximum of 120 soldiers a day in its restoration mission.

The CSC also runs the corps reconditioning program designed to restore prolonged and severe psychiatric casualties to the fighting effort. Such reconditioning is expected to require treatment of battle-fatigued soldiers for up to thirty days in the corps rear in a nonhospital setting and to involve between 15 and 40 percent of the psychiatric casualties who require intensive treatment as a precondition to returning to duty.

The final mission of the CSC is stabilization of psychiatric casualties. The stabilization function deals with those neuropsychiatric casualties who are suffering from severe mental disturbances. These individuals are sent to the Combat Support Hospital, where they are treated and their condition stabilized. They remain for three to six days while personnel in the hospital evaluate each casualty for his potential to return to duty. Those deemed to be suitable for recovery are then transferred to the CSC's reconditioning program. The most severe cases, whose prognosis for short-term recovery is poor, are evacuated to the general hospital deep in the rear of the zone of communications for extended treatment.

This brief outline of the missions of the Combat Stress Control company should make clear that the basic thrust of its function is constantly to screen the stream of psychiatric casualties, holding and treating the less severe at each stage with a view toward returning as many of them to the battle as possible. The goal is to salvage as much manpower as possible at each stage of the process in order to sustain the levels necessary to keep the combat units functioning. In past wars far too many soldiers were needlessly lost to the fighting effort as a result of poor or nonexistent screening, misdiagnosis, or needless evacuation deep in the rear. It remains to be seen how successfully the CSC will actually operate in a large-scale conventional war.

The centerpiece of the entire system is the Combat Stress Control company in the corp's medical group or brigade. The CSC's main source of support for its mission is the medical holding company. The medical holding company's primary mission is to support the treatment of casualties of the combat support hospital; its secondary mission is to support the CSC. The holding company provides 1200 cots, broken down into five 240-cot holding platoons, each subdivided into two 120-cot sections each of three 40-cot squads. There are additional tents and cots for quartering casualties not requiring hospital beds. The medical holding company provides the facilities for the CSC to recondition slow-improving battle-fatigue casualties in the one- to three-week reconditioning program. Official estimates suggest that between 240 to 480 cots will have to be made available to the CSC to support the psychiatric casualties from two divisions.

The Combat Stress Control company is expected to provide psychiatric services to two divisions. It is comprised of an eleven-man headquarters section and two forty-one-man combat stress platoons. It is also anticipated that a twelve-man section from the CSC will support each maneuver brigade by deploying forward with it. In practice, however, no more than two officers and two NCOs from this section will probably be deployed forward. Each CSC is designed to provide the personnel and facilities for a comprehensive stress-control and treatment program for its supported elements and operates the restoration and reconditioning programs. It can send specialized teams forward into the brigades to assist in mass casualty triage and emergency care of psychiatric casualties at brigade level. Each CSC platoon is organized into a small platoon headquarters, a combat reconditioning section, a general support section, and a direct support section, each comprised of twelve men. Each section is fully mobile for staff, equipment, and subsistence and has its own organic transport. Each platoon is configured to provide a therapeutic environment for treating up to 120 casualties, including sheltering and feeding. Each platoon is fully armed with small-arms weapons and is provided with common user radios to access command and support nets. They also have the capability to provide emergency stabilization care to acute psychiatric casualty cases.

Each section in the CSC platoon is comprised of twelve men, six officers and six NCOs, and is organized on a mission modular basis. The combat reconditioning (CR) section has the primary mission of staffing the one- to three-week combat reconditioning program. Additional manpower is drawn from the Medical Holding Platoon. Within the section the psychiatric nurse and NCO specialist provide general stress reduction and restorative care to battle fatigued soldiers plus specialized care and stabilization to the more serious psychiatric casualties in the unit. The occupation therapist and NCO specialist in the section provide treatment of minor injuries and general stress restorative care. They also evaluate the casualty's functional capacity and prescribe and supervise physical reconditioning and military work programs. Generally, in the CR section the officers are majors while the NCOs are staff sergeants. The CR section is equipped with a medical equipment set containing specialized neuropsychiatric medications and diagnostic and physiological monitoring equipment to be used in treating battle-fatigue casualties. The unit has its own truck and trailor, which it uses to carry food and water or to carry working parties. Part of the reconditioning strategy is to have all such functions carried out in a military environment by recovering battle-fatigue casualties.

Each of the CSC platoon's three sections has within it an Operations/ Neuropsychiatric (ONP) squad, which provides command and control functions for the section and coordinates section actions with the platoon and with supported units. Its task is fundamentally to facilitate the sections operations in treating and returning psychiatric casualties to duty. Each such squad has a psychiatrist in charge and a number of NCOs, usually behavioral science specialists.

The Direct Support (DS) section of the Combat Stress Control platoon is routinely attached to the division medical battalion and functions in the division support area under the direction of the division psychiatrist of the mental health section. The DS section staffs the battle-fatigue restoration center. Its squads may also deploy forward into medical or combat maneuver units in order to deal rapidly with psychiatric casualties. Official estimates suggest that the restoration center will have to deal with 120 to 170 soldiers a day at peak combat. Ideally, 90 percent of all psychiatric casualties that reach the restoration center can be returned to duty within four days.

Also at corps level is the mental health section of the area support medical battalion. Smaller than the division mental health section, it is comprised of two officers—a psychiatrist and social work officer—one behavioral science NCO, and six treatment specialists of enlisted rank. The section is configured to send mobile teams to the division treatment companies to augment their functions. For the most part the task of this unit is to assume responsibility for prevention programs and provide technical diagnostic and treatment help to treatment companies.

The Combat Support Hospital (CSH) at corps level also provides additional treatment of psychiatric casualties. The hospital itself has 252 beds and is dedicated to the restorative care of soldiers who have a high potential for rapid return to combat duty. Any soldier manifesting psychiatric symptoms that require hospital management is sent to the CSH where he remains for a three- to six-day period to permit stabilization. At this point casualties are separated into those who have the potential for rapid return to duty and others who will be evacuated farther to the rear. The psychiatric inpatient module of the CSC has one psychiatrist, two psychiatric nurses, and two psychiatric specialists. Thought is being given to providing it with a small neuropsychiatric ward capability. An occupational therapy officer and a NCO specialist also provide for reconditioning of casualties requiring minimal care.

The primary mission of the psychiatric practitioners of the Combat Support Hospital stabilization of psychiatric casualties with a view toward returning as many as possible to the fight. They provide for inpatient emergency treatment and detoxification of psychiatric casualties who require hospitalization. Official policy is that any psychiatric casualty whose symptoms require hospital management be presumed to have "RTD [returnable to duty] potential" unless accompanying physical wounds dictate otherwise. All "purely psychiatric" cases accordingly are sent to the CSH where a three- to six-day period of stabilization permits further separation of those who are able to return from those who will be shipped to the rear for further treatment. Those evacuated are shipped to the General Hospital in the corps rear. Those with RTD potential are transferred to the CSC company's reconditioning program.

It is of some interest to detail the caseloads that the U.S. Army projects for its psychiatric facilities to handle during periods of peak combat in a conventional war scenario. It is expected that 120 soldiers per day per division will become battle-stress casualties, a figure that does not include the number of soldiers who will suffer minor wounds, concussions, non-battle injuries, and diseases that will simultaneously manifest significant battle-stress symptoms requiring treatment. Between sixty and eighty soldiers will require holding in medical facilities. Ten will require brief hospitalization while twenty a day will enter the one- to three-week reconditioning program. Of these twenty, five will be eventually evacuated. Total loads are expected to reach 120 to 170 soldiers a day per division admitted to the reconditioning program while another 120 per division per day will be held for treatment in a central secure location. Official expectations are that between 90 and 95 percent of battle fatigue cases will eventually be restored to duty. Ratios of psychiatric to wounded in action casualties are expected to approach between 33 and 50 percent of total battle related casualties.[4]

It is worth raising the point once again that these estimates can only be regarded as "best case" estimates in light of the fact that the computer models upon which they are based are essentially updated models of World War II combat. There are, in fact, no hard estimates of the ability of either the Soviet or American army to predict with any accuracy the level of psychiatric casualties that will be generated by a high-intensity conventional war especially if chemical and biological weapons are used. What does seem true, however, is that high-intensity conventional war is likely to generate very high ratios of psychiatric to physical casualties. Whether extant medical facilities will be able to handle the load remains, at best, very problematical.

Two additional mental health facilities are available for dealing with psychiatric cases. The Evacuation Hospital located behind corps has 248 beds for use in treating all types of casualties. The Evacuation Hospital incorporates no mental health personnel on its staff. Psychiatric casualties who are shipped there are placed within the normal medical/surgical casualty stream and are treated by nonpsychiatric personnel. Patients moved from the Evacuation Hospital are sent to the 504-bed General Hospital, whose primary task is to stabilize patients of all kinds for further shipment to facilities in the United States. The General Hospital has the same neuropsychiatric staff found in the Combat Support Hospital. The primary mission of this staff is to stabilize psychiatric casualties for shipment to the United States. It also provides area support for stress casualties who may have returned to duty; a second-echelon reconditioning facility is also planned as a secondary mission.

DRUGS

The first large-scale use of psychoactive drugs for treating psychiatric casualties in the American army came in World War II. It must be kept in mind, however, that the availability and reliability of these drugs was far below what is now evident in most modern armies for the simple reason that psychopharmacology itself was in its very formative stages. Not until the mid-1950s would the "revolution in psychopharmacology," first begun in France, begin to take root in the armed forces of the West. Accordingly, those psychoactive compounds used by American forces in World War II were rudimentary in their development and untested in large-scale combat use.

The American army in World War II used both barbiturates and chloral hydrate to treat psychiatric casualties induced by battle shock. Both compounds were in primitive states of development and often produced severe unwanted side effects. Chloral hydrate, a powerful compound made famous as "Mickey Finn" knockout drops, produced a state of heavy sedation that, at times, resulted in the death of the patient. More serious was the misuse of barbiturates in the early days of the war. For example, during the attack on Pearl Harbor significant numbers of soldiers were brought to medical aid stations in states of shock. Most of these casualties were suffering from physical shock brought on by wounds or other physical damage such as concussion. Military physicians frequently misdiagnosed their condition as pure psychiatric shock and prescribed the use of barbiturates. Unfortunately, when barbiturates are administered to casualties in physical shock, they often produce a reaction in which the larynx muscles go into convulsion. This happened so often at Pearl Harbor that almost as many casualties succumbed to drug-induced strangulation as were killed by Japanese hostile fire.[5]

The Korean War saw the use of generally the same drugs for treating psychiatric casualties, though the range of barbiturates increased and the purity of the compounds improved, so that many of the most severe side effects were reduced. Nonetheless, not until the Vietnam War would the American army be able to take advantage of the broader spectrum of available psychoactive drugs made available in the twenty years of research and development since the revolution in psychopharmacology began in the mid-1950s.

During the Vietnam War, for the first time in American military history, the U.S. Army had an adequate and adequately staffed psychiatric-casualty treatment structure in place. Some medical officers would argue that the nature, type, and intensity of Vietnam War psychiatric casualties made it appear that the structure worked better than in past wars when in reality it did not. Its military psychiatrists brought to bear the full range of psychoactive drugs on patient care. A list of the major drugs that the American military used to treat psychiatric casualties during the Vietnam War appears in Table 9. In the field combat medics routinely carried such drugs as morphine, and armored fighting units carried kits containing dexidrine and benzadrine, both stimulants, for troop use. Administration of these drugs was at the discretion of the vehicle commander. For the first time as well special drug packets were assembled by psychiatrists for use by soldiers engaged in long-range missions requiring endurance. Long Range Reconnaissance Patrols, called LERPS, were issued drug packets containing stimulants for their use in the field when deployed behind enemy lines. Such stimulants as Ritalin were commonly used, and the LERPS even received special antihistamine compounds to control coughing.

Today, a number of the psychoactive drugs used in Vietnam have been replaced by more modern compounds. Their advantage is that they target certain psychiatric conditions more specifically, as well as reducing unwanted side effects. For example, most of the major tranquilizers used during the Vietnam War were phenothyazine compounds, which tended to produced oversedation. Some of them also produced pseudo-Parkinson syndrome. Since Vietnam these drugs have been replaced by such compounds as Haldol, Teractan, and Navane, compounds that are not based on phenothyazine.

Many of the minor tranquilizers have also been replaced. Many of them had a tendency toward oversedation when used specifically to combat anxiety, and some allowed the patient to build increasing tolerance. Since Vietnam many have been replaced by benzodazepines, such as Vistoril and Hydroxyzine, which allow better treatment of anxiety while avoiding the twin problems of oversedation and tolerance buildup. Many of the antidepressants used have been replaced by a breed of drugs called tricyclics, such as Zanax, which have more exact tranquilizing and antidepressant qualities. While most of the stimulants have remained essentially as they were during the Vietnam War, the category of sedative and hypnotic drugs have been replaced by benzodazepines such as Restoril and Dalmane.

CONCLUSION

The American military's plans for dealing with psychiatric casualties are perhaps the most advanced in the world. Its doctrines regarding the causes of psychiatric collapse are more humane and, it would seem, more empirically based than those used by the Soviet army. In addition, the American military has given clear institutional expression to its doctrine by establishing a psychiatric-casualty servicing structure that is certainly the most advanced—and complex—in the world. Soviet psychiatric doctrine and practice have virtually ignored the drastic changes that have occurred in the weaponry, nature, and tempo of modern conventional war. The Soviet army intends to fight the next war armed with a military psychiatric doc-

Table 9.
Psychoactive Drugs Used by American Military Psychiatrists in Vietnam

---

Major Tranquilizers:

    Thorazine
    Mellaril
    Stelazine   _____Phenothyazines
    Prolixin
    Compazine

Minor Tranquilizers:

    Equanil/Miltown
    Librium
    Valium
    Vistaril (Atarax)

Anti-Depressants:

    Tofranil
    Desipremine
    Aventyl

Stimulants:

    Amitrityline
    Dexadrine
    Dexamile
    Ritalin

Sedative/Hypnotic:

    Phenobar
    Seconal
    Amytal   _____   Barbiturates
    Nembutal
    Doriden
    Chloral Hydrate

Source:+ Interview with Colonel Michael Camp, military
    psychiatrist at Walter Reed Army Hospital, Washington, D.C.
    This table will appear in Colonel Camp's forthcoming book
    on Military Psychiatry In Vietnam which is still in
    preparation and will be published by Greenwood Press in
    1988.

trine that has remained essentially unchanged since World War I. In addition, its casualty-servicing structure for both surgical and psychiatric casualties is primitive by the standards used by most armies in the West. And the inability of the Soviet army to prevent severe manpower loss through psychiatric casualties may well turn out to be its major weakness in the next war.

NOTES

1. The list of American innovations drawn from Israeli military psychiatric practice that appears here was obtained from interviews with Dr. Reuven Gal, IDF, who headed the IDF Behavioral Research Unit for almost six years during the critical period when its doctrine and practice were being formed.

2. Lawrence Ingraham and Frederick Manning, "American Military Psychiatry," in Richard A. Gabriel, *Military Psychiatry: A Comparative Perspective* (Westport, Conn.: Greenwood Press, 1986), Chap. 2.

3. These figures are extracted from official U.S. military estimates in a draft document entitled "Interim Operational Concept Health Service Support/Air Land Battle: The Combat Stress Control Company," produced by the Department of Behavioral Sciences, U.S. Academy of Health Sciences, San Antonio, Texas, August 25, 1986.

4. Ibid.

5. This account of drug-induced deaths at Pearl Harbor appears frequently in lectures given by military psychiatrists on drug use. No one, however, seems able to document the story with a historical source. The version which appears here was told to me by Dr. Frank Jones, chief of neuropsychiatry, Walter Reed Army Institute of Research, Washington, D.C.

8

The Future of Military Psychiatry

In developing increasingly destructive weapons to wage his wars man faces a new technological paradox. War has become so destructive, so lethal, and so intense that it will generate rates of psychiatric casualties far greater than what we have ever seen. At the same time, the nature of modern war has made it impossible to deal effectively with the explosion of psychiatric casualties that it generates. But if man is to continue his fascination with the deadly business of war, this paradox cannot be allowed to stand for long. Either modern armies must find some way to deal with the problem of psychiatric debilitation or they must risk putting themselves out of business within days of going to war. If the old ways of dealing with it no longer work, then some new ways must be found. The only alternative is to admit that war has become, in human terms, truly pointless.

Unable to treat psychiatric breakdown in battle successfully, armies have naturally turned their attention to trying to prevent it. In the past armies have sought to prevent psychiatric casualties by screening the manpower pool in order to identify those individuals that psychiatric tests define as prone to mental collapse, reducing the time the soldier is exposed to combat, increasing unit cohesion, and providing realistic training. The most that can be said for these approaches is that they have worked only marginally in the past and will not work under conditions of modern war.

In most cases psychiatric screening has failed to determine in advance the capacity of a soldier to endure combat stress. Indeed, most psychiatrists involved in the screening process for the U.S. military readily agree that the tests are highly unreliable and are poor predictors of behavior under fire. For the most part, they simply don't work.

Tests to determine mental endurance are inevitably linked to the cultural values of the society administering them. Accordingly, predisposition to breakdown invariably comes to be defined within a nation's cultural context. There is no objective standard for determining endurance to stress any more than there is an objective standard for determining endurance to pain. Like pain, psychological stressors are best regarded as signals to the brain. The interpretation of these signals by the individuals, not the signals themselves, determines behavior. What we know from experience with soldiers under stress is the rather disturbing fact that all sane men break down sooner or later. Only the already mentally disturbed seem capable of withstanding the stress of combat for long periods. Sooner or later, no doubt, someone will make the case for drafting only psychopaths on the grounds that doing so will reduce psychiatric casualty rates. In other words, an army of genuine aggressive psychopaths would have fewer psychiatric casualties.

Once set in place, psychiatric screens for endurance to battle stress become self-fulfilling prophecies. The system takes on a life of its own, often with disastrous results. The American experience with psychiatric screening in World War II resulted in the loss of enough manpower to outfit fifty combat divisions. In fact, no one could really predict how the rejects would have performed under fire. They were excused from the fighting on the grounds that they had failed the test, which had become the unquestioned standard. In World War I, there was no psychiatric screening until late in the war, and there is absolutely no evidence that it reduced the psychiatric casualty rate. Indeed, the psychiatric casualty rate in World War II, after screening was introduced, was almost seven times that of World War I. In both world wars the Soviet Union did not use screening at all. Interestingly, the Soviet army's rate of psychiatric casualties was about the same in both wars, about nine per thousand, and much below that suffered by the U.S. Army in World War II. If modern armies are going to prevent psychiatric casualties, they are certainly going to have to find another means to do so.

Another way that armies have attempted to prevent psychiatric casualties is by reducing the amount of time the soldier is exposed to combat. In Korea and Vietnam soldiers were exposed to the battle environment for limited combat tours of nine months and twelve months respectively. The Israelis make much of telling their troops that their exposure to battle will, in the normal course, be for only a comparatively short time. In Lebanon, Israeli combat soldiers were often rotated out of the battle on a weekly basis. The idea behind such rotation is old. Throughout history actual combat in wars was usually confined to a single day. Even when it lasted longer, which was rare, nightfall provided a significant respite from stress and time to recoup. In World War I, the average amount of time a combat battalion actually spent in the line was about eight days. After that, it was rotated behind the lines for a week or so while another battalion took its place.

Limiting exposure to battle as a way of reducing combat stress has some validity. Unfortunately, the nature of modern war makes it impossible to rotate units out of battle on a regular basis. A major characteristic of modern war is continual engagement in the offensive. It is hard to imagine a commander on the attack breaking off the fight in order to rotate troops. It is even harder to imagine that a unit under attack will be given sufficient respite to replace its losses. After all, once one has paid the price of inflicting high casualties in the initial phases of an attack, the idea is to take maximum advantage of the defender's weakened position and drive the attack home until the defender collapses completely. In Soviet doctrine, a unit engaged in an attack that suffers heavy casualties is not pulled from the line. Rather, weak spots are reinforced with new units. The remnants of the first unit are transferred to the reinforcing unit and are expected to continue the attack. Only by such unrelenting attack can a breakthrough be exploited for maximum potential. Common practice in World War II was for Soviet units engaged in the attack to fight down to 25 percent strength, thus routinely absorbing 75 percent casualties.

Even if it were possible to pull units out of the line for rest and replenishment, there is no guarantee at all that they would not be attacked in the rear area as the enemy engages in a battle attack. Equally important, the dynamics of psychiatric collapse indicate clearly that anxiety in the soldier can continue for days before and after a battle. This anxiety can easily result in psychiatric collapse before the battle. In World War II, almost 200,000 U.S. fighting men were psychiatrically debilitated even before their units were deployed to England. These men simply could not deal with the thought of war, never mind participation in combat. Accordingly, removing men from the fight for a period of a few days will inevitably result in large numbers of them developing psychiatric symptoms as a defense against having to go back.

In World War II American soldiers who had been given leave repeatedly collapsed when told they were being returned to the front. Bomber pilots who had flown several missions often broke down back at their bases when told they had to fly again in a few days. Army Air Force medical stations the night before a mission were routinely full of pilots with psychiatric symptoms. In the early days of the war a common practice was to force them into their aircraft at pistol point. For whatever good it may do, man seems to be the only animal capable of being traumatized by what might happen. The less blessed members of the animal community restrict their worrying to what is happening to them. Perhaps that is why we attribute mental illness only to human beings.

To some the answer to preventing psychiatric collapse rests in strong human social instincts and attachments. It is no secret that men in combat groups bond strongly to one another. Military writings on unit cohesion commonly assert that the bonds combat soldiers form with one another are stronger than the bonds most men feel for their wives, and indeed this seems true at times. Military writers also often stress that a good commander must "love his troops" in order to command. Military lore requires that officers lead from the front—however impractical that may be in combat—and that officers must always eat only after their troops are fed. Young officers in every army are taught that an officer must never expect his men to endure hardships and risks that he himself is not prepared to endure. In the words of one well-known military analyst and combat officer, "a man who cannot love cannot command."[1]

There is no doubt that strong unit cohesion offers some protection against psychiatric breakdown. It also is a stimulus to acts of unusual bravery. Audie Murphy, the most decorated soldier on the American side in World War II, was once asked what moved him to take on a German infantry company single-handedly and kill them all. His response was simply that "they were killing my friends." It is also true that elite units tend to have about a third fewer psychiatric casualties than nonelite units, suggesting that strong ties to one's comrades do indeed help to ward off the pressure of stress.

But if cohesion helps, it certainly is no guarantee. It is also very doubtful that cohesion can be functionally maintained in a modern war. Most studies on cohesion use as a standard the professional, highly trained regiments of the British or German armies of the past. In those units all men were volunteers, served long periods of time together, were deployed as units, and lived together. For most armies of the world these conditions are no longer possible. In the first place no nation could sustain sufficiently large numbers of standing units of professionals without going bankrupt. As a consequence, most modern armies are either conscript armies (Germany, Soviet Union, France) or small professional armies of volunteers (Britain, the United States, Canada) that will require conscript reinforcements to keep fighting for very long once the shooting starts. Moreover, once battle begins, whatever cohesion may have existed before the war will last only a few days until the unit suffers its share of casualties. Then the combat units (platoons, companies, battalions) can only be sustained by a constant stream of conscript replacements placed as individual "fillers" in the unit. These men, quite naturally, will have had almost no time to train together and will hardly know each other. Within a few days the highly cohesive peacetime standing regiments will have been decimated and their personnel replaced at least twice. While unit cohesion may help somewhat in warding off psychiatric collapse, the fact is that future wars will not be fought by highly disciplined "bands of brothers" with a long shared experience. Rather, they will be fought by a constantly changing stream of green troops who are strangers to one another. Cohesion may help, but the conditions of modern war make it impossible to sustain for very long. Modern war will truly be, as the American army has called it, a "come-as-you-are war."

Finally, in the past psychiatric collapse has been reduced by realistic training. While there are any number of fears a man brings with him to battle, among the most disturbing is fear of the unexpected. Soldiers are supposed to be trained under realistic conditions to acquaint them with the "real" battlefield, so that they are not shocked when committed to the fighting. In the past it was possible to train troops to deal with the realistic conditions that they would find on the battlefield. Today, it is no longer possible.

Modern war is so lethal and so intense that there is no feasible way of training troops for what to expect. To be sure, it is possible, and vital, that troops learn certain procedures and skills without which they would surely become easy victims. But one cannot, as the Soviets say, "steel the will" of the soldier for actual combat without committing him to it. The Soviet army, which has the most extensive theory and practice of trying to condition the soldier to function on the battlefield, also recognizes that, for the most part, their elaborate scheme will not work when the shooting starts. Accordingly, the Soviet soldier is also told that there are spies in his ranks to report and deal with any errant behavior under fire and that he will be summarily shot if he fails to perform. As if to make the point more clearly, the Soviets point out that in World War II no fewer than 250 general officers were shot for cowardice.[2] Battlefield motivation in the Soviet army is instilled mostly by fear.

The simple fact is, however, that the circumstances of modern war will be so different that there is no longer any reasonable expectation that the traditional ways of preventing psychiatric collapse can work. The conditions of today's battlefield leave the soldier almost defenseless against the stress that it inflicts upon him. The result will inevitably be mental breakdown among very large numbers of combatants.

No government can allow such a state of affairs to persist for very long without having to admit that its huge expenditures for weapons and large standing military forces have no practical point except to provide jobs and careers. Worse, for governments to concede that armies will only succeed in generating large numbers of dead, wounded, maimed, and mad men is to concede that conventional war will fail to produce clear-cut winners and losers. Both sides will absorb such large numbers of casualties that all victories will be Pyrrhic.

Military technology abhors a vacuum, and there is no doubt that a vacuum exists between what the soldier is expected to do in modern war and what he can realistically be expected to do. Either some way will be found to prevent psychiatric collapse under fire or modern war will remain no less a mutual military suicide pact than nuclear war with the single saving grace that most of its victims will be soldiers instead of the civilian men, women, and children who are the present hostages to nuclear weapons. It should come as no surprise that the military establishments of the world are even now involved in developing a chemical solution to the problem.

THE CHEMICAL SOLDIER

The idea of trying to control the soldier's fear through chemical means is very old, although the degree of success has been low. For millennia commanders recognized that the main enemy on the battlefield was fear. Far more battles were won or lost because one side's troops had their spirit broken than by military genius or the rate of actual killing. Very commonly, the serious killing commenced only after one side broke, allowing the winners to pursue the vanquished and to slaughter them. Far more battles have been lost to fear than to the "push of the pike."

The first attempt we know of to control the soldier's fear by chemical means came 2000 years before the rise of Rome, and it remains among the most interesting examples of such attempts. Ancient tribes living on the steppes of central Russia apparently used chemical means to reduce fear and increase the fighting power of their warriors. These chemicals seem to have approached the effectiveness of the attempts of modern armies. The Koyak and Wiros tribes perfected a drug made from the *Aminita Muscaria* mushroom, a red-speckled cousin of the deadly *Aminita* "Angel of Death."[3]

The shaamans of the tribe discovered that the muscaria contained a powerful compound that, when consumed, produced a powerful analgesic effect on the body, rendering it highly resistant to pain. It was probably originally used in religious ceremonies, but it was not long before a more pragmatic military use was found: to increase the ability of warriors to do battle. The shaamans learned that if a warrior urinated after eating the mushroom, the potency of the drug in his urine was increased many times. Warriors would then store the urine and drink it on the eve of battle. After a while they hit on the idea of feeding the mushroom to reindeer and gathering their urine. Apparently, the compound passed almost unmetabolized through the reindeer's kidneys, which provided a more efficient metabolic filter, thus increasing the potency of the drug. In this way the early shaamans were able to produce a powerful chemical compound of great value.

The effect on the fighting capability of the warriors was dramatic. Apparently, men who took the drug became almost immune to pain while at the same time became capable of great feats of physical strength and endurance. Warriors were able to carry heavy loads great distances and to have the advantage of greater physical strength and stamina in battle. What is most interesting is that the drug apparently caused almost no diminution of the soldier's mental awareness and, like a natural amphetamine, might well have enhanced it for a short period of time. Equally important, the soldier was able to sleep normally.

While there was no evidence on how long the drug's effects lasted, it is clear from history that the Koyaks and Wiros became very successful military societies whose warriors were feared for their brutality and endurance in battle. Indeed, there is some evidence that their military culture may have spread as far east as India where some religious cults today continue to produce and consume a similar extract made from the *Aminita Muscaria*.

Drug use in battle has continued throughout military history. In the thirteenth century the Crusaders fought a band of Muslim warriors called "hashishim" because they used hashish prior to battle to reduce fear and control pain. The modern English word "assassin" is derived from the "hashishim" who made a practice of sneaking up upon their enemy and killing them in the fashion of modern-day Gurkas. In the sixteenth century the Spanish conquistador, Juan Pizzaro, encountered Inca warriors who increased their endurance and resistance to fear and pain by chewing on the coca leaf. Today we know that cocaine is derived from the coca leaf.

More examples of military drug use are found in the British army where soldiers have traditionally been given a double jigger of rum to steel their nerves before battle. In World War I and II the Russian army, in addition to providing vodka, made it a practice to administer a number of chemicals derived from plants to improve the fighting ability of their soldiers. Such compounds as Valeriana, a mild but effective tranquilizer made from plants, was given to soldiers to calm them. Present-day Soviet parachutist manuals recommend giving a soldier caffeine in tea or coffee to "open the pathways to the brain" before committing him to battle, to stimulate the soldier and increase his awareness. During the Vietnam War American soldiers often used marijuana, alcohol, or hard drugs like heroin, despite official regulations to the contrary, to help them endure battle stress and the conditions of military life.

The chemical solution to fear and increased battle performance has a long history. But what modern armies have in mind far surpasses anything that might have crossed the minds of earlier commanders. Biology and chemistry have combined to produce the modern science of biochemistry, which seeks to understand and reduce human behavior to chemical reactions in the body and the brain at the micro-molecular level. The ability of modern science to understand molecular bonding has brought into existence a wide range of chemical compounds that do not exist in nature. They are products of human ingenuity. Armed with this new knowledge, the military research medical establishments of the world have set for themselves the task of abolishing fear in the soldier to make him a more efficient killing machine.

Anxiety is central to the human ability to survive as a species. It provides a mechanism to protect oneself from mortal danger. Any animal that cannot feel anxiety will be unable to detect dangers that threaten its existence and will quickly meet its end at the hand of natural predators. All animals, including humans, are equipped by nature with anxiety-producing mechanisms to warn of impending dangers.

Anxiety, and the stronger emotional and physiological responses that it triggers, is a vital precondition for all animals in preparing to deal with threatening situations. Once danger is detected, anxiety rests at the base of man's ability to prepare his mind and body to deal with it. Without anxiety man would easily be destroyed in much greater numbers, which, in turn, would limit his reproduction rate and in the end threaten the perpetuation of the species. From a purely biological and evolutionary perspective, anxiety serves the same ends in all animals including man.

The onset of anxiety prepares the mind and body to engage in the "flight or fight" responses. Both responses are equally functional insofar as they remove the threat to life. Anxiety triggers a reaction in the limbic region of the brain, which sends chemical signals to the body and the rest of the brain. In response to these signals the body's blood pressure, heart rate, respiration rate, and muscular action all increase. These responses make the body a more efficient fighting machine by increasing its strength, endurance, and resistance to pain. This is why soldiers placed under stress are capable of great feats of strength and endurance. Men have been known to carry their wounded buddies more than a mile under enemy fire or, in just as many cases, flee across very rough terrain without any difficulty. For a short time the body reaches peak physical efficiency to deal with threats to its existence.

At the same time chemicals called neurotransmitters are released to facilitate the ability of the brain's nerve synapses to transmit impulses along its nerve pathways. These neurotransmitters increase the brain's ability to function, especially by increasing its state of mental awareness. Under stress, these neurotransmitters make it possible for mental functions to become extremely acute, matching the body's increase in physiological awareness. Not only do the soldier's senses of smell, sight, and sound become more acute, but the ability of the brain to interpret and assign meaning to these signals increases greatly. At this point, the whole animal mechanism is ready to do combat and, if necessary, sustain injury and endure pain.

Under conditions of short-lived fear this state of increased readiness is functional to survival, and it can be sustained for hours. Usually, once the threat has been reduced or has disappeared, the body and brain return to normal levels of physiological readiness. This reduction in anxiety is also controlled by the brain. If anxiety persists for too long, however, it is possible for the physiological effects of stress—increased blood pressure, heart rate, respiration, and so on—to become fixed at very high levels that cannot easily be reduced by the natural control mechanisms of the body and brain. In these instances, the soldier must be given medication or long periods of rest away from danger to return his body and mind to their normal state.

But life on the battlefield puts tremendous levels of stress on the soldier even when he is not directly engaged in fighting. The mind can readily generate anxiety over conditions that it expects to meet as well as over those it must deal with directly. The levels of stress under which soldiers must function are usually much higher than those found under normal circumstances. Under conditions of sustained high stress the neurotransmitters of the brain can run out of control. Too much of the chemical neurotransmitters are produced for the brain and nerve pathways to handle. A runaway series of chemical reactions is triggered by and within the brain.

When this happens, the soldier becomes a candidate for rapid psychiatric collapse, and he may suffer the onset of severe neurosis or rapid psychosis. A number of conditions may arise in the brain along with this condition. The normally circular pattern of production and reduction of certain neurotransmitters may break down, so that the brain is unable to control its own chemical functions. In other instances the supply of a critical chemical compound may be entirely depleted, and in turn the brain may be unable to sustain a complex chemical reaction cycle. In still other instances, the receptors of the brain's nerve synapses may be chemically blocked. Finally, as a consequence of any or all of these conditions the ability of the brain to produce other important neurotransmitters may cease altogether. Under any of these conditions a state of complete exhaustion may result in which the soldier becomes totally unable to function mentally.

The effects on the soldier are traumatic. Once the chemical reactions in the brain are disturbed as a consequence of prolonged and severe anxiety, the soldier may find it impossible to sleep. When he does fall asleep, he may find it almost impossible to wake up or to reach a state of full consciousness. His mental abilities fall off rapidly, and he has great difficulty comprehending even the simplest instructions. His memory, especially his short-term memory, declines greatly. The soldier becomes unable to process information and make decisions even regarding his own safety. His mental functions simply won't work normally, since the brain can no longer chemically sustain a normal level of mental awareness. Thus, the soldier is placed at risk of total mental collapse. The effects of this process can take days to emerge or, as is very common, can occur in a matter of hours or even minutes.

If the military is to prevent the onset of anxiety as a prophylactic for psychiatric collapse, the key is somehow to prevent the chemical reactions in the body and brain from becoming so acute that they produce a mental collapse. There are already a number of drugs that can be used to prevent or control anxiety. Some of the more common ones are lithium, elevil, and valium. All have major problems when soldiers use them to control battle stress. All control the onset of anxiety by preventing the brain from producing its normal level of certain neurotransmitters. While anxiety is reduced, there is an accompanying and often greater reduction in the ability of the brain to process information and think quickly. A soldier who cannot think clearly and quickly will be killed very soon on the battlefield. Another problem is that these drugs interfere with normal sleep, often producing nightmares or feelings of increased fatigue. Their effects last only a short time and often, when they wear off, result in rebound effects in which the soldier is plunged more deeply into symptoms of anxiety. In short, the price of purchasing a decrease in anxiety with the drugs we have is to dull the mental abilities of the soldier, a condition that is actually more dangerous to his survival.

The problem is to find a chemical compound that will prevent or reduce anxiety while allowing the soldier to retain his normal and vitally needed acute levels of mental awareness. Such a compound would have to work on the chemical reactions in the brain that govern the reactions to anxiety without depleting the normal function of the nerve synapses responsible for mental activity. In the terminology of the trade, the search is for a "nondepleting neurotrop." A neurotrop is a chemical compound that works directly on the transmitters and receptors of the brain's nerve pathways.

The search for such a chemical is already underway in the military research laboratories of the major armies of the world. In the last five years both the U.S. military and the Soviets have initiated programs to develop such a drug, although the details of the programs remain classified. The search has taken on increased urgency in light of the belated recognition that modern war is so stressful that it will break most normal men within a matter of days if not hours. U.S. Army estimates, produced from computer models, predict that psychiatric casualties will account for 40 to 50 percent of the casualties in a modern conventional war. It is likely that the next revolution in military power will not be in weapons technology but in chemistry that will allow soldiers to endure the conditions of modern war with its new weapons. The U.S. Army has already developed at least three prototypes that show great "promise." One of these drugs may be a variant of buspirone. If the search is successful, and it almost inevitably will be, the relationship between soldiers and their battle environment will be transformed forever. And there will be no going back.

If the military establishments of the United States and the Soviet Union succeed in developing a chemical compound that will prevent the onset of anxiety while retaining the soldier's ability to remain mentally alert, sleep normally, and process information under stress, the nature of war, already too horrible to contemplate seriously, will change once again. And once again it will change for the worse, becoming even more horrible. In solving one problem, the military establishments will create even greater ones for their soldiers and will change the psychic nature of man. For if they succeed, they will have finally done what man has been incapable of doing since he first emerged from the primal mud: they will have banished the fear of death and with it will go man's humanity and his soul.

A truly effective anxiety-controlling drug will make paralyzing fear an anachronism. With the onset of anxiety controlled or prevented, soldiers will be unable to develop deep fears for their lives or their own safety. To be sure, there will remain an intellectual commitment to staying alive, but the physiological support mechanisms that make the fear of death real and functional on the battlefield will simply not engage. No longer will anxiety trigger the endocrine system of the body to raise the pulse rate, quicken the heartbeat, raise body temperature, dilate the eyes, and stimulate respiration. Nor will the muscles spring to life at the thought of fear, which sends adrenalin racing through the bloodstream. The fear of death may remain in the conscious mind, but there will be no physiological or emotional support to make the fear real. Men may still know fear, but they will be unable to feel fear in an emotional sense. The chemical soldier will be a reality, and the reality will be a chemically created monster.

Abolishing fear on the battlefield will change the nature of both man and war, for fear has very real functions for men in battle. The most obvious effect of fear on the battlefield is that it reduces the killing power of the soldier and his weapons. Frightened soldiers don't kill very well, and in the past this has made the tenor of war manageable in human terms. It is worth recalling that in World War II only 15 percent of combat soldiers actually engaged in combat ever fired their weapons. This, of course, kept the casualties down. But if chemical preventives for fear succeed in controlling the anxiety of the soldier in only 75 percent of the soldiers, 75 percent of the combat soldiers on the battlefield will be sufficiently alert mentally to kill other soldiers, an increase in the killing capability of 400 percent at the very minimum. If one adds to this the fact that the killing power of weaponry has increased by a factor of at least ten since World War II, the increase in the destructiveness and intensity of war in the future will be enormous. And it will be achieved by simply increasing the "human potential" of the combat soldier. To be sure, a chemical preventive will reduce the rate of psychiatric casualties, but it will purchase this reduction at the price of expotentially increasing the number of dead and wounded.

Not only will more soldiers be able to kill, but they will be able to kill far more efficiently. It is no secret that men suffering physiological and emotional stress reactions have great difficulty processing information, aiming weapons, and operating equipment, all vital tasks in the killing business. At present, one of the advantages of high-tech weaponry is that soldiers can use it easily and simply by electronically replacing many of the physical and mental operations once performed by the soldier. With the soldiers' stress reactions under control, they will be able to operate their killing machines with much greater efficiency for much longer periods. The result, not unexpectedly, will be a much greater degree of lethality.

In a war of chemical soldiers, military units, once engaged, will scarcely be able to disengage. In earlier battles one side or the other simply absorbed as much death as it could until its spirit broke, and then it either withdrew or surrendered. In either case, battle had its limits and the defeated remnants at least survived. Fear put real limits on the ability of units to attack or defend and, in most cases, this element permitted victory or defeat. The chemical soldier will fight without fear limiting his ability to kill. The continuous offensive becomes matched by the continuous defensive. Battles once joined will proceed until one side has been entirely killed or wounded. Without fear, battles will be fought to the death as a matter of routine because there will no longer be any reason to stop them.

Without psychiatric collapse and fear to force defenders to surrender when all is lost, units will resist to the last man. The attacker will have to kill them all in a sterile exercise of military skill. It will be battle without prisoners. The defenders will be unable to surrender, and the attackers will be unable to offer the basis of surrender, the fear of death, because it will no longer be present in the chemically bemused minds of the combatants. In all past wars large numbers of potential dead men escaped by surrendering and becoming prisoners. Now the soldier will no longer even be afforded that luxury. He will be expected to fight to the death as the full measure of military efficiency.

In the new world of the chemical soldier there will be no military ethos. Technical proficiency measured by the body count will replace ethos. For 4000 years military ethos traditionally has set limits on the killing by requiring the victor to place himself as a fellow human being in the place of the vanquished. Soldiers have always had special codes of ethics, which guided their treatment of fellow soldiers against whom they fought. It was this empathy for fellow soldiers that led armies in the past to limit the killing. Without fear there is no basis for empathy or sympathy for the loser. Military ethos will be replaced by efficiency and the killing will go on.

The West's sense of traditional military ethos is derived from the Greek military experience, which placed human qualities over technical ones even to the point of refusing to adopt more efficient military technologies on the grounds that they were inhuman and dishonorable. For the Greeks, war remained a bloody but nonetheless the ultimate human endeavor. It was men and their actions that made war tolerable, not the mere exercise of military technique. The ends for which wars were fought and the manner in which they were fought were central to a moral view of war. It was the human dimension of war, the ability of the human being to endure in a terrible environment and to limit the killing, that gave a soldier his human and ethical worth.

For the chemical soldier military virtues will have no meaning and no function. Human qualities such as courage, bravery, endurance, and sacrifice have meaning only in purely human terms. They indicate conditions in which men triumph over normal fear. Heroes are those who can endure and control fear beyond the limits expected of normally sane men. Brave men are those who conquer fear. Sacrifice for one's comrades can have meaning only when one fears death and accepts it because it will prevent others from dying or permit an idea to live. If fear is eliminated from the soldier through chemical means, there will be nothing over which the soldier can triumph. The standards of normal men will be eroded and disappear. Man will be dehumanized and will no longer die for anything that is meaningful in truly human terms. They will just die. The military virtues—courage, heroism, endurance, bravery, and sacrifice—will be replaced in war by mere probability tables that measure the technical efficiency of "human" performance. And the standard of performance will be the body count.

In a real sense the advent of the chemical soldier will not only change the nature and intensity of warfare but the psychological nature of man himself. It will change the very basis of human emotion and action as we have always known it. A chemical compound that prevents the onset of anxiety while leaving the individual mentally alert will produce a new kind of human being, a human being who would retain the cognitive elements of his emotions but would be unable to feel emotion. The basis of all human emotion is anxiety, and without this physiological basis those elements of mental operation that give the cognitive element true meaning in human terms would no longer be present in the soldier's mental processes. Emotions are rooted in anxiety, and anxiety would disappear for as long as the chemical compound worked on the neurotransmitters of the brain. The interaction between the cognitive and physiological aspects of emotion, both vitally necessary for emotions to exist, would disappear. And along with it what we know as the soul would be destroyed.

What we would be left with is a genuine sociopathic personality induced and sustained by chemical means. A sociopathic personality is one who clearly knows what he is doing to another person, but one who cannot feel or appreciate in an emotional sense the consequences of his actions. Although sociopathic personalities are above average in intelligence, they often cannot prevent themselves from acting even though they know (but cannot truly feel) what the consequences of their actions might be. A sociopath is unable to display loyalty to others, is grossly selfish, is unable to feel guilt or remorse, or appreciate the consequences of his actions. Such persons are given to extreme risk taking and generally lack all the normal characteristics that we commonly associate with conscience. The sociopath functions only on the cognitive plane of his emotions. That is why true sociopaths cannot empathize or sympathize with those who may be hurt by their actions. To be sure, they know cognitively that they have inflicted pain, but they cannot generate a genuine emotional response to this fact. The chemical soldier will be a genuine sociopath.

Richard Hechtl, an expert in the criminal sociopathic personality, argues that his fifteen years of working with sociopathic personalities has led him to believe that it appears that significant changes have occurred in the chemical biology of the sociopath's brain operations. In Hechtl's words, "their capacity to respond normally to anxiety provoking stimuli has been diminished as to suggest an absence or paucity of appropriate neurotransmitters."[4] The sociopathic personality suffers from a chemical interruption in the brain, which prohibits the nerve pathways from chemically transmitting the physiological aspects of emotion to the brain. The physiological elements of anxiety reactions are blocked by a chemical debilitation from entering the mental processes. The sociopathic personality operates in the realm of his emotions on only one cylinder, the cognitive or purely intellectual one. He remains deficient in his ability to experience emotional responses within a human context. It is precisely these conditions that will be produced in the chemical soldier.

The real horror lurking behind the attempt to use chemical means for preventing psychiatric collapse in battle is that in order for a soldier to be able to function in the environment of modern war, he must be psychically reconstituted in a manner precisely identical to what we have traditionally defined as being mentally ill. He must be chemically made over to become a sociopathic personality in the clinical sense of the term. In short, the soldier must be made mentally abnormal in order to behave "normally" on the battlefield. If he is to function efficiently, he must first be made insane.

Psychiatric collapse under fire, it bears repeating, is not the reaction of the weak or the cowardly. Rather, it is the reaction of the normally sane to an insane environment. As the data from World War II demonstrate, only the clinically ill—aggressive psycopathic personalities—remain immune from psychiatric collapse. The chemical solution will make it possible for the sane soldier to survive psychically in an insane environment only by making him as clinically insane as the environment in which he is expected to function. Under these circumstances, abnormality becomes normality, and the psychic nature of man along with clinical definitions of sanity are altered forever. The paradox is that in order for the soldier to be saved, he must first be mentally destroyed. And with his destruction, the human dimensions of war—bravery, sacrifice, endurance, heroism—disappear, too.

CONCLUSION

On the battlefields of the future we will witness a true clash of ignorant armies, armies ignorant of their own emotions and even of the reasons for which they fight. Soldiers on all sides will be reduced to fearless chemical automatons who fight simply because they can do nothing else and because nothing else any longer "rationally" matters. The soldier will become no more than one more death-inflicting combat machine—like tanks, missiles, and guns—to be used by commanders in much the same way. Any human meaning to war will disappear. There will no longer be any way to make the loss of men in battle meaningful in human terms. Their loss will make even less sense to their mothers, wives, brothers, and children, who, safely removed from the chemically induced haze, will retain their sense of emotional balance, human judgment, and moral horror. For them, the death of their loved ones will make no sense at all. Life-and-death decisions, especially for commanders who commit their men to action, will become mere exercises in technical expertise totally devoid of human content. Men will fight and die because they fight and die. Nothing more.

Even those who fight and survive will have precious little to show for it in human terms. Battle will no longer be a fearful or exciting experience. It will be devoid of human emotion and meaning akin to that felt by a strongly tranquilized individual carelessly driving an automobile on a rain-swept winding road at high speed. He recognizes the danger intellectually, but he continues his course because the danger has no genuine emotional meaning, and his behavior is unaffected.

Under these conditions men will be able to stay "sane." They will "know" that their comrades have been killed, but it will not affect them; they will "know" that they have destroyed other men, but it will not matter; they will "know" that their actions killed innocent civilians, but they will not feel it; and they will "know" when they are about to meet their own ends, but it will not matter much. There will be no fear. The soldier will be devoid of the capacity for emotional response, and he will be left without human standards to measure or limit his actions. Amid the death, pain, and horror, the chemical soldier will simply fight on.

Nor is there any good reason to suspect that once it becomes possible to banish fear in the soldier, the search for a more efficient killer will stop. Once the chemical genie is out of the bottle, the full range of human mental and physical actions become targets for the improved mechanisms of chemical control. The search to improve the military potential of the human being will move on to press the very limits of humanity itself. Consider, for example, what can be gained in human potential on the battlefield if, once fear is banished, chemical means are found to increase the aggressiveness of the individual soldier. Today it is already possible by chemical or electric stimulation to increase the aggression levels of human beings by stimulating the amygdala, a section of the brain known to control aggression and rage. Such "human potential engineering" is already a partial reality, and the necessary technical knowledge increases every day. Faceless, well-meaning military medical researchers press the limits of their discipline with little or no regard for the consequences. We may be rushing headlong into a long, dark chemical night from which there will be no return. The paradox is that it is necessary to enslave the emotions as the means of producing soldiers who can defend a nation's freedoms.

Even the most devout military metaphysicians recognize that nuclear war has become an immoral horror, nothing short of suicide. But military thinkers and planners continue to console themselves with the belief that conventional war is still an acceptable substitute and, consequently, have continued to increase weapons technology without any significant hindrances. The result has been to develop a conventional arsenal on both sides whose effectiveness begins to approach that of nuclear weapons.

Both the Soviet and American military have developed conventional weapons that make those used in World War II pale by comparison. The explosive capacity of most modern weapons exceeds that of World War II by at least five times. Rates of fire have increased by almost ten times. Accuracy has increased by twenty times, and the ability to detect enemy targets has increased several hundred percent. On top of all this has been the introduction of weapons systems undreamed of in 1945. The overall result is that the ability of modern armies to deliver a combat punch has increased by at least 600 percent since the end of World War II. Military technology has reached a point where "conventional weapons have unconventional effects." Both conventional and nuclear war have reached a point where the combatants can no longer be reasonably expected to survive.

Confronting the real consequences of conventional war drives men mad in droves. War has reached the point where most human beings can no longer remain sane long enough to produce any military outcome except collective death and insanity. Exposure to modern war crushes the fragile mental defenses with which man protects himself against insanity. Man's profound beliefs that he can overcome danger—that he will survive, that his actions influence what happens to him, and that someone, even God, will help him get through the horror—collapse within days, often hours, of being exposed to the terrible realities of the battlefield. And with them go the last anchors of man's sanity. Insanity provides at least some escape, however twisted and bizarre.

Faced with the reality of choosing between death and insanity, most civilians engage in denial. Unable to face the realities of war, most of us refuse to think about it, choosing to leave the problems of military technology and fighting to the experts. Since even the experts have limited capacity to face the truth, they, too, deny reality on the grounds that they are only doing their jobs. As small cogs in a huge weapons machine, they would argue, it is hardly fair to hold them responsible for the consequences of the larger military system. If anyone is at fault it is the system itself. So the game goes on.

War has always had a romantic aura, and it has always exercised a strong romantic influence over the young men who fight it. For the young, visions of glory, of women who will love him for serving his country, of being tested against himself, or showing his father, older brother, or his peers that he is a man, and of proving to the women who rejected him what fools they were have always been part of the attraction. It is the mental images of war in the heads of the young that compel so strongly. In truth, the realities have never been squarely faced by the recruit. And by the time the shooting starts, it is too late to escape.

In the past wars were at least tolerable enough to allow some of the most romantic to survive. Indeed, to many soldiers a slight wound was the ultimate symbol that they had faced the challenge and triumphed. And to many an old soldier, a vital part of having survived was the opportunity to tell the younger generation how bravely he fought and how fearless he was. Having survived a war provided one with something to be proud of as the years stole one's youth and crushed other illusions. The romance and glory of war persist as realities when they are but myths.

In order to stand the killing, men have always convinced themselves that the enemy was different, that he did not have a family, or that he was less in any number of ways. In earlier times, tribes took names which meant only "man" or "human being" thus automatically defining those outside the tribe as something less than men. This made killing them easier. Today, we use ethnic, political, or racial epithets, which serve the same dehumanizing purpose. These mental gymnastics, called intraspeciation by psychologists, allow us to kill with impunity because the enemy is "not like us." One can only marvel at the statements of today's nuclear metaphysicians who work in the Pentagon's think tanks designing nuclear strike strategies. When confronted by the fact that the Russians lost 20 million people in World War II and had their country devastated, they respond that precisely because of these facts the Russians do not fear war as much as other peoples. And because they have once endured such terrible losses, the only way to make any nuclear strategy truly credible is to ensure that they know that future losses would be even greater. The mind game goes on regardless of realities.

Men dehumanize the enemy as the only way to justify their own horrible acts. Otherwise, it would be impossible to remove the blood from the soldier's hands. Once the battlefield expunges the myths that propelled the soldier to do battle, he must deal with the realities of death and destruc-

tion. And the only way to cope with them and remain sane is to dehumanize one's enemy. To recognize him as human is to squarely face what one
has done. And that is no easy task; for some it is impossible.

Societies have always recognized that war changes men, that they are
not the same after they return. That is why primitive societies often required soldiers to perform purification rites before allowing them to return
to the group. These rites often involved washing or other forms of cere-
monial cleansing. Psychologically, these rituals provided soldiers with a
way of ridding themselves of stress and the terrible guilt that always ac-
companies the sane after war. It was also a way of treating guilt by providing a mechanism through which fighting men could decompress and
relive their terror without feeling weak or exposed. Finally, it was a way
of telling the soldier that what he did was right and that the community
for which he fought was grateful and that, above all, his community of
sane and normal men welcomed him back.

Modern armies have similar mechanisms of purification. In World War
II soldiers often spent days together on troop ships on the return home.
Among themselves, warriors could relive their feelings, express grief for
lost comrades, tell each other about their fears, and, above all, receive the
support of their fellow soldiers. It provided them with a sounding board
for their own sanity. Upon reaching home, soldiers were often given parades or other civic tributes. They received the respect of their communi-
ties as stories of their experiences were told to children and relatives by
proud parents and wives. All this served the same cleansing purpose as the
rituals of the past.

When soldiers are denied these rituals, they often tend to become emotionally disturbed. Unable to purge their guilt or be reassured that what
they did was right, they turn their emotions inward. The effect can be
devastating. Soldiers returning from the Vietnam War were victims of this
kind of neglect. There were no long troop-ship voyages where they could
confide in their comrades. Instead, soldiers who had finished their tour of
duty were flown home to arrive "back in the world" often within days,
and sometimes hours, of their last combat with the enemy. There were no
fellow soldiers to meet them and act as a sympathetic sounding board for
their own experiences; no one to convince them of their own sanity. Nor
were there any parades or civic tributes. The presence of a soldier in uniform in his hometown was often the occasion for glares and slurs. He was
not told that he had fought well or reassured that he had done only what
his country and fellow citizens had asked him to do. Instead of reassurance
there was often condemnation—baby killer, murderer—until he too began
to question what he had done and, ultimately, his sanity. The result was
that thousands—perhaps more than a million—returning soldiers suffered
some degree of psychiatric debilitation called post-traumatic stress reac-

tion, an illness that has become associated in the public mind with an entire generation of soldiers sent to war in Vietnam.

In the next war there will be no need to await one's homecoming to question one's actions or emotions. The nature of modern war will force the confrontation with one's self on the field of fire itself. And in most cases the outcome will be psychiatric collapse. Past wars were often horrible enough. Modern war has become so intense, lethal, and destructive that most normally sane men can no longer endure it. The soldier's mind just won't bear the burden, and most will be driven mad.

NOTES

1. This statement is attributed to a widely respected U.S. Army colonel, Harry Summers of U.S. Army War College faculty.

2. Richard A. Gabriel, *Soviet Military Psychiatry* (Westport, Conn.: Greenwood Press, 1986), p. 114.

3. The information about the Koyaks and Wiros tribes was contained in an unpublished paper presented by Dr. Lowell Roberts of the Department of Psychology, Rutgers University, at St. Anselm College, October 18, 1985.

4. Interview with Richard Hechtl, chairman, Department of Psychology, St. Anselm College. Hechtl is a widely respected expert in the area of sociopathic behavior.

Bibliographic Essay

Until recently, the subject of military psychiatry was not the focus of serious academic or even medical concern in most countries. This is a rather odd state of affairs in light of the fact that in every major war in this century—World War I, World War II, Korea, Vietnam, and the Israeli wars of 1973 and 1982—the number of soldiers lost to the fighting for psychiatric reasons has been greater than the number killed. Nonetheless, few of the major military powers seem to have spent much time and effort in systematically assembling or conducting research on the subject of military psychiatry. What information exists, with the exception of in the United States and Israel, are bits and pieces of medical, military, and academic research, which have yet to be assembled into a coherent whole.

If any one country can be said to have attempted to chronicle its experience with psychiatric breakdown in battle, it is the military establishment of the United States. After World War II, President Dwight Eisenhower became concerned with the problem of manpower loss that he had witnessed while commander-in-chief of Allied forces in Europe. His administration funded a major research effort in the area of combat psychiatry undertaken by a staff of researchers at Columbia University. The result was the first truly comprehensive treatment of the problem from the American perspective with the publication of Eli Ginzberg's, *The Lost Divisions* (New York: Columbia University Press, 1959). Much additional information on morale, cohesion, leadership and the psychiatric condition of American troops in World War II can be found in William Stoufer et. al., *The American Soldier*, 5 vols. (Princeton, N.J.: Princeton University Press, 1949). Two very valuable works that examine the structure and process of psychiatric breakdown in battle among American soldiers are J. W. Appel and G. W. Beebe, "Preventive Psychiatry: An Epidemiological Approach," *Journal of the American Medical Association,* Vol. 131 (August 18, 1946) and A. J. Glass, "Observations Upon the Epidemiology of Mental Illness in Troops" (Washington, D.C.: U.S Government Printing Office, 1954). An excellent source covering the experience of the American army with psychiatric breakdown in World War I is found in Emanuel Miller, *Neurosis in War* (New York: Macmillan Company, 1942). Interestingly, this definitive early work was totally ignored by the American military medical community during the interwar period. Had it remained in the military's consciousness, it is probable that the military medical disasters of World War II could have been prevented. It remains an excellent original source on the subject of combat psychiatry.

Among the best and most important works in the literature found anywhere, a work whose conclusions are applicable cross-culturally, is Roy Swank and Walter E. Marchand, "Combat Neurosis: The Development of Combat Exhaustion," *Archives of Neurology and Psychiatry,* Vol. 55, (1946). Swank and Marchand were the first to detail precisely the mental dynamics of psychiatric breakdown among combat soldiers. In this writer's judgment, the work remains the best yet published on the subject. A companion work, more historically oriented, is W. S. Mullens and A. J. Glass, eds., *Neuropsychiatry in World War II* (Washington, D. C.: U.S. Government Printing Office, 1973).

The American experience with combat psychiatry in Vietnam has been only recently and incompletely chronicled. Among the best works on the subject are Franklin Jones and A. W. Johnson, "Medical and Psychiatric Treatment Policy and Practice in Vietnam," *Journal of Social Issues,* Vol. 31 (1975) and T. Keane and J. Fairbanks. "Survey Analysis of Combat Related Stress Disorders in Vietnam Veterans," *American Journal of Psychiatry,* Vol. 140 (1983). The definitive work is at the present time being written by Michael Camp, *Combat Psychiatry in Vietnam* (Westport, Conn.: Greenwood Press, in press).

If the United States has more or less adequately recorded its experience with military psychiatry, the opposite extreme is represented by the availability of relevant literature on the subject dealing with the Soviet Union. To date there has been only one book on the subject of Soviet military psychiatry published in the West. Thus, Richard A. Gabriel's, *Soviet Military Psychiatry* (Westport, Conn.: Greenwood Press, 1986), remains the definitive work. Literature in Soviet resources for many reasons is scarce and unreliable. The social turmoil and the famine that followed World War I in the Soviet Union precluded the publication of any significant source material that chronicles the Russian experience with military psychiatry in World War I. The forced collectivization efforts and the purges that followed until the outbreak of World War II prevented the publication of material dealing with the development of Soviet military psychiatry in the interwar period. After World War II, the Soviets did engage on a massive research effort to chronicle their medical experience during that war, and a whole volume was devoted to their experience with military psychiatry. Unfortunately, this work is restricted in its circulation even in the Soviet Union and is unobtainable to most researchers, even Russians. Finally, most of the scant literature published in Russian journals on the subject of military psychiatry since the war is so thickly overlayed by the necessity of the psychiatric profession to square its theory with Marxism-Leninism that it is of little help to the serious researcher. Accordingly, there are no sources worth noting that would add to the study of the subject by Russian-speaking scholars and military men.

Index

ABOUT THE AUTHOR

RICHARD A. GABRIEL, Professor of Political Science at Saint Anselm College, is a well-known scholar in the field of contemporary military affairs. Among his recent books are *Soviet Military Psychiatry: The Theory and Practice of Coping with Battle Stress* and a three-volume work of fighting armies of the world (Greenwood Press, 1986, 1983).